Being Irish

About the Editor

Marie-Claire Logue was born in 1989 and grew up on both sides of the Border in Derry and Donegal. She was educated in the Northern Ireland school system, attending Foyle College. On graduating in Law with French at the Magee College campus of the University of Ulster during the economic crash, she joined the thousands of Irish who emigrated to Sydney as an economic migrant working in a variety of law firms. After three years she won a scholarship to the University of Law in London and on graduating worked in Pinsent Mason's Belfast office before moving to McCay's Solicitors in Derry.

Her legal experience, her Northern Ireland background and her life as a migrant in Sydney and London have given her an acute interest in identity, its personal origins, its development, how it reacts to travel and the impact of external events. She is aware, as are many at home and abroad, that Ireland is undergoing a challenging period of change. As a mother of two young babies, she wonders what journey Irish identity will take in their lives over the next twenty years.

Being Irish

101 Views on Irish Identity Today

Edited by
Marie-Claire Logue

The Liffey Press

Published by
The Liffey Press Ltd
'Clareville'
307 Clontarf Road
Dublin D03 PO46, Ireland
www.theliffeypress.com

A catalogue record of this book is
available from the British Library.

ISBN 978-1-8383593-4-8

Printed in Northern Ireland by W&G Baird.

Contents

Contents

Acknowledgements

First and foremost, I would like to thank all the contributors who put much time and thought into their responses. They all saw the importance of contributing to a debate about identity at this time of change.

I am most grateful to Sorcha Pollak, Peter Lynch and Jack Byrne for their enthusiasm, ideas and introductions. I am grateful to David Givens of The Liffey Press for his interest and diligence in bringing this book to print. Thank you also to Deirdre Roberts for her publicity campaign and to Adam Montgomery of River Flow Films for his photography. I am grateful also to my editorial team, which included my husband Jonathan McLaughlin and my brother Mark Quigley. The craic we had around the kitchen table as this book progressed into a reality was a time I'll always cherish. I would thank my Dad, Paddy Logue, for his support but that would only annoy him, so I won't bother, though I am grateful to him for his Afterword.

To my entire family, but most especially my Mum Marian, for her endless support. Thanks also to the incredible women in my life, especially Ava McGillion, Karen McGillion, Deirdre O'Neill, Gretta Logue, Rachel Sinton, Rochelle Quigley, Maureen and Caitlin McLaughlin for their spreadsheets, babysitting, dinners, laughs and discussions.

I am under no illusion that this book has become a reality due to the wonderful support network who assisted me throughout this process, and I am very thankful to them all.

Introduction

Marie-Claire Logue

In 2011 I joined the great migration of Irish people following the global economic crash. After a few false starts I managed to get a job in a busy law firm in Sydney, where nobody could understand a word I said. One day, my colleagues were talking about the country being 'overrun by immigrants'. 'They're taking our jobs' a few of them agreed. I gulped nervously. 'Oh no, we don't mean people like you!' was the reply. An Aussie colleague of Lebanese descent told me afterwards how lucky I was to be 'invisible' here. I was lucky to be invisible because I was white, spoke English, and was Irish. It didn't feel like a good or 'lucky' thing in that context. It was then that I started to think seriously about identity, and what it meant to me.

It was against the backdrop of the covid-19 pandemic and lockdown, which gave many of us a chance to reflect, that I felt the time was right to take a fresh look at Irish identity, 21 years on from when the first *Being Irish* book was being edited by my father in 2000. Over Christmas, I was chatting with my family on zoom about how much Ireland had changed over the past twenty years. The year 2000 was before social media; 2000 was the time of dial up internet. On seeing the horrified faces of my young nieces and nephews, 2000 may as well have been around the time dinosaurs roamed the earth.

David Givens of The Liffey Press got the concept straight away, and so I turned my attention to attracting 100 individuals, most of whom I had never met, to give up their time to go public on their personal story of their Irish identity. I formed a small editorial group, and we began to identify a variety of contributors, contacting them and convincing them that the time was ripe for another collection of views. Most of the people I contacted were up for the challenge. They shared a feeling that Ireland and the Irish were going through a period of change unprecedented since the years of the Celtic Tiger and the Good Friday Agreement. These changes have shaped, and continue to shape, Irish identity today.

For this collection I invited people from as many sectors and backgrounds as possible and tried to achieve a balance in the age, gender and viewpoints of the contributors. The contributions come from the ranks of the famous and not so famous, people at the centre of things and people at the margins, people who live in Ireland and those who live abroad, the Irish and not-Irish-but-interested.

Contributors were free to say whatever they liked. The intention was to be inclusive and non-judgmental. I asked everyone the same questions: What does Irish identity mean to you personally? Why do 70 million people worldwide embrace their Irish heritage? Are we navel-gazing? Or are there real changes in attitude taking place in Ireland and among the Irish worldwide?

It is not an easy thing to put your personal thoughts and feelings of your identity on public record. Many of the contributors commented that this was one of the hardest pieces of writing they had ever done. Others noted that once they started writing, it was difficult to stop.

A significant number of the contributors mentioned the 2015 referendum legalising same-sex marriage and the 2018 repeal of the Eighth Amendment as being defining moments of the last twenty-one years, and as key events in shaping their Irish identity. Brief mention was made to the 2004 referendum which limited the constitutional right to Irish citizenship of individuals born on the island of Ireland to the children of Irish citizens.

We have contributions from newcomers to Ireland, the 'New Irish' who are finding their voice. Unionist voices make themselves heard strong and confident, but it was not possible to persuade Unionist political leaders to participate, understandable perhaps given the dramatic events taking place in their parties during the summer.

Many of the contributors' thoughts on identity came to the forefront of their minds when they left Ireland, and it was clear how important Irish identity is to the second and third generations of Irish people who grew up outside the country.

Recent major events such as Brexit and the covid-19 pandemic featured significantly in the articles. There was less mention of peace in this collection than in 2000, particularly among the younger contributors. Does this mean that peace is now taken for granted on the island?

Above all, the reflections in this volume show that there are many ways of being Irish. We can be Irish by birth, Irish by ancestry, Irish by geography, Irish and British, Irish by accident, Northern Irish, Irish by necessity, Irish and European, Irish by association, Irish by culture, Irish and American and Irish by choice.

In taking on this challenge, I tried to stay away from Irish cliches and stereotypes. People often joke that everyone in Ireland knows one another. It is a joke I often rebutted, only to discover during an interview with Lisa McGee that my uncle taught her at school. When searching for a contact email for the Taoiseach's office, my husband casually mentioned that his old neighbour, who once helped to put out a fire in his childhood home, is now a government minister.

In speaking to the contributors, I was struck by how easy the conversation was. How we were able to joke and laugh about things, having only spoken moments before for the first time. How I was able to take a bit of a risk with a joke, or light-hearted banter (a phrase no employment lawyer ever likes to hear) only for it to be received and returned. I admire the honesty and courage of the contributors. I thank each and every one of them. I am very happy in their company. They make me proud to be Irish.

Of all the themes that have emerged, a major one has been agreement that there is no one sense of Irish identity. Another is that Ireland has changed for the better over the past twenty years, but there remain serious issues which need to be addressed.

While Irish identity is not set in stone and is navigating a period of change, it is anchored to a few basic reference points. These include a warmth of welcome, a peculiar sense of humour, resilience in the face of adversity and the importance of the home place.

As I write this from my home place, I can hear the faint hum of band music from a few streets away. The Apprentice Boys of Derry are practicing for the annual Relief of Londonderry Parade. At the same time, my toddler daughter is singing 'Lámh, lámh eile', an Irish children's song taught to her by her Granny. She is singing the tune as she dances along to the band music outside, assuming the faint hum of the Lambeg drum is the musical accompaniment to her vocal solo, with her baby brother her admiring audience.

I wonder, not for the first time, what journey Irish identity will take in their lifetime.

For Róise and Patrick

Gerry Adams

Gerry Adams is the author of 19 books, including *Black Mountain and Other Stories* which was published in August 2021. He is a former President of Sinn Féin and a former Teachta Dála (TD) for Louth and East Meath. He was also the MP and MLA for West Belfast. He is a former political prisoner and was one of the central figures in the Irish peace process.

You get to be born Irish because of something you didn't do. Nobody plans where they are born. So I could have been born in France or India or Africa or even, God forbid, in England. I jest. But you get my point. Being born Irish is a lucky accident for those of us who are happy with that designation. We have a lot of things going for us. Ireland is a beautiful place to live in. Many of our ancient better values are engrained in our DNA. We are no better than anyone else. But we are no worse and if we were left in peace we have the wit and the intelligence and the right to shape a society to suit us all.

But we are a colonised people. That shapes us even if not all of us are conscious of the effects of the evil conquest of our island by the ruling class of our nearest off shore island. Colonisation brought with it a crushing of our native culture and native skulls, accompanied by divide and conquer martial genocide, dispossession, poverty, exile and the great hunger. As well as the counter revolution and the century of partition which followed, allied to the suffocating control and misogyny of the Catholic hierarchy. All of that has shaped us.

The wise and learned Garret O Connor, former Chief Psychiatrist at the Betty Ford Centre, was clear about this. He wrote:

> The net effect of religious persecution, land rape, extreme poverty and intermittent abuse of military power by English colonists in Ireland during 700 years of continuous occupation was to produce a national inferiority complex in Irish Catholics which I identify as cultural malignant shame, characterised by chronic fear, suppressed rage, self-loathing, procrastination, low self-esteem, false pride and a vulnerability to the use of alcohol as remission for suffering – past and present.

But we have survived it all. Proof that we Irish are no mean people. Little wonder that, despite our trials and tribulations, we are generally blessed with a good opinion of ourselves. Ready to sing and joke and have the craic even when all seems lost. But we have our faults. That's part of the human condition.

So what does it mean to be Irish today? If you are from the Traveller Community it means you are denied many basic rights, especially in the South, despite the recognition of Travellers there as an ethnic minority. This is a scandal.

So too is the failure of society to accord full citizens rights to people with disabilities.This writer believes in the basic republican principles of Equality, Freedom and Solidarity. At its core this is all about a citizen-centered, rights-based society. We have some distance to go before we achieve this, not least for citizens with disabilities and their carers. Society needs shaped to permit everyone to live our lives to the full. In fairness, the majority of Irish people support this.

So too for women who are in the majority in Ireland. After long decades of struggle Irish women are winning their basic rights but they are still under represented in the leaderships of many sectors of society, from politics and public office to commerce, academia and the media. This is a global problem but surely Ireland will be a better, fairer more decent place when women, including working class women, have full equality.

This writer welcomes those who have come to our shores to find a life here. As Imelda May proclaims in her outstanding poem, 'you don't get to be Irish and racist'. We now have African-Irish, Asian-Irish, Chinese-Irish, Polish-Irish and a multiplicity of other cultures and skin colours. That's good for us.

Our nation is global. Being Irish also includes those who live outside our island. The diaspora with its exiles' pride in their ancestors and our little island. The faith keepers with their letters and parcels and money to keep us alive, up to this day. And that indomitable element among them who fought for our freedom and funded revolution and campaigns for justice and lobbied their own governments on our behalf. Our exiled children.

But not everyone who lives on the island is well disposed to the notion of Irishness. This is particularly and aggressively the case for some unionists and loyalists. But they too are what we are. So we have to be all embracing and inclusive and ensure that the nation includes all its disparate and distinctly different definitions of identity.

Those who identify as British. Or British-Irish. Or Northern Irish. Or Irish. Or as nothing at all, whatever that might mean. No matter what any of us may think of these choices, they are the sum total of who and what we are. There is no exclusive way to be Irish. No such being as pure Irish. Being Irish doesn't mean being a nationalist.

There is a difference between nationality and political or constitutional allegiances or preferences. Unionists used to almost exclusively identify themselves as Irish. Many still do. But while the union with Britain continues it will divide us and form a barrier to a new progressive unity of people on this island. We need to come together 'oblivious of the differences carefully fostered by an alien government which has divided a minority from the majority in the past'.

Me? I'm a Gael whose ancestors were obviously Planters. With a name like Adams they could not have been anything else. And I love hurling and camogie and Gaelic games and traditional songs and seán nos music and the Irish language. But I enjoy many other non-Irish pastimes as well, if any activity can be described like this. For example I have embraced the Irish cricket team; and Country and Irish music.

And I have grown to be alert to our common humanity. No matter if we differ on many things. As long as we don't force it on others or prevent them from fulfilling their own particular dreams and passions. There is plenty of space for us all on our wee island. Women and men. LGBTQ2+. It isn't always about unionist and nationalist.

Treating everyone equally as citizens with legal rights and the ability to play a full and empowered role in society is more important than turning our noses up at someone because they define their identity in a certain way. We can all live with each other's differences. In tolerance and respect. And if that isn't possible the least we can do is to get on with our lives and let others get on with theirs. The sooner the English government accommodates this the better.

This island is big enough for all the rest of us.

Hajar Akl

Hajar Akl is a former journalist at *The Irish Times* and RTÉ Radio 1. She grew up in Dublin and studied mass communication in Egypt for two years before moving back to Ireland to pursue a journalism degree at Technological University Dublin. She was nominated for Journalist of the Year in the 2018 Student Media Awards for work published in national Irish media and is currently working as a MENA Editor.

As someone who grew up in four different countries and more than five cities, identity has always been a never-ending question that occupied my mind and shaped the person I am today. First generation children will tell you how it often feels like they don't belong anywhere, like they are not enough for either country they feel a connection to, and my experience was no different. I constantly questioned what makes someone's 'identity'? Is it their appearance, their parents, their ethnicity or their accent? And can you feel like you belong somewhere if you don't tick all the boxes?

For the longest time, my own definition of identity did not allow much room for duality. I thought if I were to belong anywhere, I had to be fully accepted as identical to those around me. As a visibly Muslim woman of Egyptian descent, this option was naturally not going to be as straightforward as I had hoped. Questions about where I'm 'really from' and how my English was 'so good' brought with them a defeated sense of frustration, constantly reminding me I will never truly belong and will forever be seen as different. But in recent years my understanding of identity has evolved into something I am much more at peace with.

Through a multitude of conversations about identity over the years, I came to the realisation that in the globalised world we live in today, it would be rather narrow-minded to limit our understanding of identity to a singular definition. I can be Muslim, Irish and Egyptian *all at the same time,* and that was the piece of the puzzle I was missing. You should not have to erase one part of who you are to accept the other. And although rather obvious, it was a lightbulb moment for me. Now, if asked respectfully and at an appropriate time, questions about my origins no longer make me feel ostracised, but remind me how diverse and interesting the Ireland we live in today is.

A big part of a person's identity is developed in their formative years, and because we moved around quite a bit, I never felt like I had roots in any country other than Ireland. While everyone else had friends they grew up with their whole life, that wasn't always the case for me. Ireland was always the one place I had a unique connection to because it was where I had childhood friends. Even in Egypt, my parents' home country and where I spent two years of my life, I felt like a stranger. No matter where I was in the world, I constantly yearned for Ireland and the connection I felt to it.

In 2020, I fulfilled a long-standing dream of mine by visiting my birthplace: Mullingar. The memory of that day is still clear in my mind. It reinforced the connection I felt to the country I have known the most my entire life. I realised that 'belonging' is not how you look or how you talk, but how you feel, and while it will inevitably hurt sometimes to feel like you aren't fully accepted somewhere you call home, I will always feel like I belong in Ireland and will forever take pride in it.

Even on a wider scale, seeing Irish people's support for those who face discrimination and oppression at a time where xenophobic, racist and Islamophobic sentiments are on the rise swells my heart with pride and joy at belonging to a country as great as this. Irish people's unwavering support for a cause so close to my heart – Palestine – is a true example of this, and a manifestation of the core values that encompass what it means to be Irish. To me, being Irish is a warmth to neighbours, a kindness to strangers, and uncompromising values when it comes to standing up for those who are oppressed. The depth of Irish history is reflected in who we are today, and I could not be more proud of my Irish identity.

It may have taken years of pondering, struggling and reflecting on the question of identity, but I eventually reached a simple answer: I am Irish because Ireland is where I call home.

I learnt that it's okay for people to be curious – it is human nature after all – but it should not come from a place of alienation, but rather that of celebration of the diverse fabric of Irish society. I learnt that all parts of me make me who I am, and one part does not diminish the other.

To me, Ireland is where I feel most comfortable, most familiar; it is where I can walk the streets and recognise the hidden spots, my favourite places. Being Irish is knowing no matter where life takes me, no matter which corner of the world I find myself in, my heart will always long for Ireland, for the comfort, charm and cheer of the place I call home.

Yaser Alashqar

Yaser Alashqar is an adjunct assistant professor in the International Peace Studies MPhil programme at Trinity College, Dublin. Born in Gaza, Palestine, he is an academic member of the Centre for Palestine Studies at the University of London. He also worked with the Glencree Centre for Peace and Reconciliation in Ireland on peacebuilding and mediation projects at the national and international level.

I am interested in exploring my broader understanding of Irish identity and drawing on some similarities between Ireland and Palestine in relation to national identity. Coming originally from Gaza in Palestine, I have lived in Ireland since 2005 and I meet people from various traditions and communities, North and South. I spent my early years in Ireland working at the Glencree Centre for Peace and Reconciliation in County Wicklow. As a peace-building organisation founded in the 1970s in response to the atrocities and the eruption of violence in Northern Ireland, Glencree has been seeking to promote dialogue, inclusion, non-violence and conflict resolution on the Island of Ireland and beyond at the international level. During my time at Glencree, I was privileged to meet and speak with people who had a direct involvement in both the conflict in Northern Ireland and the initiatives to promote political solutions and peaceful coexistence.

I started my PhD at Trinity College Dublin in 2009 and my academic research in the area of peace and conflict studies provided me with the opportunity to gain further insights into the core issues, which have shaped the national identity question in Ireland. These core issues included religion and society, Catholicism, Protestantism, secularism, Traveller communities, the relationship between the key political parties (e.g. *Sinn Féin,* Fianna Fáil and Fine Gael) and the Anglo-Irish Treaty, the subsequent Civil War and 'the Troubles' of 30 years of violent conflict in Northern Ireland. My deeper understanding of the identities on the Island of Ireland also facilitated a stronger appreciation of the British influence on certain communities, such as Unionists and Loyalists, and the role of Irish language, traditional music, pubs, national sports and literature in Ireland's cultural life.

However, identity is 'self-defence' as the late Palestinian intellectual, Edward Said, described it in a conversation with the Palestinian poet, Mahmoud Darwish. Asserting one's national identity becomes a stronger act of self-defence and resistance in situations of repression and colonialism because colonial forces dehumanise the colonised subjects and seek to eliminate their national character and right to self-determination.

> *Therefore, protecting the national identity of the colonised population and resisting colonialism become closely linked during and after national liberation struggles. This is certainly the experience of Ireland and Palestine.*

Both Ireland and Palestine were colonised by Britain and subjected to dispossession and repression. In February 2021, a century after Ireland's independence in 1921, the Irish President, Michael D Higgins, commented on the relationship between Britain's colonial history and national identity in Ireland. As Higgins observes, the Irish journey of remembering the past:

... entailed uncomfortable interrogations of the events and forces that shaped the Ireland of a century ago and the country we know today. Class, gender, religion, democracy, language, culture and violence all played important roles, and all were intertwined with British imperialist rule in Ireland.

In the case of Palestine, the role of British imperialism has also not been forgotten. Arthur James Balfour, Britain's Foreign Secretary and a former colonial official in Ireland, issued the Balfour Declaration on behalf of the British government in 1917. Through the Balfour Declaration, Britain committed itself to the policy of supporting the Jewish movement, Zionism, and to 'the establishment in Palestine of a national home for the Jewish people'. Zionism emerged in Europe prior to the First World War and wished to find a solution to the Jewish experience of European anti-Semitism. Supported by Britain as the colonial power in Palestine and the Middle East region, the Zionist movement succeeded in establishing the State of Israel in the land of Palestine in 1948. It facilitated mass Jewish emigration and settlement on Palestinian land through violent and colonial practices against the indigenous Palestinians. Taking over Palestine and expelling most of the indigenous Palestinian people in 1948 became recognised in Palestinian national history as the Nakba (meaning 'catastrophe' in Arabic).

The Nakba represents the destruction of hundreds of Palestinian towns and villages and the expulsion of 700,000 Palestinians in 1948 as a result of the creation of the State of Israel in Palestine. Commemorating and remembering Palestine prior to the Nakba remains a key element of the Palestinian national identity. 'Memory is one of the few weapons available to those against whom the tide of history has turned', as the Palestinian writers Lila Abu-Lughod and Ahmed Sa'di described the case of Palestine and forced displacement.

Partition is another important element that I believe has contributed to the transformation and the complexity of identity in Ireland and Palestine. Peoples in both countries saw the division of their land as a foreign and colonial imposition between 1921 and 1947. Partition has produced complex forms of territorial affiliation and identity. Regional labels such as 'Northern Ireland', 'North of Ireland', 'the Republic of Ireland', 'the Six Counties' and the '26 Counties' came into existence in Ireland following the implementation of partition. New identities also emerged out of partition in the Irish case: 'Republican', 'Nationalist', 'Unionist' 'Loyalist', 'Northerner' and 'Southerner'. In fact, a similar process of territorial affiliation and identity has emerged in Palestine in the post-partition era and following Israel's occupation of Gaza and the West Bank in 1967: 'historical Palestine', '48 Palestine', 'the Occupied Territories', 'Gazans', 'West Bankers', 'the *Jerusalemites*', 'the Shatat (diaspora) Palestinians', 'the inside Palestinians', 'local Palestinians', 'refugee Palestinians' and '48 Palestinians'.

In conclusion, while national identities evolve among many nations according to their social and cultural histories, Ireland and Palestine have the unresolved legacy of colonialism and partition. This difficult legacy continues to represent traumatised experiences, insecurities, fragmented identities, territorial divisions and deeper challenges concerning the past and the present. The colonial legacy has also created a permanent link between the question of national identity and resistance in the cases of Ireland and Palestine.

'Asylum Seeker'

The essay below is from a Southern African asylum seeker, currently living in Ireland under Direct Provision, who wishes to remain anonymous.

I must say, it's been very difficult being a citizen of the world, never mind being Irish.

As a God-fearing family originally from Zimbabwe, but citizens of South Africa, where we are coming from after having to deal with the sad xenophobic events that took place there a couple of years ago. After praying for years for a way out, our lives were turned upside down the day we heard from the Lord that it was our time to leave. Well, for those who believe that the Lord does not speak to people in this day and age, our story will blow your mind.

When we traveled to Ireland exactly one and a half months after hearing the message, we had no idea we were travelling into a worldwide pandemic. We had been prompted by the Holy Spirit to travel quickly without delay to our new destination, Ireland, but we didn't imagine the reason for the urgency was to arrive before the whole world totally shut down. We had never had Ireland on our radar, so the message to travel to Ireland came as a total surprise to us.

On arriving, things appeared quite normal at first until the pandemic struck, bringing a fast end to our Irish experience. We have now spent 16 months in Ireland, but can't really say we have experienced what it really means to be Irish. Of those 16 months, 14 have been spent in lock down, hiding from this monster virus called covid-19.

This Irish lockdown has transitioned us rather strangely into Irish life. Being Irish has given me a closer spiritual connection with my Lord and Saviour, Jesus Christ. I have spent most of my 14 months in isolation, getting to know the creator of this beautiful, yet complicated world. I have spent time reflecting on who I am as a spiritual being, reflecting on what is important to me as a citizen of this world. I can confidently say, this has been the most amazing year of my entire life. We have never felt more content.

Being an immigrant to Ireland has allowed me to find inner peace. Ireland represents not only a new life, but new beginnings on a whole different level. Being Irish represents hope for my family; peace of mind from all the turmoil, violence, anger, human rights violations, and uncertainties faced in our own country.

We lived a life of constant fear, always afraid for our lives, and that of our children, young adults who have never had the opportunity to just be young adults. Even though we find great peace here in Ireland, we find ourselves faced with fears of a different nature – delays in the Direct Provision system mean our future is in limbo, our independence compromised, but the Lord has given us the strength to press on.

We will live our best life and show Ireland that we have so much to offer, while being completely humbled by this beautiful country and its beautiful people and warm hospitality. Ireland has allowed us to believe in mankind again, despite all the chaos we face in this world. Direct Provision is not the ideal system to live in, but we are grateful for the provision. We will persevere and hold on to the promises of our dear Lord. After all, our hope is in Him.

Sinéad Blaché-Breen

Sinéad Blaché-Breen (she/they), who writes and performs under the name Sin Blaché, is a Black Irish musician and author. They have been writing horror and sci-fi stories all their life, only recently finding a vulnerable freedom in nonfiction essay writing. She's currently working on her first novel. She lives in the North West of Ireland and can be found obsessing over obscure folk instruments, becoming a reluctant saviour to feral cats, and playing too many video games.

When I was very young I was obsessed with my father's blue eyes. When I was a child, right before we moved to Ireland, I just thought that they were amazing. Over my years of living in Ireland, I've heard a lot about what people consider true markers of 'Irishness'. Around the world, Irishness seems to be simplified down to being red-headed and freckled. Bright eyes. Green and grey and brilliant blue. A pale milky skin that looks soft to touch, like silked-cotton or warm, fresh sheets. But once you're on Irish soil, the idea of Irishness becomes a little harder to pin down. It shows up in the ability to take a joke, and how quickly you can serve it back. How well you can catch a lie, the good-natured ones, and how loudly you laugh when the truth comes out. Irishness looks like singing with friends, making up words to songs you half-know but love all the way through. Irishness looks like everyone having the same stories about their granddad even though they come from different families.

And, even with those vague and most authentic proofs of Irishness, it always seemed very important to have piercing blue eyes. There are songs written about lost loves with blue eyes from the Emerald Isle. Girls from Galway. Paintings of druidic heroes, their ethereal sapphire-blue gaze arresting you where you stand. There is a sense, even here, where you might think everyone's used to seeing them, that my father's eyes were something special. Something extremely Irish. Something old, séan-nós, like the songs and the land and language.

I was born in America, but I grew up here. I know the songs. I've been complimented on my wit. I can both take a joke and can recognise it when someone is taking the piss (a gift I attribute to growing up in North Dublin). I can speak Irish, though my fluency is waning – atrophying like a forgotten muscle.

When I was very young I wanted to feel Irish more than anything else in the world.

Friends and family, knowing I got upset about what people would call me without knowing me, would assure me that I was Irish. Just as Irish as them, they would say. I never felt like that was anything more than platitudes, because all my markers for Irishness weren't the obvious ones. My curls weren't loose like poetry. My skin wasn't something that looked delicate to others, no matter how soft and vulnerable I felt. I didn't have my father's eyes.

I updated my definition of Irish as I grew up, just as I imagine everyone else in my situation must have done. In school, people were proud of their long, silky-straight hair in high ponytails or, conversely, bafflingly ashamed of the constellations of freckles that dotted their skin. As we moved from Dublin to Donegal, and I from one gaelscoil to another, I started to learn about regional dialects of Irish, and how fierce people would grow talking about their kind of Irish versus another. I was told that the Irish I had learned in Dublin wasn't as Irish as the kind in Donegal. Nonsense, of course, but all of it deepened the profile of Irishness and what that meant to other people.

The feeling of being Irish seemed so tangible to them. When I asked about it, since I have never felt like anything but an outsider even while ticking so many boxes that might indicate otherwise, their definitions always described who they were. Answering the question led to them describing themselves, not the idea of their people. Nor did it lead to a discussion about the history of the language, or the land, or the songs. Irishness shifted to include everything they were. And how lucky, I thought, that they had that ability.

All of us on this island have recently had to face up to the fact that being Irish doesn't look like milky white skin or fiery red locks. The fact that Irish can look like me, sometimes. Mixed race and *líofa* and possessed of a foot placed firmly in the storied past of the island.

Because Irish looks like the children who are born here with Nigerian names and thick Cork accents just as much as it looks like old lads in flat caps nursing pints and swapping jokes.

Irish looks like turning turf, looks like children of Chinese immigrants who came here to start a new life, just like the Irish have done all over the world for hundreds of years. Irish sounds like *Mincéir cant* weaving into hip hop beats, the songs their way into virality online, into the hearts of people all over the world.

Irishness shifts to fit the person in question and doesn't have to be defined by blue eyes. I carry that knowledge inside me, now, fragile and hard-won. I'm happy to live in an Ireland that's learning to realise this, instead of the Ireland I grew up in, the Ireland that made children like me feel separate.

David Bruce

The Rt Rev Dr David Bruce is Moderator of the General Assembly of the Presbyterian Church in Ireland

Three days before Michael Collins was killed at Béal na Bláth, County Cork, my father was born in Bellaghy, County Derry. It was August 1922. The struggles for Irish independence would not have occupied his young Presbyterian mind as he grew up in the new state of Northern Ireland. Like his father before him, he was British first, an Ulsterman second, with barely a mention of Ireland, although he was neither an Orangeman, nor an Apprentice Boy. My father's Britishness was expressed not by parading and beating a drum, but by the quiet affirmation of the values of plain decency and hard work. The struggle for his family had less to do with the high politics of national freedom from colonial British rule, and more with the daily grind of scraping a living from the soil of their small holding. He imbibed from his parents a strong work ethic which would make him restless all his days. So he embarked on a lifetime's journey which would lead him off the farm, into grammar school, on to university and a career in medicine where he excelled, both academically and as a gifted physician.

For myself, the youngest of three children, being Irish in Belfast during the 1970s was not a natural self-description. The violence of those days, including the IRA murder of a close friend, cemented in my young teenage mind that 'Irishness' was alien and even malign. There was certainly a season in my younger days when I had little personal affection and no political affinity with counties beyond the bordered six I called home. There was nothing to challenge my thinking on this within the bubble of my Protestant existence, other than a few sandal-wearing bearded-types who rabbited on about peace. In fact, the rough cadences of Paisleyism and the certainties of fundamentalism seemed more to my liking, at least for a time.

But the seeds of a change were sown in 1977 when over that beautiful summer I rode my bicycle the length and breadth of this island. From the stark beauty of Fair Head in Ballycastle I followed the coast west and south, pitching my tent in whatever field took my fancy, talking to the locals and other fellow travelers along the way. In Balliosadare I fished for salmon in the Owenmore River and dined like a prince on the fruit of my labours. I sang rebel songs in the pubs of Ballina and Westport, and caught a whiff of a history I had never been taught at school. In Leenane I fell slightly in love, and on the cliffs of Moher I stood transfixed, feeling the pull of wings about to unfurl from within me.

At Glencree in County Wicklow, a new Centre for Peace and Reconciliation had opened in an old British Army barracks, and I joined a gang of youngsters helping to re-build the place. Faith and Life intersected in ways they never had before, and presented me with a new vocabulary to describe the possibility of being both Presbyterian and Irish.

The magic of that sparkling but deeply challenging summer has never left me.

Perhaps, then, it was no particular surprise that as a young and newly ordained Presbyterian minister, myself and my wife Zoe moved to Dublin in 1987 where we lived for five happy years. These were days of recession, but with the first hints of a growling Celtic Tiger about to pounce. Dublin was buzzing and beginning to shake off the dust of the decades. We hung on tight as the eighties gave way to the nineties, sensing rather than knowing that the changes coming would not be cosmetic, and would go to the heart of what it means to be Irish.

I couldn't have guessed at what was to come – the damage done to the witness of the Christian churches through the unspeakable evil of servants of the church who behaved like monsters.

I couldn't have hoped for a solution to the political impasse which was the script of my life up to then, until in 1998 we witnessed Agreement of a kind which stood the twin tests of international acclamation and mutual acceptance on both the Falls and the Shankill Roads.

I couldn't have imagined that Ireland would kick over the traces of its Christian past with such a gleeful lack of discrimination at what was good and what was not. Perhaps the roots were not so deep after all?

And yet, if asked, I have no hesitation whatever in saying what my old Dad could not. I am of Ireland. This is my home. And as time runs on I know that for Protestant, Catholic and Dissenter, and now also New Irish who know little of our terrible beauty and have not shed its blood, that this is where I belong.

Teresa Buczkowska

Teresa Buczkowska is a migrant woman living in Ireland. She is an Ethnologist by education and a migrant rights' activist by profession. Teresa was appointed to the board of the Arts Council of Ireland, and most of her professional career she spent at the Immigrant Council of Ireland. She has published both in Ireland and internationally on racism, integration politics and diversity in leadership.

What makes us Irish? Is it our birthplace? Ancestors? A distant line of blood? How far in history shall we look back when tracing branches of a family tree? How long does a family tree have to grow in Irish soil to be considered New Irish no more? Can Irish be Black? Can Irish be of a non-Christian faith? Can Irish speak with an US accent? How about an Eastern European intonation, just like mine? All of these questions make me wonder: what gives Joe Biden more rights to call himself Irish than me?

The 46th US President's ancestors left Ireland nearly two centuries ago. When he visited Ireland for the very first time in his life, he was praised for declaring *Ireland will be written on my soul.* I have been living here nearly half of my life, immersing myself in my local community day in and day out, but when I say I am Irish, people ask, 'but where are you really from?' This question to some may seem to be just asking out of curiosity, but to me this question is a challenge to my feeling of Ireland being my home.

I can't remember when my sense of identity started to evolve, but I remember the first time I thought of Ireland as home. It was February 2015 and I was on board a plane flying back from attending a learning exchange in New York. When after six hours of flying we entered the Irish air zone I saw beneath all of the shades of green on the chessboard of Irish fields. I breathed a sigh of relief, thinking; *ah, finally home.* I surprised myself with that sudden thought, but I was pleased that I arrived at a point where I could call my place of living a home.

What does it mean to be home? I think we all have a similar idea of *home* that we share. Home is a place where we breathe at ease, having a sense of familiarity with daily life practices, people and spaces. It is the confidence of knowing what to expect when we step outside our front door. Moments of feeling united with your neighbours in communal joy or sadness when we experience a collective win or loss is what makes us feel at home. It is a place where we see ourselves living in years to come. Home is where our future is, not only where our past was.

For more than 16 years I have been living and breathing Ireland in all aspects of my life. I nourish an Irish strong sense of community, and in return I give that love and care back. I have here my go-to places when I need a mental rest, and favourite spots to meet my friends. I participate in Irish daily rituals even when I am not here because these habits are now mine. It took time to learn, but now I enjoy my tea strong with a dash of milk, I discuss the weather with strangers and friends alike, I practice the *ah-sure-it'll-be-grand* attitude to life. I felt such a pride of place when we collectively said *Yes to Equality* and *Repeal the 8th.* I can say that Ireland is written on my soul too. This all means to be at home, and if I am at home in Ireland, I am Irish then.

Calling myself Irish does not mean the need to renounce my Polish roots. Being a migrant means I am bridging both identities, and I do not have to choose only one.

Identity and sense of belonging can be a space defined by collective experiences, common interests and connections, not by the concept of nationhood limited only to borders, land or blood. The traditional understanding of nationhood is a quickly expiring idea that demands declaring our belonging only to one people, one culture, one place. How can this belief still stand in our constantly intertwining world, where the cross-border flow of ideas, people, culture and thoughts is the staple of our times?

I was born in Poland so that's where I am partially from. That's where my childhood happened, that's where my past was. When I arrived here, at first I didn't plan to stay. Ireland was an adventure that turned into a permanent home. My whole adult life has been here, and I am planning to stay for good, so I am from Ireland too. Having two places that I can feel a strong sense of belonging to isn't as confusing as it may seem. It is quite simple though: if Joe Biden can be a hyphen Irish, so can I. I am Polish-Irish because Poland is where I was born, but Ireland is now my home.

Gerald Butler

Gerald Butler is a historian and co-author (with Patricia Ahern) of *The Lightkeeper*. Descended from lightkeeping grandparents and parents, he followed in their footsteps, serving as a lightkeeper in numerous lighthouses until automation brought his career to a close in 1990 (he is still employed as a part-time attendant lightkeeper at Galley Head lighthouse). For more than thirty years he has lectured on the history of Irish lighthouses.

The present moment is our only reality, and yet to define what it means to be Irish today requires reflecting on the past.

We stand on the shoulders of our ancestors and draw from the legacy they have left for us. Theirs was a bitter story of starvation and exploitation. They were famed for their religious beliefs: Irish religious scholars founded monasteries and schools and furthered education across the world. To stand on their shoulders is indeed humbling. But what might they have to say to us today? 'Ouch … my shoulders are hurting.'

The Catholic faith is entwined with our Irish identity. As the grip of the Catholic Church is loosened, so is the discipline that goes with it. As a parent raising three children, I had to accept the changes to my own traditional ways, which now give way to a new sense of Irishness. But I feel this modern sense of Irishness needs a firm foundation if it is going to stand the test of time. Now, as I think about what it is to be Irish today, I am looking at a broader picture.

As always, times are changing and it bodes well for us to examine carefully what we are doing. I do not go around thinking of my Irishness as I carry out my day's work, but since some of my work involves dealing with holiday guests from overseas, I am made aware of our friendliness by their comments. Being Irish, I like to think this is in our DNA. However, we are also known for our coarse language and the more of this I hear, the more I question, 'is this part of our Irishness'?

History tells us that change has always been part of our evolution. The exponential growth of technology means that our lives are changing at a quicker pace. As a parent and grandparent looking at our next generation, I find it difficult to see how I can pass on a sense of Irishness to their tiny minds that are wired for electronic technology. Given the power of social media to which every child has access, I feel lost and left behind. I believe we can control change and keep our own direction, but we cannot put old heads on young shoulders.

Change may very well bring out a new sense of Irishness that has lain dormant until now. During the last twenty years we have become accustomed to seeing people from all over the world living among us. Being a small, insulated island, I never thought we could accept this change so quickly, but we did, which speaks well of our openness.

My name, Butler, is of Norman origin, and though not from a line of the Gaels, the Butlers have become more Irish than the Irish themselves. I see this as giving great hope to the migrants who have come to live on our shores. Being Irish has to be about the people – perhaps more than about the island itself. To see the children of migrants learning to speak Irish at school and joining local GAA teams, or taking up Irish dancing, brings to life the meaning of being more Irish than the Irish themselves.

Every day the road less travelled lies before us. Living on this island during the last twenty years has shaped our sense of Irishness perhaps more so than ever before. In this time of change I do not ever want to change who I am. Some things, yes, but I can only go with the ebb and flow of life. All in all, I am happy to be Irish.

Geraldine Byrne Nason

Ambassador Byrne Nason is the Permanent Representative of Ireland to the UN. She previously served as Ambassador to France and as Second Secretary General in the Department of the Taoiseach. She led Ireland's successful campaign for a seat on the UN Security Council, which she now leads for the 2021-2022 term. She was Chair of the UN Commission on the Status of Women for 2018 and 2019. Ambassador Byrne Nason is married and has one son.

Irish tradition suggests that we are a tribe of wanderers – 70 million people in our global diaspora testify to that tradition. As a diplomat, I embody that Irish wandering. From Geneva to Helsinki, Vienna to Brussels, and most recently from Paris to my current base in New York, I've wandered many parts of the globe in the last four decades, speaking about Ireland, promoting our interests, our trade policy and culture, as well as our values, including critical issues such as human rights and humanitarian principles.

I've spent my career representing Ireland, mainly off the Island, so 'Being Irish' is almost my profession. But it could never be a job or a title. It is so much more than that.

My Irish identity expresses itself in two distinct ways. The first is an extraordinary pride in that small peripheral island that is my home. And the second is a sense of limitless possibility, ambition and hope for future generations of Irish people.

My pride in Ireland might well be genetic. My grandparents fought for our independence. My parents were part of the brave and industrious generation that helped build a new Ireland in the 1950s and 1960s. I was lucky enough to be born into a new phase of Ireland's evolution – one that knew conflict on the island, but also benefitted from new developments, like free education and a refreshed sense of social and economic potential. I grew up surrounded by a very palpable sense of hope.

One of my prevailing memories from my early teens is when Ireland joined the European Economic Community in 1973. We had a sense that we were on the verge of something new. A conviction that Ireland would blossom in Europe, that it was an unparalleled opportunity. As we built our relations with continental neighbours and took our place as equals with UK and others at the EU table, being Irish took on a new gloss. I felt immense pride in the country my grandparents and parents helped build, knowing that now we were stepping up to another level of confidence and potential for our island as an EEC member and future EU Member State. Even as a young woman, I recognised the exceptional momentum EU membership brought to gender equality in Ireland. Being Irish and being European at the same time unlocked so much.

And of course that pride has grown as the years went on. As an adult I've watched Ireland break through the conservatism that defined the early years of our State and embrace what I see as a welcome social revolution. Ireland has expanded in diversity and removed barriers to inclusion. Whether as a woman, a person of colour, irrespective of creed or sexual choice, we all can now all proudly celebrate our Irishness in its fullness.

The second facet of my Irish identity brings with it a sense of the limitless possibility, hope and faith for the next generations of Irish people. We are a small country, but our culture and our global presence are disproportionately influential. We have a type of superpower, culturally. My cultural identity is neither limited to Drogheda nor the Island. I don't think of it as linked to place or time. Rather, it is an identity with a global passport. Irish identity is about passion for human rights, about empathy for others, about marching to the beat of your own drum. Irish people are deeply linked in a unique way to a hard past, but we have retained an extraordinary ambition for our future. We stand up, we stand out.

This distinctiveness is rooted in our culture. My earliest memories of how I expressed myself are cultural – I was an Irish dancer, I studied and speak our own Irish language. Others play our music, and recite our beautiful poetry.

Irish culture still illuminates my work as a diplomat and has helped me connect with people all over the world, whether I'm Ambassador in Paris speaking about Samuel Beckett, or here at the United Nations standing beside the late Eavan Boland discussing Irish suffragettes.

Our culture is a global asset that brings people together.

In my current role – representing Ireland at the United Nations and on the Security Council, I regularly pass a photograph of Ireland's first Ambassador to the UN and the only Irish diplomat to preside over the General Assembly – Ambassador Frederick 'Freddy' Boland, Eavan Boland's father. In 1960 he was elected as President of the General Assembly, just five years after Ireland joined the UN.

In the 1960s Ireland had a golden era of Irish identity on the global stage: not only did Ireland have an Ambassador leading the great assembly of nations, but also an Irishman in the White House in President John F. Kennedy, and a much beloved Irish-American Princess of Monaco in Grace Kelly. Our far-reaching, global ambition was cause for immense pride – symbolic of our limitless possibility, it seemed. My childhood was imbued by that sense of possibility.

I grew up in an Ireland that awoke to its own possibilities, and bred in my generation the faith and confidence in our capacity to deliver on it. Whether I'm in a yellow cab here in Manhattan, in a café in Paris, or on the streets of Helsinki, that faith stays with me.

I suppose you could say that as I work for Ireland and I'm a professional Irish woman wandering the globe, I carry my island with me always: in my head and in my heart.

Jack Byrne

Jack Byrne was born in Liverpool in an Irish family. He worked in engineering and industry for most of his adult life and went to the University of East Anglia to study English at the age of forty. He is married with two children and his debut novel, *Under the Bridge*, was published by Northodox Press in February 2021. Set in the Irish diaspora of Liverpool, the story deals with issues of class, nationality and identity.

Ghost in the Room

My Irishness came late, it was delayed by tragedy, and a commitment to class. The idea to which we attach our identity is not always chosen freely at first. It comes from the water we swim in, the road we travel along, and the events and people we meet. The identity we finally accept is in our hands, we determine who we are, not where and when we are.

By the mid-seventies, I had chosen. I stood at the bus stop in Speke council estate, briefcase in hand, waiting for the bus to a posh grammar school. My parents had left for work before we got up, two sisters were next to me waiting for the bus to a local factory. I remembered Ted Heath saying, 'It is the government or the miners' and being happy the miners won. A shop steward brother introduced me to Paul Foot and the Ragged Trousered Philanthropists. I couldn't decide between Slade and T Rex but did decide the Communist Manifesto spoke for me. The working class is still the spectre haunting Europe.

One of the events on my road was the suicide of an older brother in Ebrington barracks in November 1975, three days before my fifteenth birthday. He used the rifle issued by Her Majesty's Government to kill an Irishman, himself.

Our father left Wicklow, like tens of thousands of other social and economic migrants, after WWII. He moved to Liverpool where he met my mum. As a seaman, my mum's dad, also from Wicklow, was already shipping out of Garston.

My brother wasn't the first Irishman to die in the British army; in earlier times he would have been escaping poverty in Dublin or Belfast, and later the rest of the UK.

The defining things about Peter were his love of sport, Everton Football Club, and English nationalism. Maybe it was youthful rebellion, or the lack of Irish as opposed to a Catholic culture, but he became a supporter of Enoch Powell. The army was an escape from factory work or the dole, but also a mission to serve his queen and country. From the moment of his death, we could not talk about, share or enquire of anything Irish, in fear of raising his ghost. I know our family's loss is just one of thousands on all sides; there are plenty of ghosts.

I wrote a poem called 'A Mirror Cracked', which is long lost, but the central idea was the distorted image Peter must have come to have of himself. In Derry he saw the same terraced streets and houses as Garston, he saw the faces of neighbours, family and friends, and the names were as Irish as his own. Whether it was a sudden realisation, or a growing awareness of the disparity between who he was and what he was doing, doesn't matter. What matters is that it was finally resolved by taking his own humanity.

The tragedy of an English-born son of Irish parents going to die in the British army in Northern Ireland came to encapsulate for me the failure not just of the Northern Irish state, but of the Southern state that was torn from the UK in fire and fury and cost the lives of so many, only to see the welfare functions of the new state handed over to the Catholic church and the economy to a new breed of Irish capitalist.

> *The newly independent Republic failed my father and the tens
> of thousands like him who became migrants. Fleeing Ireland
> were many of the victims of trauma from the industrial schools,
> the laundries, the mother and baby homes, or women escaping
> the social constraints imposed by rigid catholicism.*

These past twenty years of the Good Friday Agreement were an opportunity to overcome the political divide, the walls and the barrier of armed struggle to create a new country. The success has been the absence of war, the failure is the absence of a common experience. The material interests, and the sectarian culture that sees a layer of politicians and criminals making a good living atop the crumbling edifice of the northern Irish state, means it will not be an easy transition. There is enough blood in Irish soil to incorporate the celebration and commemoration of all traditions. Truth could have led to reconciliation. The working class on the Falls and Shankill, in Derry and Garston, have always had their exploitation, and now food banks, in common. The hope of many was that the removal of guns could lead to unity in the recognition of common class interests.

Ireland for my kids is catching crabs off Parnell bridge in Wicklow, or dodging the surf in Brittas Bay. I hope in the future they are not visited by Brexit-shaped ghosts of the past.

Tony Connelly

Tony Connelly is an Irish journalist and author. He is Europe Editor for RTÉ News and Current Affairs.

Researching a story about the Slazenger family as a feature-writer at the *Irish Independent*, I stumbled upon an anecdote from Ralph Slazenger in a 1969 newspaper profile. He was asked the difference between being Irish and being English.

Slazenger, whose sportswear family had recently bought Powerscourt, was racing to catch a train in London, managing a cliff edge leap onto the departing locomotive. He was immediately rebuked by the train manager who let him know how dangerous it was and how lucky he was not to be fined.

A few weeks later Slazenger found himself, once again, leaping on to a departing train in Dublin. He braced himself for another dressing down as the Irish train manager approached. Instead, the manager beamed: 'That was a great race!'

That stayed with me as a handy code-breaker. Being Irish, relative to being English (and what other relativity is there?), meant not taking life too seriously, admiring ill-judged bravery and venal rule-breaking.

The Ireland of 1969, however, is not the Ireland of today. The Irish have learned the hard way about the perils of cutting corners and trying to game the system. Perhaps there was more than a whiff of jumping onto a moving train in the Anglo-Irish Bank catastrophe.

As a young democracy Ireland had to succeed, and being Irish meant wanting to be liked. Affirmation by foreigners became a subconscious national fixation. That was why the banking crash was so hard. Not only would the economy be wrecked, people might not like us anymore.

Growing up in Derry, being Irish meant not being British. As a teenager, there was a vague set of negatives: not being unionist, or in the Orange Order, or loving the Queen. But what were the positives? Summer holidays in Donegal or Achill or Kerry, craic, the gaeltacht, scenery, pints, pubs, Irish music, an easy going sense of humour, an escape from the oppressive sectarian politics and violence of the North.

I went to Trinity College in the 1980s, but the economic climate in Dublin was so grim that my sense of being Irish was tested by lived experience. I recall fretting that the South had to get its act together (economic, social, political) or being Irish would never appeal to unionists, who preferred being British.

After graduating I lived in London. The late 1980s were an awful time in Anglo-Irish relations (the Birmingham Six, the Guildford Four, the Gibraltar Three, the IRA bombing campaign) and the anti-Irish mood in tabloid Britain was unsettling.

Yet, I felt part of a new generation of university-educated Irish. We would play U2 covers at parties and quote Seamus Heaney. We were the fun-loving, all-drinking, all-singing, new Irish, raised on Planxty and Monty Python. Being Irish could suddenly be an asset, not a handicap.

But being Irish meant obsessing about what being Irish meant. I returned to Dublin just in time for the Celtic Tiger. Suddenly, my undergraduate fears were swept away. Ireland was great. We could do this. We could become a modern, prosperous, socially progressive republic.

In 2001, I landed in Brussels as an RTÉ correspondent. Now I had a whole new set of adjacent identities and histories against which being

Irish might be measured. Being Irish soon left me feeling somewhat small. We like to think of Irish monks in the sixth century, or of how European power struggles might pivot on a seventeenth century Irish battle here, or a botched invasion there. But I realised, when I wrote a book on European stereotypes, that Ireland was a small piece of the European jigsaw.

Figuring out stereotypes meant wading through thousands of years of bloodshed and battles, great tidal surges of empire and religion that killed and displaced millions, and redrew boundary and tribal identity every half century.

Ireland certainly punched above its weight in European history, and the famine was a true horror relative to other shameful episodes, but being Irish usually meant only having to figure yourself out relative to the English. Still, being Irish opened doors. People liked the Irish, as if we were the friendlier, more europhile versions of Brits. UK broadcast journalists sought Irish passports because they meant less hassle at borders.

Once, crossing the frontier between Montenegro and Albania during the Kosovo war, a Serb military checkpoint asked what country we were from. When we said Irish, the commander declared: 'The Serbs and Irish are brothers.'

Then the crash happened. German officials were initially sympathetic to the Irish banking collapse (one told me that the Celtic Tiger was a case of 'over succeeding'), but the Anglo-Irish Bank tapes betrayed a mortifying ugliness.

Now, we have largely recovered, and with the UK gone, being Irish in Europe means being Nordic: fiscally responsible net contributors, who still need to learn a thing or two about climate change (and corporate tax), but with the ability to psychoanalyse post-Brexit Britain and open doors to the Biden Administration.

Being Irish still means being blessed by friendliness and the gift of the English language, and an ability to blend business with informality that (mostly) pays dividends. Constrained by experience, we probably have to be less Irish than we used to. Or maybe we have all become post-Irish.

Louise Cooney

Louise Cooney is an Irish fashion model and lifestyle blogger from Limerick.

Growing up just outside Limerick city, I didn't think much about my identity. It wasn't until I spent time in America that I started to reflect and think about *being Irish*.

I have always been drawn to America, particularly New York. I've been over and back many times, and every time I go there I have a different experience. I have spent periods with my family who emigrated to Connecticut, and I was also one of the many young Irish people who spent a college summer on a J1 visa in New York. It was during these experiences that I became aware of the ways in which we were different, and it made me appreciate what being Irish means.

After college I worked for Tourism Ireland, one year of which was spent in their New York office. My colleagues became like family to me. Although not everyone was Irish, there was a distinct 'Irish way' in the office – we all looked out for one another. I soon realised that this was not normal office culture in New York. Going into work was like a little piece of home in the middle of New York city. The Irish have a strong ability for drawing us all together with the Irish community abroad thriving.

Being a blogger has opened many opportunities for me, especially travelling and meeting people. The nature of my job means that I could essentially be based anywhere. But the thing about an Irish audience is that it is deeply engaged and naturally inquisitive. Maybe it's because we're from a small island, where we feel everyone is our neighbour or we have a connection to someone. My most recent trip to New York in 2020 was when I contemplated adapting to try to fit in with the more commercial New York culture, such as changing the way I speak, my accent and the phrases I use. It made me realise how proud I was to be Irish, and to have those quirks, and that I didn't want to change. Such simple things like ending every sentence with, 'do you know', saying 'now' when I've finished a piece of work, and the many different uses for the word 'grand'. It's all so Irish.

Now, that I have returned home, I am genuinely delighted to see and enjoy all the familiar things I grew up with. I love the sense of community and how we wave at each other when passing in the car on a narrow road. Even our tourism industry benefits from our habit of speaking to everybody. Last year very few tourists could come to Ireland due to the travel restrictions, and so the majority of the tourists were Irish. I went on a hike one day and every single person I passed spoke and said hello. I thought to myself that I was going to be hoarse by the time I finished!

I am incredibly proud of how far we have come as a nation. We have become more independent in how we think. We are not as deeply associated with the Catholic Church. We dramatically declared our support for the LGBT+ community and for women's rights; we have adopted environmental standards and sustainability goals, for example, the plastic bag levy.

Our awareness of and support for mental health care has increased enormously in the past 20 years. My parents growing up wouldn't have known what mental health was, and now the stigma is reducing and support is more readily available. Whilst there are still challenges and changes to be made, we have become a nation which is open to change.

I'm optimistic for Ireland, especially its young people. They have had a hard time during the pandemic. They have a lot more life to live and I believe they will come out of this stronger. A whole generation has become comfortable and efficient working online. When I was a teenager, there were lots of things abroad that weren't available in Ireland. That's no longer the case and with many multinational companies now based in Ireland there are more opportunities to stay at home.

We have qualities that make us unique. We are not the only nation with these qualities, but we are the only nation with this collection of qualities. It is the sum-total that makes us unique. We are warm and friendly. In my opinion we are the friendliest nation in the world (I may be biased, of course!).

We are resilient – we can come through hard times; we have patience, and we don't give up. We are ambitious, we get things done, nothing is outside our abilities. We are generous. One small example of our generosity is when I was part of a fundraiser for Pieta House just as the Covid-19 pandemic hit. People didn't know what their future held, if their job was secure, yet they still dug into their pockets and we raised €90,000 in a very short space of time, which shows the best of Ireland and its people.

Jack Coulter

Jack Coulter is an Irish artist. He is widely known for his paintings and the visceral quality within his work. In 2020, *The Financial Times* described Jack as one of the most popular abstract painters emerging today. In 2021, *Forbes* featured Jack in their 30 Under 30 list.

I was born in the Royal Victoria Hospital, Belfast, on the 20th of April, 1994. The city where I've grown up, and where I'll forever be proud to come from. My mother and father are from working-class families; they always instilled in me that working hard was a necessity, as well as a skill in itself. I think this is quite an innately Irish mindset and something I am very thankful for.

My mother ensured that I was exposed to great art, music and literature throughout my childhood. I'm indebted to her for enriching my youth with such wonderful experiences, especially within the world of visual arts, and I felt personally addressed by it. My first perceivable memories were formed through frequent visits to museums and galleries. There is a photograph of me in a pram outside the Tate Gallery, London in 1995. There is another photograph taken in 1998 where I'm staring at the Pompidou in Paris when everyone else is looking at the camera. Those photographs speak volumes; my sense of awe at the Pompidou, memories of being wheeled round the Tate in my pram. These memories together with many more similar experiences shaped the person I am today. In 1998, I vividly remember one day after school my mother taking me to a Yoko Ono exhibition at the Ormeau Baths Gallery in Belfast. I still remember writing my wish and hanging it on Yoko's Wishing Tree. In fact, I did the same thing many years later at the MoMA in New York.

I went to a small nursery school near my home in Ormeau Park shortly before attending one of the few integrated primary schools in Belfast. My grandparents were born in the 1920s, my mother grew up in Armagh City and my father in Irvinestown, County Fermanagh. My paternal grandfather was born in Scotland, and I still have lots of relatives there, many of whom work in the film industry. For example, Michael Coulter (cinematographer for films such as *Notting Hill* and *Love Actually*).

I never really thought about my cultural identity much while growing up and I was never socialised to judge anyone by their religion. Growing up in Northern Ireland, inevitably the question was asked what religion you were, and I could never answer that question, as my family didn't adhere to any religious denomination. Hilariously, my introduction to religion was watching *Father Ted* with my dad. The integrated schools I attended exposed me to different cultures, religions and backgrounds. They shaped my identity in very important ways.

My personal identity has also been shaped by many different experiences. My aunt Christine (my mother's sister) was an abstract painter-printmaker whose influence on my artistic growth was vital. She had an intense understanding and knowledge of art, and instilled in me the core belief that the manner in which I expressed myself naturally was *right*. I remember 'hearing' colours at her exhibitions as a child, in particular the tiny red dots indicating that the paintings had *sold*. In secondary school my art teacher, Jaqueline Rogan, always encouraged me. After seeing one of my life drawing homeworks she asked, 'Have you always painted like that?' The rest of the art class had drawn bowls of fruit or their pets. I had saturated my double page in second-hand house paint and watercolour. She was an abstract painter and I felt she understood my form of expression. The type of art I was creating was affirmed by three inspiring Irish women – both at home and in school. My mother, my aunt Christine and my art teacher, in different ways, gave me confidence in myself as an artist. My Irish identity was formed from a basis of *feeling*, and although a sense of cultural identity can sometimes be seen as a divisive thing in Northern Ireland, I see myself first and foremost as an artist.

Initially my art began to be publicly recognised around the age of 20 or 21 and I do feel being Irish helped that process. At that time, London in particular embraced my work. Then the US simultaneously. At 21, I was being covered by press outlets such as *The Independent, The Guardian* and *The Huffington Post*. Early on, that rapid attention was creating serious opportunities, projects and collaborations. I was back and forth to London, working intensely hard.

> *Having ambition and a yearning to travel has always been part of the Irish story. Being Irish did set me apart, and I am very thankful for that. Belfast is forever in my heart, always. Big dreams felt real growing up, I knew the history of great people within pop culture associated with Belfast. My goal is to be added to that list as the painter who was born there.*

One thing that crystallised my sense of Irishness happened quite recently. In June 2021, I was invited by Hilary Weston to have tea in her London home. She had a private viewing of my painting in Sotheby's, London, a week or two prior to our meeting. Normally, it would have been quite a daunting experience, meeting someone of her reputation and calibre. However, Hilary is Irish and, as such, I just knew we would share a lot in common apart from the love of art. For obvious reasons, we lead very different lives. Yet, I felt there was always going to be some commonality because of our Irish roots. I asked Hilary about her childhood growing up in Dublin and her eyes truly lit up as she told some incredible stories. Even through just the simple things, such as knowing the names of places in Ireland, we shared a connectedness. Coincidently, my mother had also told me that Hilary's younger sister had attended the same school in Armagh as her and my aunt Christine, in fact, my aunt was in the same class. So, the cliché is true, in Ireland we all know each other in some way.

I could write a thesis on the intricacies and wonders that come with having a sense of Irishness; I think Ireland's the most special and beautiful place on earth. Never in a million years would I want to be from anywhere else.

All over the world the Irish are known as the kindest and most generous of people. Many Irish writers describe the beauty of the land and its people, and I love this quote from 'The Lake Isle of Innisfree' by W.B. Yeats:

> I will arise and go now, for always night and day
> I hear lake water lapping with low sounds by the shore;
> While I stand on the roadway, or on the pavements grey,
> I hear it in the deep heart's core.

Lisa Cunningham Guthrie

Dr Lisa Cunningham Guthrie is a Consultant in Emergency Medicine and Prehospital physician. She is also Chief Medical Officer of the Order of Malta Ambulance Corps. She holds the rank of Commandant, the youngest and first female to do so. A proud Mayo woman and a lover of the Irish Language, she is the team doctor for the Mayo Ladies Gaelic Football Team.

My reflection may be slightly skewed. I've returned from the UK, after one year. I feel my sense of being Irish is at an all-time high!

My definition of Irishness is the sense of or relating to Ireland, it's people, culture or language. I think there are many parts to what it means to be Irish for me.

Firstly, the epitome of being Irish, is the sense of pride of Irishness. A collective community, a meitheal – local, national or international – that we are all so proud to be involved in.

Locally, it's the pride when the community gets *le chéile* to win the Tidy Towns competitions. Getting a picture in the local newspaper *agus* a mention on the local radio station, which is the higher echelon of showing your local pride.

Nationally, it's the clubbing together of a county to support and encourage a local person. It's the posters in the window for that person, the chats on the street about that person! The garda escort for the person returning to the parish with their achievement celebrated by the whole *contae*. How proud we all are of our own counties!

Internationally, it's the sense of pride we have watching our fellow compatriot represent us so well on the international stage. How we cry watching them receive their gold medal, while thinking of how proud their family must be. But also feeling part of that *clann*, despite never having met them.

We are a family, umbrellaed by the joy and delight for another person for whom our hearts could burst with fulfilment for their achievements – because they are Irish.

Secondly, I feel being Irish is a sense of being non-sensical. It's our quirks and our oddities that make complete sense to us from tradition but gives us secret delight to explain them to a person who cannot make head nor tail of them. I cannot explain but I can use examples that people will nod to. While reading, imagine saying this to someone that has never experienced it before.

- Putting a headless Child of Prague out under the bush for the good weather for a wedding, and then arguing over whether the child has to be headless or the head intact.

- Scoffing at the *scéalta* of fairies, the *pishéogs* and folklore, but in the same breath you would never cut down a fairy bush as you heard of someone who did and their fate was not good.

- Meeting another Irish person abroad and going hell for leather for three minutes until you find some connection, even if it is a butcher you both know in another Irish town. You feel a sense of relief that you've come to some closure.

Thirdly, our language. People will read this as a lecture about Gaeilge – which is another innate thing of being Irish, the negative association with our own language. There is almost a delightful hatred about the way it was taught in schools, whilst also happy to have a general conversation about how lovely it is as a language, the conversation normally ending in, 'but sure I would love to learn it again'. We take pride in our Gaeilge and it is blossoming as a language. A whole generation is now being 'taught it differently' and we are already reaping the rewards of gentle inclusion of Gaeilge in our lives. Like the *cúpla focail* I've thrown in here, *fite fuaite*.

However our other language, our English-speaking dialect, also shows our uniqueness of being Irish. Living in the UK for the year, I was constantly told about how bad my grammar was. It delighted me to educate my fellow colleagues about our dialect of their language, Hibernio-English. Right down to the history of how it came about. In the end, my English colleagues spoke a few words of Gaeilge, learned from me, sat and watched our national sport and wanted to learn more about it, entertained me in their interpretation of our Irish dancing and even perfected the making of my cup of tea. Most of them had some sort of ancestry from Ireland. In quiet moments, they would chat with me about the areas from Ireland they knew some history of from their family, expressing a desire to visit at some stage. Despite being born in the UK, the pride of Irishness transcends generations and still has the pull over people.

The *grá* and desire to feel this is welcomed by us Irish. This is because we know how lucky we are to be Irish and want to break off a *píosa beag* and share it with the whole world.

Alison Curtis

Alison Curtis moved from Canada to Ireland in 1999. She now lives in Dublin with musician husband Anton Hegarty and their 10-year-old daughter Joan. Alison produced the *Ian Dempsey Breakfast* show for nine years, and is currently presenting one of Today FM's biggest shows, the *Weekend Breakfast Show* on Saturday and Sunday mornings. Alison lectures in radio and has a regular parenting column with the *Irish Examiner*.

Love Letter to Ireland

I love Ireland. I fell in love with the country before I even moved here on a trip during summer holidays while I was still in university. A close pal and I travelled through England, Wales and on to Ireland where we were so blown away by the charm and beauty of the country and its people that I subconsciously must have made up my mind then to move here.

Fast forward a few years and the plan was to pass through Ireland again on my way to complete a Masters in Glasgow. I never got to Glasgow. Instead, I got a room in a house in Glasnevin in Dublin and a temp job as PA to the then CEO of Today FM.

That job was short lived as my tea making and note taking skills were awful and I wanted a job on a show, which happened to be a defining moment of my life. My first radio gig was on *The Ian Dempsey Breakfast* show and 20 years later I am still loving creating and presenting shows for radio.

Life in Dublin and in radio was exciting. Way more exciting and social than even my 'college years'. Immediately I noticed that you could go out any night of the week, find a crowd and have the most fun. Irish people are social, they are welcoming, they seek out a good time and I really felt included from the first few weeks I lived here.

Things were very different to Canada. Canadians in general are a bit more reserved and certainly less spontaneous. I loved when a few drinks were mentioned on a Thursday and what was meant was going out that actual day! Not a few days or a week from then.

There are a lot of cultural and social differences between Ireland and Canada which I had to learn to navigate during my first few years living in Ireland.

When I first moved here, I noticed Irish people tended to be private and bounce the focus off of themselves in conversations. I also really got the sense that people were living for the moment. Not for tomorrow and not for a month's time. I felt people lived for today and to make the best of it. I really admired that and pushed myself to be more like that.

I also had to learn to let go a lot when I moved here and not take everything so literally. I had to learn to joke and to tease and not worry about being on time! When someone suggested meeting at 8.00 what they really mean is 8:30 and that it is totally okay.

I also had to stop asking for a ride and replace it with a request for a lift. Gradually my language changed and so did my expressions. My accent may have remained pretty solidly Canadian, but I most definitely converse like an Irish person now.

I also learned the true meanings of the word 'grand'. That sometimes people use it to move the conversation along and to respect that. Other times what they really meant was things aren't so good and after a little while you might get to the bottom of it with them. People might also say it with an expression of sarcasm or sincerity, all of these tiny readings of people helped me become Irish too.

During the years when everyone was leaving the country and so many people were taking up residence in Canada, I was repeatedly asked why am I still here? It made me sad to see, that for some people they no longer saw what I saw in this wonderful tiny nation.

Thankfully, that shifted after a few years and hundreds and thousands of people returned 'home' and that sense of Irish pride grew again. People started setting up creative businesses, helped local communities flourish again, start their own families in towns and villages they grew up in and it was wonderful to see.

Then in 2013 after a good bit of paper and leg work I became an Irish citizen. It was honestly one of the proudest moments of my life. To become part of a collection of people who look after one another and have one of the strongest senses of national identity I have ever come across.

We Irish have pride, we have innovation, we are independent thinkers, we are hilarious and we are unique. I am proud to be Irish.

Emma DeSouza

Emma DeSouza is a law reform advocate in constitutional law. She successfully reaffirmed the identity and citizenship provisions of the Good Friday Agreement by securing legislative changes to domestic UK immigration law. Emma is a writer, public speaker, political commentator and civic rights campaigner.

'You can't stop the suns from setting'

For most people, their identity is not something that can be taken away or questioned. Described as 'the condition of being oneself' and protected in countless treaties worldwide, identity has been long accepted as a human right. It was paramount to the Good Friday Agreement, which is where it carries an even greater significance and weight.

Since 1998, there have been significant shifts in cultural and political identities, with more and more people moving away from the historically binary identity politics of the region. The post-GFA generation continue to subscribe to a more plural concept of identity, with recent polling from both the Northern Irish Life and Times Survey and Lucid Talk revealing significant generational divides. Results from the NILT survey displayed that only 14 per cent of those aged 18-24 describe themselves as British, compared to the 49 per cent of those aged 65 and older.

The survey also demonstrated that 34 per cent of individuals between ages 18-24 hold an Irish identity, while 36 per cent hold a Northern Irish identity. The many diverse and varied birds of the Galapagos developed unique traits and characteristics resulting from the innumerable influences of their environment over many generations. So too has a plurality of identity developed in Northern Ireland. The recent growth of a Northern Irish identity is often misinterpreted to imply tacit support for the partition of Ireland. This deliberately myopic mindset once again breeds a desperate grasp at labels, most of which only fit the outdated socio-political divisions of the past. A Northern Irish identity is not synonymous with any-one view on the constitutional position of Northern Ireland. Rather, it is a manifestation of an attachment to one's homeplace, and given the rich culture unique to the North, such a manifestation is entirely natural.

The growth of those identifying as neither unionist nor nationalist has also been on the rise. The broadening community is of particular interest to many within both unionism and nationalism, with the 'others' being perceived as so-called 'kingmakers' in any referendum on constitutional change. However, the enigmatic nature of the community has left both unionism and nationalism struggling to understand the group. Nonetheless, both will undoubtedly be vying for their support.

Perpetuating the narrative that the people of Northern Ireland merely file into one of two communities often still sparring with each other is not representative of the current state of the region, but rather is a depiction oft used to suit a political agenda. Despite political inaction, and a failure to fully implement many of the rights-based provisions of the Good Friday Agreement, the people have embedded for themselves the true meaning of reconciliation.

There remain fragments of the past strewn throughout even the most mundane of our everyday interactions. Language, for example, may still be misinterpreted as an indication of one's political beliefs – an oftentimes subconscious practice for most, while other times a strategic choice deliberately weaponised by those stuck firmly in the past. In my own recent experience, I was told by an individual on social media to stop using the term 'Northern Ireland' unless I 'support partition'. This egocentric motivation to project one's own personal connotations on to the verbiage of others completely ignores subjectivity in the misguided pursuit of political correctness. Forcing others to only use prescribed language which they perceive to align with their own ideals ignores the all-important nuance inherent in each individual's life experience.

In this region, our relationship with words, titles and places can sometimes feel as personal as our own identity. Like many, I consciously try to refer to our province by all of its many names: 'the North', 'NI', 'Northern Ireland'. I do this deliberately to be as inclusive as possible and have personally never associated any connotation with the term 'Northern Ireland'. My use of this denomination does not define nor reflect my position on the constitutional question. I can support constitutional change and still use this term; in the words of Seamus Mallon, 'I don't care what you call this place, as long as you call it home'.

The importance of identity, and its complexity, lay at the centre of my own lived experiences after I was ensnared in a half-a-decade long court challenge with the British Home Office over the right to be accepted as Irish.

Referred to as the first human rights case of the Good Friday Agreement, the case resulted in legislative changes to UK immigration law. To pursue the case, I had to forensically dissect my Irish identity, its value, worth and substance. Being Irish was never a choice or a decision – it is integral to my culture and heritage. Being a part of the Irish nation is to belong to a community that knows no borders or boundaries. It is a rich and storied history of embrace and generosity; that is what being Irish means to me today, generosity of spirit and inclusivity.

We are all products of our environment, born to our respective plots of earth, with our beliefs, morals and choices in-turn borne of the million tiny slices of life we slip through as we grow old. Identity lines in Northern Ireland are shifting, the island of Ireland is on the cusp of transformative reinvention and Brexit is likely to speed-up that process.

To quote a lesser-known Skywalker, 'You can't stop change any more than you can stop the suns from setting'.

Martin E. Dempsey

General Martin E. Dempsey recently retired after 41 years of military service. In his last assignment he was the 18th Chairman of the Joint Chiefs of Staff, the highest ranking officer in the US armed forces and principal military advisor to the President. He was one of *Time* magazine's 100 most influential leaders in 2015, and in 2016 was inducted into the Irish-America Hall of Fame.

The Irish-American General

In 2013, in the middle of my time as Chairman of the Joint Chiefs of Staff, one of my international counterparts asked me if I knew what made America great. I hesitated. He didn't. 'I'll tell you what it is,' he said, 'it's the dash.'

He went on to explain that in the eyes of the rest of the world, America is unique because we have somehow figured out how to take different races, different ethnicities and different cultures and convince them that they all belong and all have something to contribute in our country.

'That is a source of great strength,' he said.

I agree. My dash is that I'm the Irish-American grandson of four Irish immigrants.

One of them, Grandma Bridget, was the larger-than-life figure in my childhood. Bridget had traveled to America on her own from County Mayo when she was 16. Six years later she married John Og Devenney from County Donegal who had come to America in the early 1920s.

When he died at 44, she was left a young widow. With his life insurance, she purchased a small, two-family house on 3rd street in Bayonne, New Jersey. She lived upstairs; we lived downstairs. In the years before we were old enough to go to school, or later when we had a school holiday, she often cared for us. In doing so, she was determined to make sure we knew that we were Irish, Catholic and American. In that order.

One day in 1958, when I was six years old, my Grandmother took me by the hand and walked me to Mary Jane Donahue Elementary School in Bayonne. She worked at the school part time as a janitor. On this day, like many others, she would open the gym and give me a basketball so that I could entertain myself while she fulfilled her responsibility to clean the school. Sometimes I wearied of the basketball and I would wander the corridors until I found her somewhere in the school diligently accomplishing her responsibilities. I remember the care and attention she took even in the most menial tasks. There were no short cuts in Grandma Bridget's life. She found true joy in an honest day's work.

My parents, Moe and Sarah, both worked. Both of them had to work 'to make ends meet' as they described it in their matter-of-fact way. Moe as a warehouseman for the Esso Oil Company, and Sarah stocking shelves in a convenience store in Jersey City. Neither ever missed a day of work in my memory. Despite their diligence, the ends didn't always meet. On those occasions, an aunt or an uncle would show up at the house with bags full of groceries.

Weekends, especially Sundays, were family affairs. After Church of course. As far as I could tell, at least until I became involved in intracity sports, everyone in Bayonne was Irish, and it seemed to me that I was related to most of them. Later I discovered that the Irish population in Bayonne was concentrated from First street to Eighth street in the southern end of the city. But in those eight city blocks, I learned about music and dancing, about sports, religion and politics, and, of course, about the 'old country'.

In the summer of 1961, when I was 9 years old, Grandma Bridget took me to Ireland for the first time. We stayed with her sister Ellie and her family on their farm in Castlebar in County Mayo. There were seven of us in an 800 square foot three-bedroom cottage with neither refrigeration nor plumbing but with an abundance of joy. Each day, the cows had to be milked, the hay in the fields needed to be cut and bundled and brought in for the winter, and about every other week, someone would have to make a trip in the ass and cart to cut turf to fire the stove for heat and cooking. Every day was a new adventure, and every evening a different relative would drop by to meet the young 'Yank' come over from America.

> *Early in our month-long visit, my great grandfather took me into Castlebar to his favorite pub to show me off to his mates. When we returned to the farm, Grandma Bridget said something sternly to him in Gaelic. The unmistakable smell of cigarette smoke on my clothing had quickly spoiled our little secret. He just laughed.*

When we boarded the airplane to return home, I cried.

To me, being Irish is about faith and hope, humility and hard work, family and music, good humor and the good kind of stubbornness.

I reflect on my Irish roots often. In those moments, I sometimes hear the distant echoes of lilting brogues, the voices of those who worked so hard to give me so many wonderful opportunities. They remind me that 'if you're lucky enough to be Irish, then you're lucky enough.' So true.

Flossie Donnelly

Flossie is a 14-year-old marine environmentalist and climate activist in Ireland. She set up the charity 'Flossie and the Beachcleaners', which raises awareness of plastic pollution, along with her Mum, Harriet, when she was 11.

To me Ireland is a country of unity and hope!

I'm a 14-year-old marine environmentalist and climate activist in Ireland and I worry about the climate and weather, also how the changes we make have a good or bad effect on the climate!

I've been beach cleaning for five years because we have such a beautiful biosphere and our marine life which spans from lobster and crabs to basking sharks to visiting humpback whales and so much in between. So it's unthinkable that our marine life is being strangled by pollution and sewage-filled water!

When I was 11 my Mum and I set up a charity. We do workshops and teach junior school kids and Transition Year students about plastic pollution, and also connect to schools and conservation trusts in Indonesia and other countries on the other side of the world where Climate Change affects them first-hand. We see how much children want to save their planet from the workshops we give, and also how much they enjoy saving their planet!

I live in Sandycove with my family and since I was born, Ireland has been constantly changing and having to readjust as we are faced with different emergencies. It could be politics, Covid or climate change, and this is why when I think of Ireland I think of 'unity', because when a crisis falls on Ireland we work together to fix it! Our solutions may not always be right, but we continue to try to fix the problem until we find the correct solution. Look at Covid – it hit the world and no one knew what was best for their country so they all separated and tried different tactics to try to keep their country safe. Covid isn't over yet but we have all come together as a country to try to stop it; we have made changes that three years ago we couldn't have even imagined, all to keep one another safe.

We are all constantly trying to work out how we can solve climate change which is hard because it's a global problem which is still not being viewed as one. Some people still don't believe in climate change, either because of a lack of education or they are scared. My Mum and I believe environmentalism should be taught as a core subject in junior and senior school.

Because let's face it, my generation is being handed a broken planet unlike the past generations and we are the ones who are going to fix it, but for that to happen we need to understand climate change and how to stop it. That's why if environmentalism was a core subject in Ireland it would focus on how to actively help the climate instead of just charts and graphs which young kids cannot understand and older kids can find overwhelming!

Future generations will look back on us and will either see us as villains who had a chance to stop climate change and ignored it or heroes who saw a problem and decided to fix it. The clock is ticking and soon we will only be seen as villains… Covid has given us a very small reset, but we need everyone to work together now and treat climate change as they treated Covid… we have a chance to change, we have to take it.

When I think of Ireland I think of hope because we came together as a country, all four million of us, to stop Covid-19 so I have no doubt that we can do the same for climate change. Before Covid I always tried to be optimistic about climate change and how we can solve it but a part of me was always scared as Ireland was one of the worst countries in Europe for climate change and so many people still don't believe in it but now I know we can solve it. After all, Ireland is an incredible country filled with incredible people like Mary Robinson who has an amazing quote which is the charity's motto, 'Fear Paralyses, Hope Energizes', or Dara McAnulty who constantly writes beautiful books about his love of nature, or Henry Denny who invented the bacon rasher, and Mr Tayto who created Ireland's favourite crisp and all of the Irish Gretas who are constantly trying to stop climate change!

I'm proud to be Irish because we are blessed to live in this beautiful country which has the most incredible marine life from our playful seals to our basking sharks and such supportive and kind people. This is a country that truly understands teamwork and when abroad support each other like no other country. This is a country of hope, this is Ireland!

Lola Donoghue

Lola Donoghue is a contemporary Irish artist. Her work is held in private collections around the world.

I'm not sure that I felt particularly Irish growing up; at least it wasn't something I was acutely aware of. The Holy Trinity of being Irish – religion, GAA and an awareness of a complicated history with the English had largely passed me by. We weren't overtly religious, my siblings weren't particularly into football or hurling and as for the English, there was nothing complicated about how I felt. My granny had married an Englishman whom I adored and summers were spent in their always sunny, perfectly English garden, shopping in large department stores, discovering the High Street shops and getting the bus to town, all very civil and proper and a world away from the stone walls, green fields and shop streets of the West of Ireland. It was on those sepia-toned holidays I first became aware of being Irish as I repeated phrases for my English cousins who smiled indulgently at my lilting Irish accent.

When I travelled abroad, I again became aware of my Irishness. Firstly as a people, we are beloved by everyone, or so it felt, everyone I met proclaimed some Irish heritage and being Irish was nearly a buy into any group, an automatic reference as you will. Secondly, the banter, self-deprecation and slagging I had grown up with was uniquely Irish, most other people can graciously accept a compliment, don't answer a greeting with the requisite 'grand', and can complain with confidence if service or meal doesn't meet muster! Through my work, I no longer need to travel to feel that Irishness. I am reminded time and time again of my Irish identity through the countless dm's and emails from people all over the world who want a little piece of Ireland in their home, who feel a connection to Ireland through my paintings. They might have studied in Galway or had parents from Donegal, or maybe fell in love with an Irishman and can't wait to visit, so it's hard not to feel a sense of pride at being Irish, to feel a little bit special.

Not having grown up with the GAA gene, it was through my fiancée Trevor, a former Mayo captain, that I experienced the true love Irish people have for their national game, the pride felt for club and county and the instant respect and regard this earned him; it spoke of his character and was a commonality and connection felt by most Irish. Now I spend my weekends on the sidelines of my children's first foray into football and hurling, the lure of one day playing for your club, a seed planted at an early age, planted and nurtured through ritual, tradition and community, guaranteed to thrive as parents proudly watch on. The same sense of commitment and volunteerism that was the backbone of the church in Ireland is what keeps the GAA thriving.

My first real experience of religion or Catholicism in Ireland was the Sisters of Mercy. After my parents' separation, we moved from the rural countryside to the urban setting of a three-bed terraced house in the town of Tuam. Being the youngest, they took particular interest and I wanted for nothing growing up, took part in all the extra curriculars and while they may not have halted my gallivanting around town, those extra eyes on me ensured I didn't get up to too much. My first and one of my favourite art teachers was a lovely, engaging and open-minded nun. They kept up with my progress throughout college, celebrating every win as their own, and even now as an adult, a week doesn't go by that Sister Geraldine doesn't check in with my Mother to see how we are. It's safe to say their kindness and interest has greatly influenced who I am today.

I realise that everyone has a different experience and any good the Catholic Church did is certainly not a popular opinion right now.

Almost 800 children's remains are buried in a septic tank across the road from where I grew up. It's hard to marry the actions of a church that committed such atrocities in the past to the caring individuals I grew up with.

Past sins are being uncovered, repentance is slow but times are changing. While I am sad that my children will not have those extra eyes on them as they gallivant, I am hopeful for the future of an Ireland where my daughter will never know the phrase 'getting the boat to England', the home babies of Tuam will hopefully have been acknowledged and public recourse paid to them and their families in as much as it can be, and hopefully, we will have a National Maternity Hospital where patient autonomy is key. My children will grow up without any of the bias of my youth; they live in a multicultural society, study world religions and have choices that previous generations didn't have.

What does it mean to be Irish? We are a nation of tea drinkers who have embraced the takeaway coffee, a people who still thank the bus driver as we disembark, a people who repealed the Eighth, voted for love and equality on the 16 November 2015, reflected in the history making leadership of our country yet still wonder who did bring the horse to France. We don't offend easily and take pride in a good slagging match; in fact, it is safe to say we'd rather an insult then a compliment .We are a nation of drinkers and poets, we have a way with words, we are likeable, never ones to go above their station but if we did we didn't brag about it. We have a national holiday, Saint Patrick's Day, its famous parade introduced by the US diaspora to remember home, and now celebrated internationally. A cynic might say it is a marketing dream as famous landmarks around the world cast an emerald hue on the 17th of March each year, but for a small island nation it's hard not to feel pride, to feel a little bit special, and know that we have left our mark globally in more ways than one.

Brian Dooley

Brian Dooley (@dooley_dooley) is a human rights activist and author of books including *Choosing the Green?* about the contribution of second generation Irish people to Irish history, and *Black and Green: The Fight for Civil Rights in Northern Ireland and Black America.*

More than 20 years ago, for the first edition of this book, I wrote about growing up as a London Irish teenager during the 1970s and 1980s. We weren't living The Troubles anything like the way kids in Belfast were, but the conflict threw a constant shadow over us, and largely defined our Irishness.

Two decades on, although much has changed about what it means to be Irish, expressing that identity is still often an uphill struggle. Irish (and British) people regularly question the authenticity of second generation Irishness. The Plastic Paddy charge now has a fresh new energy since the surge in Irish passport applications following Brexit, and a proposed referendum about letting us vote in Irish presidential elections.

We're routinely asked to prove what makes us Irish, tested again and again to meet a standard never asked of people with Irish accents.

Believe me, you can end up doing all sorts of things proving how Irish you are. Some people represent London at GAA (I did that), or earn a silver *fainne* for being able to speak basic Irish (I did that too), or write books about the diaspora in Irish history (I even did that), or get a tattoo across their chest *as Gaeilge* of the place where their family is from in Kerry (I really did).

But for some people it will never be enough. You could win the Eurovision for Ireland, kick the winning point for Kerry in the All-Ireland final, and head the goal that beats England to win the world cup. You could take a lap of honour in the Olympic stadium draped in the tricolour after taking gold for Ireland, invent a new Taytos flavour, and parade around wearing de Valera's glasses and Michael Collins' wolf slippers, but unless you *sound* Irish it won't really count.

I've learned that when saying you're Irish the question, *But where were you born?* usually means, *Why do you sound like that?* The bigotry around accent is often coded in questions about birthplace.

But really no one questioned world cup legends Paul McGrath's Irishness, or David O'Leary's, although both were born in England. Because they have Dublin accents that was okay, but for Irish soccer international Steve Finnan (born in Limerick but speaks with a London accent) there were suspicions.

Soon after my last essay for the *Being Irish* book Roy Keane made a spectacular outburst against Mick McCarthy during preparations for the 2002 world cup. Early reports said Keane had told McCarthy he was 'a crap player' and 'a crap manager', and that 'you're not even Irish, you English cunt'.

The shocker was the use of the E word, because in a Plastic Paddy context there can be no greater insult. Maybe Keane borrowed the slur from another angry young Cork man 80 years earlier.

During the explosive Dáil debates on whether to accept or reject the Anglo-Irish Treaty of 1921, Michael Collins lashed out at second generation TDs fighting the deal. Spying Constance Markiewicz, Éamon de Valera and Erskine Childers on the opposite benches, he searched for the ultimate insult. 'Deserters all to the Irish nation!' he sputtered. 'Foreigners – Americans – English!'

Irish people with London, Liverpool, Glaswegian and other British city accents played a leading role in the founding of modern Ireland.

Many of the Volunteers who first stormed the GPO on Easter Monday 1916 were second generation. For some their first visit to Ireland was to fight in its revolution.

They have been largely airbrushed out of popular histories of the Rising and the War for Independence. You know that scene in the epic biopic *Michael Collins* where Collins (played by Liam Neeson) gets smuggled into police headquarters in Dublin's Brunswick Street and spends the night locked inside a small room, going through police intelligence files on Sinn Féin? It really happened, in April 1919, but Collins was with Sean Nunan, and there's no place in the film for the boy from Brixton with the south London accent.

It can be hard to identify as Irish when you sound Cockney. I can speak English in a very passable west Kerry accent, but really, why should I? Why the hierarchy of Irishness? The only one of the 40 shades of green to matter should be the one on your passport (and even that's purple).

The wonderfully bonkers 1971 film *Flight of the Doves*, about two young Liverpool-Irish kids escaping back to Ireland, includes a massive parade in Dublin's Phoenix Park where a dazzling ensemble sings, 'You Don't Have To Be Irish To Be Irish', as though Being Irish is a state of mind. It's a great idea, if tricky to argue at passport control in an airport.

For some of us, it turns out that Being Irish is often pretty complicated, and involves a lifetime commitment to constantly proving it.

See you in 20 years for updates on how it's going.

Colum Eastwood

Colum Eastwood was elected Leader of the SDLP in November 2015 and as the MP for Foyle in 2019. At the age of 27, he became Derry's youngest ever Mayor, and has also served as a Derry City Councillor and MLA in the Northern Ireland Assembly. A firm believer in social justice and human rights, Colum has been an enduring advocate for the Bloody Sunday families and those whose loved ones were murdered in their campaign for truth and justice.

It is difficult to overstate the scale of change that has taken place in Ireland over the course of the past decade. Our island, known across the world for the warmth of our welcome and the generosity of our people, has changed beyond recognition and it has undoubtedly changed for the better.

When *Being Irish* was originally published, we were right in the middle of a real revolution in Irish politics. The culmination of the talks that led to the Good Friday Agreement, the subsequent referenda across the island and the end to violence in the pursuit of political goals was an incredible moment that lifted the spirits of people and communities across Ireland, regardless of background, class or creed. It was at that time that I first became politically active, joining the SDLP as a teenager to campaign in the referendum on the agreement in the North. Anyone who knocked doors during that seminal moment in Irish history got a real sense of the ambitions, hopes and desires of ordinary people who had lived through an extraordinary period. Without fail, every person

I spoke to conveyed the deep rooted values of modern Ireland – care for their neighbours, compassion for people they share this island with and, above all else, an unshakeable desire to build a better country for everyone.

In spite of our contested past, I think that spirit of reconciliation is a fundamental part of the Irish experience. I was confronted, very literally, with it again as a young man in Derry. It was the end of a long and difficult summer that had seen clashes between people from different traditions during the marching season. Tensions were high, tempers were flared and there seemed to be no space for healing between those who occupied our shared towns and cities. I was in the diamond, in the centre of Derry, with SDLP members as a loyal order parade was passing. And as a foolish and hot-headed young man, I muttered something unkind or uncharitable.

What I wasn't banking on was John Hume, Nobel Laureate, MP, MEP, SDLP Leader and one of my heroes, hearing me. He took me by the shoulders and I'll never forget him saying, 'Colum, if the people of Derry, this great nationalist city, can't demonstrate to our unionist neighbours that they are a valued and valuable part of our community, what chance do we have of ever uniting this island?'

It was a stark reminder, from a man who lived the values of care, compassion and reconciliation every day, that we all have to work relentlessly to accommodate one another and build our shared home place.

Today, I think those values remain. We've had a fair few referenda since the Good Friday Agreement in 1998 but at all times, in every campaign I've experienced, people have been overwhelmingly motivated by their desire to look after their neighbour. Marriage Equality and the campaign to repeal the Eighth Amendment of the constitution clearly demonstrate that a society which has been repressed and oppressed over the course of centuries, when given the chance to take a stand for the rights of their friends, families and neighbours, will not hesitate to do the right thing. The images of planes, boats and buses filled to the brim with young Irish men and women travelling huge distances to cast a vote to secure rights and dignity for people they may not know, or ever meet, was a moment of liberation for our island.

For me, that's at the heart of what it means to be Irish. It's a strong sense of empathy and compassion for others, it's what motivates the depth of our generosity and the warmth of our welcome. It is living the maxim that there is so much more that unites us than could divide us. As an island with a contested past, we haven't always lived up to those values. But in this new century I believe we have an opportunity to redefine our island, recommit to those values and build a home that we all share, together.

Linda Ervine

Linda Ervine was born into a working class Protestant family in east Belfast. She is the first Irish Language Officer to be based in a loyalist area. The centre is now one of the largest providers of Irish language classes in Belfast. In 2013 Linda received the Roll of Honour in the Aisling Award for her work promoting the Irish language. In 2015 she received the CRC Civic Leadership Award, in 2020 she received the Eastside Community Champion Award and she was recently awarded an MBE.

When I was a child no one ever sat me down and told me that I was Irish, it was something that I just always knew. It was as plain to me as the fact that I was a girl and that I had blue eyes and blonde hair. It was just who I was.

When I was young I spent a lot of time with my grandparents. My Nanny was a typical Belfast matriarch and my Grandfather, a quieter personality, was from Essex. He had come to Belfast in the 1930s, making it his home after marrying my Nanny and going on to have a family of five sons. When my Nanny and Granda fell out, according to her, he was that 'bloody English man' which distinguished him from us as we were Irish.

My first husband had joined the Irish Rangers before we met and he served three years in the British Army. On his army papers his nationality was recorded as British/Irish. He was a young Protestant man from the Newtownards Road in east Belfast, who told me stories of how he proudly wore the bunch of shamrock that was presented to all of the Rangers each St Patrick's Day. Celebrating St Patrick's Day was just as important to him after leaving the army as it had been during his years of service. I also have many happy memories of St Patrick's Day parties when we celebrated our patron saint and our Irishness. Imagine my shock when in my thirties someone tried to tell me that I wasn't Irish and that this isn't Ireland! And this was something that occurred in my life post the Good Friday Agreement! Suddenly there seemed to be this new mindset that we are not and never have been Irish. For me it was like being asked to say that black is white and white is black.

How can you live in a place with the name Northern Ireland and yet be convinced that it is not nor never was part of Ireland? To be au fait with the Church of Ireland, the Presbyterian Church in Ireland, the Methodist Church in Ireland, the Irish Football Association, etc, etc, and yet to deny the Irishness of Northern Ireland? Strangely, some people are convinced that partition changed the geography of this place.

So why am I confident of my Irishness even though I hear these dissenting voices around me? Well, I am Irish because I was born on the island of Ireland. I'm as Irish as my two grandmothers, one a Protestant, Annie Watson, the other a Catholic, Kathleen Kelly, both born in Belfast in 1910 before Ireland was partitioned. I'm Irish in the same way that people born in other parts of the UK claim their regional identity as well as their over-arching British identity. If someone in England is English and British, or someone in Wales is Welsh and British, or someone in Scotland is Scottish and British, how can anyone deny that I am Irish and British? To deny my Irishness is to suggest that I do not belong here, that I am a usurper, that I have no right to be here. The opposite is true, I am a native of this place!

Sometimes I feel that as northern Protestants we are the forgotten, ignored Irish. We're not Catholic, we're not southerners, we're not what literature has portrayed as Irish, but that doesn't make us any less a part of this island or any less Irish.

Learning the Irish language has created within me even more of a sense of belonging to this place. Knowledge of the placenames has enriched me and given me a new insight and awareness of the place that is my home. I have discovered that I live at 'the mouth of the sand back Ford' close to 'the fort of the foals' and 'the hill of the rabbits'. And some people might be surprised to discover that it was my introduction to Irish that introduced me to the beauty of Ulster Scots, which we also see in our placenames, for example, every brae, burn and whin is of Scots origin.

The phrase 'Tá Gaeilge agam' literally means I have Gaelic and it is how you would say that you are an Irish speaker. I remember thinking that I would like to be able to say, 'Tá Gaeilge agam', that I would like it to be part of who I am. Ten years later I can do exactly that.

Even though I am still very much a learner and a struggler with the language, I have enough of it to now be able to say 'Tá Gaeilge agam'. The language has become part of my identity. I use it every day in my worklife, speak it with my friends, read it, write it and continue to learn it. For me this is an example of how identity is not a separate element which you can box and label; it is complex and fluid, multi-faceted and rich with nuance. My identity draws not only on my own lived experience but that of the generations who came before me. I embrace and celebrate it all as part of both my Irish and British identity.

Sinéad Flanagan

Sinéad Flanagan from Adare in County Limerick is the current Rose of Tralee having won the title in 2019. She qualified as a Physiotherapist from the University of Limerick in 2014 and subsequently studied Medicine in University College Cork. She now works as a doctor in a Dublin hospital.

As an Irish woman who can trace back her ancestry for several generations, I have always had a strong sense of my Irish identity. However, my perception of 'being Irish' certainly evolved with my Rose of Tralee experience. I have long been fascinated by the connection the International Roses have with Ireland, many of whose ancestors left Ireland decades or even centuries ago. One American Rose in my 2019 group became aware of her Irish heritage solely through a commercial DNA test, but was in fact one of the most passionate Irish people I have ever encountered. The women who participate in the Rose festival are striking ambassadors for the desire of their families to keep Irish heritage alive overseas. This enduring pull to an ancestral home from which emigration long preceded their birth prompted me to consider my own perception of my 'Irishness'.

The contradictory nature of many aspects of our Irish identity fascinates me. As a people, we love our native shore and yet we love to travel the world. Our wander lust and adventurous spirit takes us to the four corners of the world but yet at every opportunity we identify our Irishness and proudly portray it. Not alone do we show off our Irish identity but also treasure 'I loves me county' even more when abroad.

A lot of us like to believe that as Irish people we share many common traits. Yet many people of my generation believe we are very much individuals with important contributions to make on the international stage. In some senses we celebrate the nostalgic preservation of our traditional Irish identity, and at the same time we welcome the homogeneity and heterogeneity of globalisation. Even though wary of generalisations, I sense that Roses with more distant links with Ireland are very comfortable with the traditional Irish identity, whilst those with more recent associations are keen to portray a more modern Irish outlook.

Another fascinating contradiction in Irish people is our humility and our confidence. A *New York Times* feature on the 2019 Rose Festival stated that part of what makes the event so quintessentially Irish is the premium everyone places on humility with a disdain for 'showing off'. Yet all the Roses were, and are, confident and ambitious young women eager to achieve their potential. Interestingly, as a nation, we are fiercely competitive in a sporting sense and as a proud Limerick woman this is a trait I greatly admire. Ultimately, I believe, as Irish people we dislike pretension and prefer our confidence to be low key.

We are an optimistic nation and I witness the power of this optimism daily in my working life. However, endearingly or otherwise, we retain a healthy scepticism which allows us to be critical and pessimistic often cloaked in humour.

My Irish identity is rooted in a few key areas, such as friendships. I believe we are a friendly people with a huge capacity for making and keeping friends. Friendship is the major component of the Rose of Tralee success story over 60 years, and is the aspect that I have found most enjoyable and sustaining. Since the festival, I have formed enduring friendships with many of the 2019 Roses. I acted as bridesmaid for one of the girls last summer and look forward to the favour being returned in 2022!

Wit and humour are also key components of our make-up. Our disposition to see the funny side of things, the gift of gentle self-deprecation and the ability to 'slag' or more importantly 'take a slag' are all at the heart of our Irish identity. Having the 'craic' continues to be a very Irish trait and is, arguably, the aspect of our identity that attracts most people. The ability to deliver a 'party piece' remains a much admired talent.

> *There is, and always has been, a community solidarity associated with 'Irishness'. It is based on kinship and family values and is a powerful force in Irish life. From this solidarity, I believe, comes our generosity of spirit.*

During my medical training, I witnessed first-hand the generosity of Irish people through fundraising efforts for the Surgeon Noonan Society, a charity providing medical aid to healthcare centres across Africa. As a Rose, I was privileged to witness the extraordinary work of Irish people with the Hope Foundation in Kolkata and Chernobyl Children International. I have also been honoured to be involved in other fundraising activities, all of which illustrate that our traditional caring and generous spirit is alive and well.

Ultimately, I believe our Irish identity is centred on community. That community is a diaspora of over 70 million people worldwide who cherish their Irish heritage, a heritage that celebrates our sense of place, our sense of origin and our sense of pride.

Eileen Flynn

Senator Eileen Flynn is the first Traveller/Mincéir to serve in the Houses of the Oireachtas. Her background is in community development and activism on behalf of Irish Travellers and in solidarity with other ethnic minorities. She was one of the first in her family, along with her twin sister, to attend university earning an Honours Degree in Community Work from NUI Maynooth. She lives in Donegal with her husband Liam and young daughter.

When I was a child, a young Traveller growing up in the halting site in Labre Park in Ballyfermot, being Irish was all about music and culture, about family and community. In many ways, that is still what it is about for me.

My father was an extremely good accordion player and I know a little accordion – my father taught me – though I wouldn't be great at it now, to be honest. But I grew up in that kind of household, listening to traditional music and musicians, going to Mass on Sundays, taking family trips to Glendalough and to the lakes in the Wicklow mountains.

We loved the GAA from a very young age, wearing the Dublin jerseys and Kilkenny jerseys. We had the best of both worlds when it came to the GAA because Dublin would always win the football and Kilkenny would always win the hurling. And the atmosphere around All-Ireland day, no matter who was playing.

We went to a lot of matches at Croke Park and standing on Hill 16 makes you pure Dublin as well as Irish, that kind of a way. I had the opportunity to travel as a younger person and have been to Brazil and also to many European countries. But my favourite city in the world is Dublin. And I feel like crying, even saying that.

Going to school in Ballyfermot and not learning the Irish language was a bit disheartening, but I don't think that makes me any less of an Irish person, nor does it make me any less of an Irish Traveller. I speak Cant, or Gammon, though I wouldn't be fluent. That's part of what being Irish is to me, too.

Being Irish means you're privileged. If we look at Ireland today, it's good to see the diversity, it's good to see inclusion and the embracing of other cultures. And I think for us as a nation we have to understand that – we did enough emigrating ourselves, and we are connected nearly all over the world. It's that sense of connection as well that to me is about being Irish.

I remember my mother always saying to treat everybody equal and that's where I get this from. Never judge a person. My mother said – and I've said this many times – nobody knows the shoes cutting them, only the person who's wearing them.

Having that level of empathy is what's nice about being Irish – not being judgemental and looking at people who are in difficult situations and knowing it could be you.

Sometimes we say Ireland is the friendliest country in the world, and a lot of the time I don't see that. There are an awful lot of people in Ireland who are left behind and don't have equality of opportunity, and that includes migrant people, refugees, Traveller people, people with disabilities.

I can't forget living the experience of discrimination and unfortunately that's part of my being Irish – having those memories as a child and feeling less than your peers. It has been people in my life, good people, who have empowered me.

Even though things seem to be changing, we need representation of all people across all of Irish society and that's something we're missing. We are missing vital voices.

That's why I stand up for human rights and equality, because I know what racism and discrimination feels like. 'Taking care of our own' is a statement I don't use. I may be born and reared in Ireland, and am so privileged to be born and reared in Ireland, but that doesn't make me more Irish than the person who wasn't born in the Coombe Hospital. People who live here, belong here.

We can't speak about being Irish and not mention the terrible way women were treated in the mother and baby homes. That's a shameful part of our history.

I also think of the great women I know who have helped to shape Ireland, great activists like Nan Joyce and Bernadette Devlin, Dr Hannah McGinley, Ailbhe Smyth – we have made some progress and I just think that is so important to recognise, though I do think we've got an awful long way to go.

We should keep lifting up people to do better and to engage with people in all communities in the Oireachtas, in Leinster House, in Stormont.

I know I may not see it in my time, but I would love to see a united Ireland. A united Ireland for me means an Ireland where all people are treated with dignity and respect, where there is an understanding that everyone is different, but should be treated as being of equal value and worth. An Ireland where everybody has equal opportunities, where there are no people in homelessness, where we treat people fairly.

Olwen Fouéré

Photo credit: Kevin Abosch

Born in Ireland of Breton parents, Olwen Fouéré is an actor, writer/director and creative artist working internationally in theatre, film, the visual arts and music.

These bones of sand

Sitting in a three way
waiting to be called
what does it mean
Identity:
Irish

not until birth
no Irish blood
not even a drop
post-war torn
from another edge
of Europe
with a tongue
only vaguely related

Olwen Fouéré

on the run

it's complicated

A name from the Mabinogion
translates
a trail of white flowers
or white foot print

facing west to the ocean
the first ground touched
by the baby foot
is Ireland
of that there is no doubt
of love there is abundance
of place
there is belonging

of place

these bones of sand
granite quartz and feldspar
this water of salt

and then
and then
the floating riddle of sound
called language
in silence found
true language
impossible to communicate
assimilate
or imitate
until the cowboy became indian
and vision grew
from land and sea
how much was due

Identity
human:
destroyer
forever
in debt
to an
other
species of being
restless
circling
question
to live in the question
a nomad

while war explodes
the island
a past and present
unresolved
impossible to turn back
so treacherous span
of time and place

and how to navigate the other chaos
unfolding secret
power greed and inequality
the curse of private property
the entitled few
the dispossessed
the no address

another riddle

for everybody must answer the sphynx

Olwen Fouéré

each step a word
a mark
a passing through
the inevitable

each footprint mine

and these bones
will be buried in sand
beside my bones

John Froude

Dr. John Froude is a practicing physician and Infectious Disease Specialist who graduated from Guy's Hospital London and has worked in the UK, Nigeria, Uganda, Zimbabwe, Saudi Arabia, Oman and the United States. In the USA he has worked at the Rockefeller University and New York University. Currently he works in upstate New York out of semiretirement for the Covid-19 pandemic. He is a Fellow of the Royal College of Physicians.

Privilege

My mother was born in Trillick, County Tyrone. One significance of this statement passed me by for fifty years.

I had been working in New York City for a decade or so and I was sitting one evening in Eamon Doran's bar with friends. A famous scientist at the Rockefeller University, whose mother came from Annalong, County Down, said to me in the course of a conversation on matters Irish that I would know all about that *being an Irish citizen*.

'Nah, come on mate,' I replied suavely, 'O gor blimey, stone the crows, leave it out, I'm bleeding English, in I?' My mother had travelled to England to be a nurse, where she met my father.

'Oh yes! Didn't you know? If either of your parents were born on the island of Ireland, north or south, you are automatically an Irish citizen. Whether Catholic, Protestant, Muslim, Hindu or Jain. If they were born in Ireland there's a welcome on the mat for their chisellers.'

'Begorrah,' says I.

It wasn't quite that simple.

Documents.

Two years later, with the assistance of relatives living in Ireland, it arrived. My Irish passport. I waltzed around my mailbox in upstate New York. I was elated. *The silver apples of the moon, the golden apples of the sun.*

It was another year before I went to my new home, the Republic.

At Dublin airport I stood in the Irish line at Immigration. The officer, a young man of forty, saw me clutching my Irish passport open at the photo page expectantly and waved me through.

'Aren't you going to stamp it?' I implored.

'No, it's all electrical these days.'

I drew myself up. 'This is an important moment for me, officer. I am entering Ireland as a citizen. With a passport. For the first time.'

In kindliness, he took the little brown booklet, looked at it upside down and handed it back.

'Privilege,' he said.

Taxi to town. Checked into an airbnb in Upper Baggot Street.

Privilege.

What did he mean? Well obviously he meant it was a great privilege for me. With which I wholeheartedly agree. But didn't he mean a little something extra? Maybe it's only 10 per cent but wasn't he saying it was Ireland's privilege for the son of one of the Daughters of Róisín to have taken up his birthright?

In any case, it was now time to celebrate my Irishness. I shall go unto a public house and I shall avow it there. Now it's Sunday night and ten p.m. Where will I find a pub under these circumstances? I had to walk nearly a hundred yards. It was William Searson's Public House. There were photographs of Flann O'Brien, Patrick Kavanagh, Samuel Beckett, my *countrymen*, by the main entrance.

I walked with purpose to the bar, and with full Irishness I said to the curate, 'I will take a *pint*.'

'A pint of what?'

'You're not Irish are you?'

'No, I am Italian, from Milano, how did you know?'

I struck up a conversation with the man leaning against the bar to my right. He was drinking half a pint of Guinness. He was German, visiting the city for a business meeting. In the corner an assembly of young men were singing rugby songs. They were Welsh, over for the International.

James Joyce has got his way. Dublin is a European capital.

I finished my pint and walked out past Toner's bar, past O'Donohues to St Stephen's Green. Past the Shelbourne Hotel to Grafton street. I walked down Grafton street towards Trinity College and stopped to watch the last of the buskers that night, a young man wearing a flat cap, with a guitar singing 'Raglan Road'. Then on towards the Liffey.

Privilege.

Niall Gibbons

Niall Gibbons is Chief Executive of Tourism Ireland. He oversees the marketing of the island of Ireland across the world, leading a team of over 160 staff in 21 markets. Niall is a business graduate of Trinity College Dublin and a Fellow of the Institute of Chartered Accountants in Ireland. He sits on the Irish Government's Export Trade Council, is a member of Culture Ireland's Expert Advisory Committee and an Honorary Fellow of the Institute of Hospitality in Ireland.

In my time working for Tourism Ireland – the organisation responsible for promoting the island of Ireland overseas as a compelling holiday destination – I have had many opportunities to reflect on what 'Being Irish' means to me and to others.

In my role as Chief Executive of Tourism Ireland, I have come across many people around the world with Irish connections and have spoken with them about their heritage. With an estimated 70 million people across the world claiming links or affiliations with the island of Ireland, we are extremely fortunate. In fact, we are the envy of many other countries in having such an influential and committed Diaspora. That Diaspora has reached every corner of the globe and I have met them in the most surprising of places, as well as in countries with a long history of emigration from Ireland, including Britain, the United States, Canada, Australia and New Zealand. It is clear to me that the three standout Irish characteristics, from a tourism perspective, are our warm and friendly welcome, our rich unspoilt and natural landscape and our culture. Our culture finds many forms of expression through music, poetry, dance, literature, theatre and many more. Dublin has been recognised as a UNESCO City of Literature. Yeats, Beckett, Heaney and Shaw have won Nobel Prizes for literature. From a contemporary perspective, our theatre and music festivals are still global magnets for tourism (obviously, in normal non-Covid times).

Our inability to travel freely around the world over the past year, due to Covid-19, has made many of us stop and think about our identity – from our appreciation of our own locality and our culture to the many things we have *not* been able to do, enjoy or see. For those of us who identify as Irish and those who have not been able to travel home, it has perhaps heightened the importance of our heritage. The bonds between Ireland and those who cherish their Irish heritage have never been stronger. And, for many people living overseas, particularly in distant countries such as Australia, the lack of opportunity to travel home and be with friends and family has been particularly difficult. A recurring theme through our international research during Covid-19 has been 'wholesome reconnection'. This found its expression through people who have swapped the dream of a once-in-a-lifetime braggable holiday for the opportunity to travel to familiar destinations that are closer to home and to reconnect with their friends and family whom they have missed during the pandemic.

All around the world, how we define our national identity is complicated and often fluid. When I stop and reflect on what it means to be Irish, I have asked myself the question, has the core of who we are changed over the decades? The question of how far we have come is often considered and, in my view, we have come some distance. But it is also clear that the Irish conversation around the globe is at different points in time. Emigrants to the United States in the 1950s hold a different view of Ireland than the people who left in waves for Canada and Australia during the global financial crisis around 2010. However, at the core, there is still a strong bond and pride in the sense of place.

I have been blown away by people's commitment to our Irish heritage and identity through the support for Tourism Ireland's annual Global Greening during St Patrick's Week. Every year, this initiative sees hundreds of iconic landmarks and sites around the world light up green to celebrate the island of Ireland and St Patrick. Our Global Greening first began in Australia – when the Sydney Opera House went green on 17 March 2010. Since then, it has gone from strength to strength every year, with a record 725 iconic landmarks in 71 different countries taking part in the 2021 Global Greening.

While Tourism Ireland has undoubtedly led the way on 'greening' famous landmarks for St Patrick's Day, the initiative could never have achieved its current global scale without the support of many of the millions of Irish men and women who left these shores and have gone on to make their mark on the world. So many of the 'greenings' have materialised simply because the people responsible for making the decision had a special place in their heart for Ireland. Our Global Greening project is a powerful symbol of the impact of our Irish abroad and is an expression of our reach, our shared values and our ambition. Global Greening, like our Diaspora, stretches across the world, to every continent, going beyond our historical connections into where we can now be found.

> *Being Irish also means having a capacity for humour – which is just as well, since in 2011, Tourism Ireland took credit for the 'greening' of London's Big Ben, when in fact the bell tower on Big Ben is always green!*

On my travels overseas, I have met many people who forged a special connection with Ireland following just a short holiday here, sometimes remembered from many years ago. Their experience has always been one of great hospitality and an extremely warm welcome, the kind of welcome that lasts long in the memory and encourages people to keep on returning again and again.

Equally, I meet people who deliver that warm welcome – thousands of highly experienced and skilled professionals across the tourism industry. This is an industry that has been deeply impacted by the pandemic, but an industry that is primed and ready to show what we have to offer to visitors from all over the globe.

Tourism Ireland was established after the Good Friday Agreement to promote the island of Ireland overseas. Tourism has endured many crises over 20 years – including 9/11, the global financial crisis and terrorist attacks in North America and Europe. However, it also serves as an example of how compromise and goodwill between people can build a stronger future for us all. 'We face a deficit of tolerance. Tourism brings people together; it opens our minds and hearts,' said former United Nations World Tourism Organization Secretary General, Taleb Rifai, at a recent conference. We must continue to build on the achievements of the Good Friday Agreement, continue to build hope for the future across the island of Ireland and a growing and sustainable tourism industry is key to this.

Mervyn Gibson

Mervyn is married to Lynda with two grown up daughters and five grandchildren. A former member of the Royal Ulster Constabulary, retiring after 18 years, he is presently minister in Westbourne Presbyterian Community Church, East Belfast. He was one of two DUP negotiators at the Haas Talks in 2013. A lifelong member of the Orange Institution, he is currently Grand Secretary of the Grand Orange Lodge of Ireland.

'I am who I am', a product of geography, choice, history and context. My identity is not fixed, it can change and adapt through influence and by experience, with one notable exception. I am a Christian, a follower of the triune God. As a Christian I belong to Christ and no longer to myself. However, God has placed me in this world to live my earthly life and he has given me free will, a conscience and example to follow in the form of Jesus Christ.

Within the Christian tradition I identify with the Reformed faith and would describe myself as Protestant, as I believe the authority of Scripture alone teaches us that Salvation is by grace alone, through faith alone, in Christ alone and to God alone be the glory. Within the Protestant family I would identify as Presbyterian, initially by birth and family tradition, but now by choice.

I am British by birth as I was born in the United Kingdom, although comfortable being referred to as Irish as I was born on the island of Ireland. However in such cases I often delineate that I am from Northern

Ireland to highlight that there are two distinct jurisdictions on the island. I am proud that my father and grandfather were Donegal men, which underscores my credentials as an Ulsterman. Therefore, I share my ethnicity, as British, Northern Irish or Ulsterman depending on the understanding of who is asking.

It was Oscar Wilde who said, 'Most people are other people. Their thoughts are someone else's opinions, their lives a mimicry, their passions a quotation.' This template for identity sums up Irish Republican and Nationalist views of my British identity if I would only recognise and embrace their version of Irishness. I should become the other, as my opinions are not my own, I am merely imitating being British. Nationalism on the island of Ireland often fails to recognise that my Britishness is as real and valid as their Irishness.

My political identity is Unionist by antecedents and conviction, as I favour the continued unity of England, Scotland, Wales and Northern Ireland as one sovereign state. In shorthand in the context of Northern Ireland, Unionism rejects Irish nationalism by embracing Britishness, however Unionism is much more than the rejection of Irish political nationalism; it is a rich identity that has been shaped by the Union, its values, history, culture and the plurality of identities found within.

It is said 'memories are the architecture of our identity', this being the case Unionist identity for many, not least my own, has been strengthened not only by the experience of Irish Republican terrorism in living memory, but over four centuries of Irish nationalistic intransigence of failing to embrace the reality of the presence of others.

The historic Nationalist line was that the only valid identification was 'Irish' and a United Ireland is the only solution. As Billy Hutchinson summarised it, 'They think unionists are deluded Irishmen.' My Unionist identity becomes even more precious when Nationalism attempts to delegitimise it.

The question arises is when does the planter become native? The Ulster poet John Hewitt offers a response when he penned the words,

> Once alien here my fathers built their house,
> claimed, drained and gave the land the shapes of use.

Once alien here, but no longer, the sentiments of the Woody Guthrie song come to mind, 'This land is your land, this land is my land'. Being Irish and British requires the acceptance and toleration of others.

Two other identities I would claim are that of Loyalist and Orangeman. Loyalist and Unionist were once synonymous and interchangeable terms, however nowadays Loyalist is often used by the media to describe Unionist working class communities as distinct from the rest of Unionism. I subscribe to the original interpretation as someone who is Loyal to Queen and country and reject the attempt to load the term 'Loyalist' with class overtones. My Orangeism embraces faith and politics, it seeks to promote the Protestant faith, maintain the Union of Great Britain and Northern Ireland, and displays its loyalty to the Crown. It provides a framework and public display for my identity.

On 28 September 1912, a poem was published in the morning papers, 'The Blue Banner' by Rev WF Marshall, Presbyterian minister, UVF member and Orangeman. It linked the Ulster Covenant and the struggles of the Scottish Covenanters. The concluding verse embodies some of who I am:

> For all they died for gladly in the homeland o'er the sea,
> For blood-won rights that still are ours as Ulsterborn and free,
> For the land we came to dwell in, and the martyr's faith we hold
> God grant we be as loyal to these as were the men of old.

Cathriona Hallahan

Cathriona Hallahan is a Non-Executive Director, Coach and Business Transformation Consultant. She recently retired after 35 years in Microsoft, becoming Managing Director in 2013. Her work has been recognised with several awards, including the Woman's Executive Network Hall of Fame in June 2015. In 2018, Concern Worldwide presented her with its inaugural Women of Concern award, set up to recognise leaders who promote gender equality.

Looking back over my own upbringing in Dublin and my 35 years working at Microsoft Ireland, I feel privileged that I have been able to experience it all in Ireland.

Living in this country I have always felt encouraged not to underestimate my potential, and to appreciate the value of an honest day's work. This started as far back as when I was a child, born to a working-class family in Dublin. My father was a mechanic and ran his own small business and my mother was a housewife.

My father died when I was young, after which my mum returned to work as a cleaner to support three children under 13. Her resilience and dedication instilled a great work ethic in me, and not long after I secured my first job as a shop assistant in the local newsagents.

My mum left school at 13 so great value was placed upon the importance of myself and my siblings finishing secondary school, which we all did. This was helped in no small part by the introduction of the free post-primary education scheme in Ireland in 1967, a huge turning point for so many children and their families in Ireland and a significant marker of progression and maturity in Irish society.

After secondary school I wanted to support my mum and so instead of attending university, I went to work for a small family business. I spent three years with them before joining Microsoft's fledgling operation in Ireland in 1986 as employee number 24.

From the beginning of my career at Microsoft, I came to realise the importance of believing in yourself and harnessing new opportunities. Having failed to get a role early on in my career because my boss thought I had not shown the aspiration, I made sure not to let an opportunity pass me by again. This experience has not only shaped my own career pathway leading to many roles and opportunities within Microsoft, but also instilled in me a passion for supporting and mentoring others to reach their full potential.

My deep belief is that to build an equal and inclusive society where everyone can reach their full potential, Ireland must equip its people with the right skills to participate and succeed. It is with this ethos in mind that I look back with pride on some of the programmes we delivered in Microsoft to equip everyone with the digital skills required for the jobs of today and tomorrow.

From Youth2Work, an initiative launched after the financial crisis, which equipped over 13,000 young unemployed people with the skills that they need to succeed in the IT sector, to Microsoft Dream Space which continues to provide young people with digital experiences to help open their minds to careers in STEM-related industries. Programmes like these have meant that thousands of people in Ireland have been given a new opportunity to help shape our digital world.

That focus on opportunity first emerged in the 1980s with Ireland's opening up to foreign direct investment (FDI). It helped to bring about positive change to our economy and society. This led to the development of a more creative, confident and outward looking nation in the 1990s which provided a platform for new leaders to emerge.

As a founder of Connecting Women in Technology (CWIT) and a member of the 30 per cent club, I have also had the opportunity to be a voice for change in this space by encouraging more women to take on business leadership roles and to consider an exciting career within STEM.

Leading global teams from Ireland throughout the 1990s and into the 2000s gave me a deeper understanding of the vital importance of cultural diversity and in creating an inclusive society with equal opportunities for all. This became a reality for our small nation when being Irish was given a whole new meaning when Ireland voted yes in the marriage equality referendum in 2015, and the protection given to women through the repeal of the Eighth Amendment in 2018.

Although Ireland has transformed and emerged as a progressive nation in recent decades, it has been heartening and humbling to see our community spirit remain intact. Our collective response to Covid-19 is a prime example of this.

Over 60,000 people answered the HSE's appeal to Be on Call for Ireland in the early weeks of the pandemic, a response which set the tone for other responses to the pandemic at individual, community and company level. To me, giving back and helping others is something that is practically ingrained in the Irish psyche.

When you're born in this country, being Irish isn't something you choose. And yet, having reflected on what it means to be Irish against the backdrop of recent seismic changes in Irish life, I realise how lucky I am to be part of this generous, compassionate, self-challenging, hard-working and inclusive national community. A community that is now open to new ideas and which strives to empower every person – irrespective of their background or ethnicity – to succeed in whatever path they want to take.

Marina Hamilton

Marina Hamilton is a renowned Irish artist from Donegal. Her gallery featuring original paintings and sculpture is located on the family farm in St Johnston. As a former jockey she is also well known in equestrian circles and is married with three daughters.

I like to think I have followed a unique path in life as a proud Irish Presbyterian living in the shadow of the border over the past five decades. That is because during that time I have played in an Orange Flute Band and later went on to help set up and play for a ladies GAA football team. I'm not sure too many others could claim to have taken that same untraditional route.

It all started in 1971 when I was born in Derry to Donegal parents. It was at the height of the troubles but it seemed a sensible move as my parents Tom and Rebecca didn't want me to be burdened with the same paperwork they needed to cross the border on a daily basis.

We as Protestants were on the front line back then as the violence spilled over the border. My aunt and her family were forced to leave their home in St Johnston and move into Derry after their home was targeted. It was a toxic time and it damaged relations among neighbours who all of sudden were expected to take sides.

Those Protestants who didn't leave and cross the border felt isolated and at times under siege, and that shaped much of my early childhood. I often faced questions from others about whether I considered myself British or Irish growing up, which I resented.

Thankfully we stayed and I have been able to live all of my fifty years on the family farm in Maymore. It overlooks the River Foyle which separates north from south and so the border has been a constant in my life. The first thing I see every morning and the last thing I see at night. This is a magical place which has given me so much; it is my sanctuary and my sense of place.

That was brought home to me in letters I read as a child which I will never forget. They were written by my great aunt in her latter years who had left Maymore in her twenties to start a new life in Canada. She wrote how she walked the fields of Maymore in her mind every night and how she wished she had never left the sight of the Foyle. But she was proud to say she never gave up her Irish passport. That lament and those words stuck with me and I decided then never to leave.

I attended the same Protestant National School at Castletown where my mother went, before then going on to enrol at the Catholic secondary Raphoe Vocational School. It was an unusual move as most Protestant children attended the Royal in Raphoe but for me it helped broaden my horizons. I have so many fond memories and the staff went out of their way to ensure I didn't feel isolated as the only Protestant in the class. They made me feel very welcome and at home in the school, which in turn meant I was always comfortable mixing regardless of faiths or background.

After leaving Raphoe I continued my education in Derry and Belfast and finished up after six years with a Diploma in art and degree in Ceramics. I also picked up a husband along the way, Enda McClafferty.

You've probably guessed by the names it is a mixed marriage and in a mixed marriage there are two big issues to consider – what religion you bring up your children and where do you get buried. When asked the first question we like to say our three daughters Kellie, Jade and Chloe are hybrids, as for the second question, time will tell.

In keeping with my untraditional route we decided to christen the girls Catholic and send them to Protestant schools. Like me, they have benefitted from a broad perspective in life mixing from such an early age. I like to think they have had a life free of orange and green.

But I on the other hand have managed to mix orange and green. Like most teenagers I went through a patriotic phase and joined the newly formed local Orange flute band in St Johnston. We paraded both north and south during some very difficult years. At the time joining a band was the traditional path for Protestants, but I was never one for keeping fully with tradition and the restrictions which came with it.

Keeping the sabbath free from all other activities was one of those traditions which I rebelled against when I became jockey and raced all over Ireland on Sundays. Once again, as a girl I was in the minority.

This time in my life gave me a real sense of what it was to be Irish far away from the border as I travelled around every corner of the Island to places like Dingle and Lisdoonvarna where I experienced the music and culture. That eventually brought me to play GAA for Downings in Donegal at a time when ladies football was a real novelty. It was always about sport for me; politics or religion didn't matter.

Thankfully, Ireland is a different place now and as an artist I meet people from all corners of the country and from all backgrounds, and feel that we have more that unites us than divides us.

That is why I am proud to be Irish and, more importantly, from Donegal.

Patricia Harty

Patricia Harty is an Irish-born American journalist, author and editor. She is the editor-in-chief and co-founder of *Irish America* magazine, based in New York city.

I am remembering a June day back in the early seventies. My mother is driving me across the county to say goodbye to a friend.

We are silent for long stretches as my mother navigates through the country roads of Tipperary passing from North Riding into South. She is never comfortable driving, always has both hands on the wheel as if propelling the car forward by sheer force of will. It's beautiful farm country, lush green fields, and roads yet to be widened with EC money. There is little traffic. Ireland back then had a sleepy air to it; those who had jobs went about them quietly – those who didn't, emigrated – there was no hint of the industry that was to come.

'There's nothing for you here,' my mother said, as if reading my thoughts and giving me a final push out of the nest. She had brought us up with the maxim that 'travel broadens the mind', and I was about to begin my journey.

And so it was on July 4, 1972, that my brother Henry and my cousin John picked me up at JFK airport. We drove through Harlem on the way to the Bronx and I remember watching children dancing in the spray of water from a fire hydrant. It was strange and magical.

That first night I spent in a basement apartment on Briggs Avenue. It was the home of Nora Barrett from Mayo, sister of my brother's roommate, Tony, and it would become my home too. I would leave for Atlantic City for the summer, and then spend three months traveling around the country. Then it was November and back to the Bronx and sharing with Nora and later, her sister, Philomena.

The apartment was next door to The Ranch, the local bar that served as the center of our lives. It was here we stopped after our shifts as waitresses and bartenders, construction worker and sandhogs. It was where we got news of home and heard of work and received advice on how to navigate our way in the new world.

I had never travelled much outside the boundaries of my own county, but in New York I met lads from Connemara and girls from Leitrim, and a girl whose brother was interned in Northern Ireland. You could say that in America I truly came to know Ireland.

By the end of that first year, I would also come to know something about Irish America.

As summer work in Atlantic City drew to a close, I paid $99 for a Greyhound bus ticket that allowed unlimited travel for three months.

You could get on and off wherever you liked in the United States and Canada, and we did just that. Three girls from Fermoy in County Cork and myself. Our first stop was Toronto. Arriving on a Sunday morning we passed by a church as the parishioners were exiting. We were bold enough to talk to the priest who, as it turned out was Irish. He introduced us to one of his flock, a woman named Mary, who took us home with her – we stayed for a week – and showed us around the city. It was a good start to what turned out to be an incredible journey.

We went to Medicine Bow, Wyoming because I had a crush on Trampas (Doug McClure) one of the stars of the TV series *The Virginian*. We danced the two-step with real cowboys in Montana and had our photo taken for the local newspaper in Walsenburg, Colorado – because we were 'real Irish'.

We travelled south to New Orleans, north to Montreal, as far west as California, and along the way we met a lot of people who told us they were Irish, most of whom had never been to Ireland. They were descended from ancestors who had come over a long time ago, and they were happy to meet young people from what they had come to think of as a mythical place.

I knew little about the Irish in America before I left home. We had been told about the Famine in school and the 'coffin ships' that ferried the starving Irish to the New World, but they didn't tell us what happened when they got here. No one mentioned how many died on the journey or that thousands were buried in mass graves on Grosse Île and all along the St. Charles River in Canada. They didn't tell us that in New Orleans the Irish died of yellow fever building the canals, or that there's a statue there to 'Margaret', an Irish woman who built an orphanage and supported it with a bakery, though she could neither read nor write.

They didn't tell us about the Irish who fought in the American Revolution, the Civil War, and all the wars since, earning more Medals of Honor citations than any other ethnic group; and they didn't tell us that the Irish helped build the railroads, and skyscrapers, that they panned for gold, and worked in the copper mines in Butte, Montana, that they would go on to become the face of public service, and even become legends of stage and screen.

And no one told me that there were then 40 million Irish in America, so that I needn't worry, I would always feel at home.

Everywhere we went there were signs that other Irish were there before me – the Irish Bayou in New Orleans, the towns of O'Neill in Nebraska, and Dublin, Ohio. Years later, in 1985, when I helped found *Irish America* magazine, it was the people who I met on that trip in 1972, people who carried Ireland in their hearts, who had treated us like family – they were the ones I had in mind as the readers, the ones I wanted to reach out to.

At the end of our travels, in November of that year, we arrived back in the Bronx and my friends departed for Ireland. I stayed on. I have never regretted that decision. Every July 4th I celebrate what I've come to call 'my Independence Day'.

I love America. I am grateful, too, that when the going gets rough I can find that place called 'Irish America' and know the support and caring and the comfort of being amongst my own.

Those early Irish immigrants, as Brian Moynihan, CEO of Bank America, whose own ancestors came over in those hungry years of the 1840s, reminded me when I interviewed him back in 2009, knew: 'It doesn't all break your way all the time, so you've got to just power through it.'

His words ring through in these uncertain times. This is a great country and the Irish who helped build it were not quitters. We can take strength from that, and from those ancestors who would say to us that it's a time to look to family and community and 'power on through it' together.

Pete Hogan

Pete Hogan is a well-known visual artist, who specialises in paintings of Cityscape and Seascape. Born in Dublin, and educated in both Dublin and Vancouver, he has travelled extensively. He has spent periods in both Canada and Australia, but now lives in Dublin. He built a boat in Vancouver, sailed alone around the world by way of Cape Horn and wrote a book about it, *The Log of the Molly B.* He is married to Micaela and they have two children, Clara and Joshua.

In the immortal words of Roddy Doyle's character Jimmy Rabbitte in *The Commitments*: 'The Irish are the blacks of Europe, Dubliners are the blacks of Ireland, and the Northsiders are the blacks of Dublin.'

These days it is becoming difficult, even risky, to speak or write about such things as ethnicity, nationality, race, preferences and even attitudes. One runs the risk of offending someone, somewhere, somehow. I would include the claim to be Irish in that. We have many 'national characteristics' – drinking and fighting, poetry and literature, sentimentality, friendliness. It's probably okay to write about the good characteristics, but less so to examine the negatives. Who wants to read a lot of clichés about Church and State? Who wants to read about alcoholic families, laundries, recipes for brown bread, whiskey priests, mighty hurlers, ballrooms of romance and dancing at the crossroads? There is another Ireland. It's the Ireland of leafy suburbs, fee paying schools, golf clubs and Sunday roasts which is just as valid. It happens to be from where I hail.

I have the credentials to call myself Irish – a mother from small town Mayo and a father from rural Tipperary. They settled in Dublin in the post war move to the cities and I came along in 1951 – Irish in name, religion, schooling, culture.

I tick all of the boxes. I was born in Ireland, my parents were Irish. Their parents were Irish, going back to the time of the Normans and beyond. I went to the local school, across the fields in my bare feet, bearing the sod of turf and the apple for the teacher! I got all that religious stuff. I made my first Holy Communion and Confirmation. I never washed my teeth. I failed miserably to learn the Irish language. No one ever told me about sex and that sort of thing. I wore woolly jumpers from Dunnes stores. I'm fair with grey blue eyes. And crucially, I couldn't wait to get the hell out of Ireland. When I finished school, my Irish education, Trinity College included, I considered Ireland a mediocre, priest-ridden, gombeen-infested, sodden homeland. Off I went overseas the first chance I got.

It was while living away from Ireland that I became Irish. No one much on the south side of Dublin spends their time thinking about whether they are Irish or not. They are more concerned with what car they drive and where they live. But when you end up in London, New York or Sydney it tends to concentrate the mind.

I found myself frequenting the public library waiting for the next edition of *The Irish Times* to arrive. (Before the wonderful WWW.) I think I am not unusual in that regard – the homesick Paddy. And In my case I came home.

That I built my own sailing boat so that I could come home was a bit unusual. But I was always conscious of the fact that I was a 'Paddy building a yacht'. I even named the boat 'Molly' after James Joyce's unfaithful wife of Leopold Bloom. *The Mayo News* announced that I had 'returned to see my Granny' when I sailed into Westport, County Mayo. And it was a strangely proud moment when I flew the tricolour on the back of my yacht in Cape Town, Sydney, or Auckland and people noticed it.

To be a visual artist and be Irish is a bit of a contradiction. There are the writers, the poets, the playwrights who are revered in Ireland. There are the musicians. Often it is said that there is no tradition of visual art, especially of painting, in the country. The ancient Irish had no paintings. Perhaps they might have hung carpets and tapestries up on the walls of their banqueting halls. But there is no tradition of software engineers either. Things have to start somewhere.

So I became a visual artist. Perhaps the contradiction and the difficulty appealed to me. Maybe it was a process of elimination. I had tried just about everything else. A long forgotten, supressed, memory of a childhood workroom in a big house in South Dublin came back to me and, in a way, defined my life. There I was happy, there I made things, there I flourished. Like Titus Groan I went forward, out into the big bad world, and I have been trying to return to that silent, safe, place ever since …

You might as well be from somewhere small if you have to be from somewhere. A minority grouping, an outlier, somewhere on the other side of the tracks. Such a place is Ireland. In this globalised world it's good to have a home base and to be comfortable in one's skin.

Billy Holland

Billy Holland is second on the all-time list of Munster rugby players with 247 caps. He captained his province 47 times and has also been capped by Ireland. Billy retired from professional rugby at the end of June 2021. Billy and his wife Lanlih raised over a half million euro for children's health care in 2020 in honour of their late daughter Emmeline. The money was donated to Crumlin's Children Hospital, CUH Children's Wards and to the Ronald McDonald House.

Irish supporters can see your soul on a rugby pitch. They can sense your commitment to the cause, appreciate you putting your body on the line. They saw it in me, a man who wasn't the tallest, or the biggest, but never took a backwards step.

Munster is a club that I grew up supporting, idiolising many of their players, some of whom I actually got the opportunity to take the pitch with, such as Paul O'Connell and the late Axel Foley. When you start playing with Munster you are entrusted with a responsibility that you don't quite understand at the beginning.

It is all consuming and it took over my life but what I got back was so powerful. It became my identity. I had the privilege of visiting hospitals, helping charities and was stopped by strangers just to chat. One day in Crumlin children's hospital, a child in his surgical gown ran up to me in the corridor. He told me he was on his way in for heart surgery and he couldn't believe he was meeting me in real life. He skipped off again and

I sat in disbelief that I, Billy Holland from Cork, could have the honour of making that much of a difference to his day. Sport in Ireland is more than just a game. It is community, passion, loyalty, connection, pride and family.

The most important role I have is to my family; as a son, a brother and now a husband to my college sweetheart Lanlih, and as a father to Emmeline, Matthew and with a third on the way.

I could not have imagined growing up that my family would now have such a rich blend of cultures. Lanlih's mother, Wahmay, is Taiwanese and married my father-in-law, Gerry from Duagh, County Kerry, who was working in Taiwan at the time. She has told me about the culture shock she got when arriving in Ireland in the eighties, in the depths of winter, to a cottage with no central heating, and with very little English. She describes feeling 'like an alien' as she looked distinctly different to anybody that was around her.

It is a joy to watch all four of Emmeline and Matthew's grandparents provide them with such love, in their own unique ways, gifting them parts of their own childhood with every song, nursery rhyme and game that they share.

Instead of using the word 'hug' my son will only reciprocate if I use the word 'Bao Bao' (Taiwanese for embrace). I am so proud of being Irish and I absolutely adore that my children have their own unique culture.

Our first-born child, our daughter Emmeline, was born in 2018 and I instantly felt so much love, pride and an overwhelming need to protect her. She was born with a heart defect so we spent the next few months between Crumlin Children's Hospital, Cork University Hospital and a few precious weeks at home in Cork. We felt such joy doing the most mundane things. Going for a walk, as a family of three, was a gift every time. Emmeline adored cuddles and I spent every possible moment with her in my arms or watching Lanlih and Emmeline together. I was only but a bystander to the love and connection that they shared.

Emmeline died in May 2019; a day shy of six months old. To not have her here today is a pain that is beyond any words I could possibly share. There is a piece of me that died with her that day, connected to her forever.

To have a seriously ill child is to enter into a world that you can never fully leave. People appeared to help us before we even knew we needed them. We decided to fundraise as a way to thank them and show our solidarity to other families. Also, Irish people, men in particular, have often shied away from talking about grief and their feelings. Emmeline gave me the courage and the bravery to open up.

Lanlih and I appeared on *The Late Late Show* in January 2020 where we spoke about our precious little girl. We received thousands of messages of support and the generosity of the people of Ireland meant that we raised over half a million euro in less than a week.

Emmeline's legacy is now that she has changed the lives of sick children in Ireland, and their families, for generations to come. A fitting tribute to our darling girl and that was the gift the people of Ireland gave to us.

Merlin Holland

Merlin Holland, the only grandson of Oscar Wilde, is an author living in France. For the last thirty years he has been researching his grandfather's life and works. He is currently working on an account of Oscar's 'posthumous life' which will show that he caused even more trouble after his death than when alive. After Oscar's conviction in 1895, his wife, Constance, and their two sons were forced to move abroad and change their name to Holland. The family has never reverted to the name Wilde.

Be(com)ing Irish

I first set foot in Ireland in the summer of 1962. I was sixteen and I spent a week hitchhiking with a school friend from Dublin to Tipperary via Limerick and back. Michael knew the ropes since he'd done it before and there was a strict pattern to be followed for the first twelve hours: night-boat from Holyhead to Dun Laoghaire; early train into town and straight to the Shelbourne where we left our small suitcases in the cloakroom (not rucksacks, you note, or they would have given us away); shaved, cleaned up and snoozed in the hotel lounge until midday as though we were proper paying guests. That was the last bit of comfort for a week. It was also the last time I would cross the Irish Sea for twenty-nine years.

I never did understand why my father couldn't have given us a few introductions to the people he knew there. He was a lifelong friend of Shane Leslie with whom he had been at Cambridge; he and Liam O'Flaherty had been irresponsible bachelors in Paris in the 1930s; and there was his more recent friendship with Micheál MacLiammóir (Irish admittedly by design rather than by birth). Perhaps he thought that as a teenager I might disgrace him, though it was more likely to have been my mother's suspicion, which I only found out years later, that Michael and I might be gay which prevented him. The idea was absurd but had it been true, and given who my grandfather was, it could have made for some juicy gossip in Dublin.

I don't even recall thinking that I had Irish blood in me at the time or that this teenage jaunt was some sort of atavistic need to retrace my origins. Oscar's letters, which would later play a significant part in his rehabilitation, had only just been published and I was discouraged from talking about the family association. As a result, I didn't feel any real connection to Ireland, apart from taking the side of the Irishman in those derogatory jokes of the time because he had a refreshingly oblique view of life and, significantly, always had the punch line.

When I finally did return in 1991 it was at the invitation of a Trinity College professor of medicine, Davis Coakley, who was giving his inaugural lecture as president of the 'Bi', the TCD students' Biological Association, and breaking with the tradition of talking on a medical subject, he planned to talk on Oscar Wilde. It was through his extensive knowledge of Sir William Wilde's place in the history of Irish medicine that Davis had started to take an interest in his son, and he asked me to supplement his lecture with a brief talk of my own. I told the audience that my presence might be seen as verging on the fraudulent as I was only part Irish and not medical, but afterwards several people made the point that with the ancestors I had, I should allow myself to be as Irish as I was comfortable feeling.

That weekend Davis made me understand just how much my grandfather had unwillingly eclipsed the achievements of his two parents in Irish history, both of whom were still revered in Dublin, she for her ardent nationalism and he for his contributions to medicine. As I wrote to him afterwards, 'I felt in a strange way as though I were coming home after a long absence; maybe there is more to blood ties than we would like to believe,' but it was not a sentiment that I dared to express more than very privately and it left me somewhat confused. I took a cynical view of American Presidents paying semi-regal visits to small towns in County Cork to gain Irish-American votes back home, and I had an instinctive horror of Plastic Paddydom, yet both circumstances and Dubliners seemed to be encouraging me to claim the little that, in an inexplicably self-effacing way, I myself was wanting to deny. In the end, feeling comfortable with it would take another twenty years and it was largely through Irish generosity that it happened.

The reassessment of my grandfather's place in literary history was gathering momentum at the start of the new century, but with it came the unwanted attentions of his fan club who insisted on covering his tomb in Paris with lipstick kisses. The Office of Public Works in Dublin became aware of the problem and offered to help clean and protect it, an impossibly large expense for me alone. Despite the economic downturn, they were as good as their word and shortly after, in 2013, as a mark of gratitude and respect, I asked for and was given Irish citizenship. It felt as though I had been granted membership of a special club more by invitation than by application.

I still wonder if there's anything in the idea of genetic hard-wiring and if I can thank my ancestors for some of the ways I think and speak and respond to situations. If there is, then I'm especially grateful to the Irish for giving me their understanding of the beauty and music of language.

Eamonn Holmes

Eamonn Holmes is the world's longest serving breakfast television anchor, having amassed 26 years with GMTV and Sky News. He debuted at the age of 21, hosting Ulster Television's *Good Evening Ulster,* before being chosen by the BBC for its national daytime launch team. His interests includes everything from current affairs to sport to light entertainment. Proudly Irish, he has always maintained a home in Belfast while working in England. In 2018 he was awarded an OBE for Services to Broadcasting.

It is evident by my Christian name and my accent that I'm Irish. Look closer and there's so much more that's a giveaway, such as my attitude to life, my nature and personality. We are a social nation and people seem to like us for it.

Why in general are we so outgoing? Why are we such good mixers? Is it our emigrant tendencies, the need to get on with new people, to integrate? I latch on to other Irish emigrants wherever I am around the world. I need the reassurance of their story, their journey and why, like me, did they leave home. Home is a great word for the Irish. We all know what it means. It's our common bond. So strong was that call of Home that I kept a house in Belfast even though most of my time is now spent in England because of work.

I come from a particularly complicated part of the Emerald Isle – Northern Ireland. Some people from those six counties feel Irish, some feel British, but an awful lot more feel Northern Irish. Legally, citizens of Northern Ireland are entitled under the Good Friday Agreement to hold dual citizenship. It may sound complicated, but it's not for so many. I point out these distinctions which are strongly held by many to highlight one thing:

Whatever flag some fight over, the irony is the rest of the world doesn't really care about our nuances. They don't see us as Irish, Northern Irish, Unionist or Republican; to them we are all Irish, pure and simple.

Another irony is that many of us can be more Irish abroad than we are at home. Sometimes others can determine how we see ourselves.

As I write this, I'm sitting outdoors in rural Fermanagh, reckoned to be the wettest county on the Isle. Historically, we send our people to American shores and have done, especially since the time of the potato famine, but since time immemorial the American continent has been sending rain collected right across the Atlantic Ocean to us. Around me there are people I have never met before and amazingly there has been no rain, not just today but for all week.

Rain or sun it wouldn't have stopped us talking though. Talking as if we've been friends for years. None of us are related but give us long enough and somebody will find a connection because we are Irish and by and large we are a happy people.

Being Irish is a privilege. I am proud to be thought of as such and being an export myself I am not alone in exporting key elements of what I am and what we are as a people. I see being in the public eye as having a duty and obligation to promote the Emerald Isle.

Ireland is a modern evolving country and although Leprechauns and shelelaghs are part of our makeup and culture, so too is literature, the arts, dance and song, research and development, pharmaceuticals and an intelligent and educated workforce.

Being Irish can often be a passport that gains access not just to countries, but to the hearts and minds of so many different people and cultures. It is an amazing calling card and it is a badge I wear with pride.

LeAnne Howe and Padraig Kirwan

LeAnne Howe, born and raised in Oklahoma, is an enrolled citizen of the Choctaw Nation. She is the Eidson Distinguished Professor of American Literature in English at the University of Georgia. Her awards include the inaugural MLA Prize for Studies in Native American Literatures; a United States Artists Ford Fellowship; and a Fulbright Scholarship to Jordan. She received the American Book Award in 2002 for her first novel, *Shell Shaker*.

Padraig Kirwan is Senior Lecturer in the Department of English and Creative Writing, Goldsmiths, University of London. His first book was *Sovereign Stories: Aesthetics, Autonomy and Contemporary Native American Writing* (2013). He recently co-edited *Famine Pots: The Choctaw Irish Gift Exchange 1847–Present* with LeAnne Howe (2020).

Padraig Kirwan:

Over the past number of years, LeAnne Howe and I have been researching the meaning of the gift that the Choctaw tribe made to the Irish in 1847, during An Gorta Mór. To my mind, this single charitable act might do much to help us consider some of the significances of being Irish, and what it means to be recognized as Irish and identify yourself as such.

First, a little about the gift itself. At the height of the famine, news of starvation and hardship in Ireland reached Skullyville, a small agency town in what was then known as Indian Territory and is the state of Oklahoma today. The Choctaw gathered around, acted quickly and spared what they could in the wake of their own displacement just over a decade earlier. This was an act of supreme generosity, and although it is the case that famine-time donations arrived from numerous places, it is fair to say that this particular gift resonates; it has been long remembered by the Choctaw Nation and the Irish.

That depth of remembrance in Ireland reflects, I think, the fact that the donation spoke to a wide set of historical and cultural experiences, many of which have helped to shape the Irish as a community and nation over time. As inhabitants of a small island, we have certainly viewed the gift as an eloquent reminder of the importance of being an outward-looking, open-hearted and empathetic country. While it is not always easy to maintain those principles, or protect those ideals, we could say that many of these values were visible during the pandemic, when huge numbers of Irish people contributed to the Navajo & Hopi Families Covid-19 Relief Fund. Just as importantly, the gift speaks to enduring cultural values and the opportunity to share stories, as well as the memories of more troubled histories.

In considering the Choctaw tradition of mound-building and the tribe's ancient laws, one might think of the ancestors who shaped early Irish landscapes and developed the *Feineachas* (Brehon Laws). We might also think about forms of acceptance, recognition and solidarity, as well as the importance of privileging those above moments of sectarian division or intolerance; in Ireland, we have seen the value – and the price – of both attitudes to the world around us.

The Choctaw donation reminds me of the values, histories and experiences that led to our friends and allies helping us in times of need. More than that, it prompts me to think deeply on the responsibility that we all bear, as citizens of Ireland, in upholding those principles and honouring the gift.

LeAnne Howe:

Thank you, Padraig Kirwan for those powerful words. My tribe, the Choctaw Nation, has long loved oration and storytelling. It is something our two cultures share, the love of a good story told well. Over the years I've written about the Choctaw gift and honour my mother for telling me the story of the $170.00 gift that the Choctaw people gave to the Irish for famine relief. As Padraig discussed, it's an amazing story. But even more important to me is that my mother and I were together, I think working in the kitchen, when she casually said something like, you know our tribe sent money to the Irish when they heard that the Irish people were starving. (I must have been in my late 20s.) I was gobsmacked, amazed, astounded, all those emotions were bouncing around in my body.

'Why have you never mentioned this before.'

She shrugged and said something like she hadn't thought about it in a long time.

'Anything else you haven't thought about in a long time.'

'No.'

I kind of reckoned that wasn't completely true, but didn't press her. However shortly before Mother passed away in 1999, she looked at me from her hospital bed and said, 'I have a lot more stories to tell you.' I knew what she meant. She was trying to say that I would learn through her spirit, even after death, if I listened for the words blowing on the wind.

One thing I learned through my research into the Choctaw Irish connection from 1847 was that our cultures are indeed kindred spirits.

This is something that sculptor Alex Pentek investigated as he was making his famous sculpture, 'Kindred Spirits', located in Midleton, County Cork. When Padraig and I were working on our 2020 book, *Famine Pots: The Choctaw–Irish Gift Exchange*, a collection of essays by Irish and Choctaw scholars, we traveled to Ireland to see it. It is a beautiful piece of art inspired by the gift that celebrates the bond that still exists between our two nations. Somehow, I know my mother is proud that I'm telling the story that she told me. *Ome chi pisa lauchi ke.*

Eileen Ivers

In a 30+ year career, Grammy-winning and Emmy-nominated Eileen Ivers has performed with Sting, Patti Smith, and The Chieftains. She has guest starred with over 50 symphony orchestras to date, and was the groundbreaking musical star of *Riverdance*. A former member of the Hall & Oates band, she was a featured instrumentalist on *Back to Titanic* and film soundtracks including *Gangs of New York*. She is one of the most awarded ever All-Ireland Fiddle and Banjo champions.

'My Navigator'

What does 'being Irish' mean to me? Quite simply, it is my silent, and at times not-so-silent, life's navigator. Being born and raised in arguably Ireland's 33rd county, County Bronx, I am a first-generation Irish American. I love my country of birth … her ideals, her freedoms, her hard-fought history and proven spirit, and I am a proud American. I also embrace and embody my Irish heritage, and it fuels my daily life.

When asked to be a contributor to this book, the inquiry fell around St. Patrick's Day 2021 … the second straight year of not being able to represent and share Irish music and culture on stage because of the global pandemic. I've been blessed to have a career – a calling, a passion – in performing Irish music through the years on many of the world's great stages. This career is not only performance-driven, but comprises being a composer, producer, band leader, educator – and I love it! Since the stages went dark on March 12, 2020, I found myself at a loss, unable to represent my Irishness through music on another St. Patrick's Day, a day that is obviously known for showcasing one's love of Ireland. My fiddle was silenced from stage performance, but I found myself wanting to share my Irishness. I *needed* to show it – I never felt that need so strongly before.

That St. Patrick's Day morning, on the way to visit my mother's senior day care center with my fiddle, I stopped to pick up something green, something to scream 'I'm Irish' for my mom Annie. Years ago, it wouldn't have been my thing to buy someone a shamrock-ladened teddy bear. This year I did … the greener the better! Annie loved these Irish reminders and basked in the 'Happy St. Patrick's Day' greetings she received all day long. It even brought back happy memories of receiving the annual, card-pressed, real live Irish shamrock that lovingly came from her own mother and mother-in-law back in Ireland in the 1960s.

Travelling and touring the world through the years, I have always relished finding 'pockets of Irishness', the many folks enjoying Irish pubs that dot the world from Australia's outback to Singapore to Trinidad … Irish dance schools from Anchorage to Missoula to Moscow … incredible traditional Irish musicians playing in a Tokyo session or jamming in Tonder Denmark … some old fellas sportin' green-dyed beards riding their Harleys in the Omaha Nebraska St. Patrick's Day Parade … the woman who ran from her audience, met me as I was fiddling in the crowd, and while she was jumping and clapping in tempo screamed, 'I love this music, and I'm not even Irish – I'm Mexican!' These folks may not have a DNA connection to the Emerald Isle, but they celebrate 'being' Irish.

When performing our 'Beyond the Bog Road' concert in Brookfield, Wisconsin in 2012, I met an extraordinary African American woman named Lydia. She was never exposed to much Irish music or stories of Irish history. She was in the front row, eyes so wide, grin so big … I noticed her getting emotional at times throughout the concert. In the lobby afterwards a long chat ensued, and the start of a cherished friendship was born. We discussed the similarities and struggles of each other's heritage. One of my musical passions in my recording and performing career is showcasing cultural similarities that parallel the

Irish experience. In particular, my 'Beyond the Bog Road' record and subsequent tour spoke of the parallel journeys of various immigrant groups, and how elements of Celtic, African, European, and Native American music are at the heart of Americana roots music. Many Irish came to America in refurbished slave ships … our journeys intersect in numerous ways. One could argue that great American artforms like jazz and tap dance grew from Celtic and African traditions. If the integration through immigration never occurred, these and other artforms may never have been born. After being touched by Irish music and history, Lydia was moved to visit and experience Ireland, even visiting my family's own neck of the woods there – a pre-famine village in Mayo. My husband Brian and I built a holiday home on one of my family's fields there around twenty years ago. Lydia loved Ireland, and all things Irish.

All things Irish is who I am also, how I was raised, and how we raise our son, Aidan. The Irish sense of tradition, faith, resiliency … the Irish love of literature, art, music … the innate Irish way of taking care of one's neighbor, the land, trying to take life slower and not so seriously – these encompass 'Irishness' to me.

Many Americans still identify themselves with what was once a hyphenated adjective: 'Irish-American, African-American'. The actual hyphen is not so widely used these days, but the adjective preceding American helps define who we are. I am grateful that I was given the opportunity to know my ancestral heritage. I am proud of my Irish adjective. I am proud of all the heartache, sacrifice and hard work that my parents went through to gift my sister Maureen and I a wonderful life of opportunity in a great nation. The adjective has helped me relate to others, and for me, music is the perfect vehicle for inclusion. Perhaps in America 2021, more focus of this ideal is needed. We can embrace the adjective, enjoy the diverse palette it represents and how it fuels us to be who we are meant to be, but realize at the end of the day we are far more similar than different … we just might navigate through life differently.

Roland Jaquarello

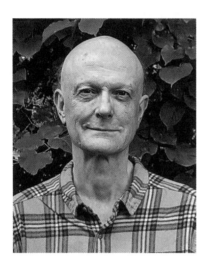

Roland Jaquarello is an Englishman who's lived in Ireland north and south for 13 years and has been connected with its culture since 1964. Former Director at The Abbey Theatre, Artistic Director at Lyric Theatre Belfast, Artistic Director at the Green Fields and Far Away Theatre Company and Senior Producer, Radio Drama, BBC Northern Ireland, he is the author of *Memories of Development: My Times in Irish Theatre and Broadcasting.*

Ireland is a very different to place to the country of my student days in the 1960s. Then the idea of a black actor playing Christy in *The Playboy of The Western World* at the Abbey would have been regarded as fanciful. A belief that abortion and same sex marriage would be enshrined in Irish law would have been greeted with hilarity. These days Ireland is a fully-fledged member of the EU, having shed its colonial yoke and gained both prosperity and national confidence. Of course, there are still challenges, but Ireland is in a much better place than in days of yore, when the Gardaí were prowling around Trinity Players concerned about a play which included a gay kiss.

In fact, my introduction to Ireland was at Magee College, Derry. At that time, Protestant Presbyterianism dominated the North. Sundays in particular seemed like the end of the world. Shops, cinemas and pubs were closed, as were, surprisingly, parks. This led to one student remarking that 'Paisley would have the legs of ducks tied as well, if he could get away with it!' Despite convivial Derry hospitality, at weekends students often preferred to go south to avoid such gloomy scenarios. Although the Republic was ostensibly more liberal, ultimately it was also dominated by religion and the conservative interaction of church and state. Getting contraception was a nightmare and when I moved down to Trinity, a girl friend was admonished by a doctor for making such a request. A friend observed that these oppressive restrictions 'made having sex like committing murder' so it became even more exciting! As the late 1960s-70s evolved, the predominance of British popular culture via the Beatles and company began to influence cities like Dublin. Nightclubs like Sloopy's and Zhivago ('where love stories begin') were heaving as the Abbey became more adventurous, presenting not only early Friel and Murphy but Gunter Grass, Fernando Arrabal and even a rock musical in Gaelic.

Despite such developments, the troubles remained the elephant in the room. The days of attending parties in the Bogside where we all sang Bob Dylan songs seemed a long way off. Bloody Sunday created understandable anti-British feeling. After I witnessed the consequent burning of the British embassy in Merrion Square, an eminent writer warned me that 'we could be in the Weimar Republic shortly'. The IRA and the UVF gathered momentum. Positions hardened and the island became more divided and the British government more inflexible. Nonetheless, nobody had abused me personally for being an Englishman in Ireland. Similarly, in the UK in the late 1970s, when I ran a touring Irish theatre company, audiences remained relatively unaffected by IRA bomb attacks and responded positively to our work. Nonetheless, the Hunger Strike of '81 accelerated tension. It was as if the Thatcher government responded without any understanding of the place of such sacrifice in Irish history.

Still, after such violence and tragedy, green shoots eventually grew. The Anglo-Irish agreement moved peace closer but maybe football also played a significant part. Billy Bingham's World Cup success with Northern Ireland in 1982 and 1986 was followed by Jack Charlton's Ireland beating England 1-0 at Euro 1988 and a triumphant march to the

World Cup Quarter Finals in 1990. The game seemed to cross the divide and often embraced a wider diaspora, including many of Irish origin forced to emigrate through economic circumstances. I also noticed that regardless of sectarian allegiance, many in the North also supported Charlton's Irish team. In memory of these times, a Dublin friend still sends me a card with a picture of Ray Houghton's iconic Euro winner!

These major sporting landmarks put Ireland centre stage and helped later cultural enterprise. Mary Robinson, one of my Trinity contemporaries, became the first female President of Ireland. *Riverdance* turned out to be a worldwide phenomenon, Irish writers got more internationally recognised and divorce finally became legal.

Meanwhile, while I was working in Belfast, the landmark Good Friday Agreement brought hope that there was some kind of resolution to the Troubles as Van Morrison sang of 'Days Like This'.

Since those heady times, the Celtic Tiger crashed in an orgy of speculative greed. It was if the consequences of earlier Thatcherite excess went unheeded. While the economy recovered, the church's power diminished through horrific sexual abuse revelations. A divisive UK Brexit referendum with no citizens' assemblies led to an immature debate. The consequent result has meant that a border poll is more likely and a united Ireland no longer seems just an aspiration.

However, it remains to be seen whether there'll be sufficient flexibility to absorb not only the Protestant tradition but the concerns of ethnic minorities to make it a reality. If this can be achieved, Ireland will have fully succeeded in becoming a united, diverse, multi-cultural state.

Helen Johnston

Helen Johnston is a policy analyst with the National Economic and Social Council in Dublin. She is also the chairperson of the Centre for Cross Border Studies. She is originally from a farm in north Antrim.

They say you are lucky in life if you are fortunate enough to do work which you believe in and which you think can make a difference in people's lives. I have been fortunate that for most of my life that has been the case, and my current job involves working on a project which I ardently believe in … and that is researching the concept of a 'shared island'.

Nearly 7 million people live on this island, which is less than the population of London or New York City. We are living in two jurisdictions with increasing diversity in both parts of the island in terms of race, ethnicity, religion, culture and traditions. While we are governed by different institutions, how can we best live together as good neighbours, respecting difference, celebrating each other's traditions and achievements, and cooperating, where appropriate, to the benefit of us all?

I grew up in a Presbyterian farming household in north Antrim. A beautiful part of the world with its scenic coastline and mixed farming landscape. Mutual support among farmers trumped religious division with farmers helping each other out with seasonal tasks and respecting each other's traditions. I participated in the cultural and social events of the area with my family and peers – mainly band parades and young farmers' club activities – which were a great social outlet for an adolescent at the time. We were taught British history at school and it was only as I progressed through college that I became more aware of Irish history. A key part of my school and young farmers' club activity involved sport – playing hockey and soccer. It was through my sporting activity that I first travelled to the 'Free State', as we referred to Ireland at that time, taking part in school hockey tours to Dublin. The novel experience was being away from home and we took little notice of cultural differences.

It was at University, in Coleraine and Belfast, that I became more politically aware. There I studied with, played sport with, and made life-long friends with people from different backgrounds and from various parts of the island of Ireland. Divisions became apparent during the 1981 hunger strike and Irish politics were debated in the relatively safe space of summers spent working in the USA.

Living in Belfast and working in the Northern Ireland civil service I began to understand the underlying nature of the divisions which existed. My work involved researching disadvantage in Northern Ireland and evaluating community relations projects. On a day to day basis our bags were searched going in and out of shops, we were often asked to evacuate the building because of a bomb scare, and there were limited venues which were felt safe to socialise in. It was only when I moved to Dublin in the early 1990s that I felt a sense of freedom and was aware of the oppressive nature of Northern Irish society at that time.

As a northern Protestant living in Dublin I have felt fully accepted in southern society, in both my work and social life. I worked for 14 years in the Combat Poverty Agency, an organisation responsible for delivering part of the EU funded peace programmes, jointly with Pobal, in the border counties of Ireland, following the 1994 ceasefires. This work gave me great insights into the experience of living in a border region, but also the wide range of projects and programmes aimed at peace building and reconciliation, much of this based on 'being able to put yourself into someone else's shoes.'

Being a regular north-south traveller, over the years and especially since the 1998 Good Friday/Belfast Agreement, changes started to emerge. In the early 1990s, the roads on the northern side were of much better quality than on the southern side, but as the South became more prosperous the roads on the southern side greatly improved. This was only one of a large number of changes which have taken place over the last 30 years. The economy in the Republic has boomed with job opportunities and returning emigrants, dampened only by the economic crash of 2008 and the recent pandemic.

Perhaps more progressive has been the social liberalisation of the South where it feels like a much more inclusive place to live. It seems like the North, with its superior and mostly free public services, has been somehow left behind, accentuated by the fall out of Brexit.

In the current circumstances it is even more important that we learn how to share this island and cooperate to mutual benefit. Whether we see ourselves as Irish, Northern Irish or British, the most important underlying principle should be upholding the peace and ensuring that our young people have opportunities and futures to look forward to, whether through maintenance of the *status quo,* through some type of confederate arrangement or through a united island – whatever is the desire of the majority of the population.

Returning to the reason I first travelled from north Antrim to Dublin – for the sport of hockey. The Irish women's hockey team is an all-island team whose captain is from north Antrim. In 2019 they were silver medallists at the World Cup and in 2021 they are competing in their first Olympics in Tokyo. Their commitment, passion, talent and enjoyment of representing Ireland encapsulates for me what being Irish is all about!

Alex Kane

Alex Kane is a political columnist and commentator based in Belfast. He was formerly a director of communications for the Ulster Unionist Party.

The next part of the journey is for those without baggage

There are moments when I think I should feel Irish. My adoptive parents were born before partition into an Ireland that was united, albeit as part of the United Kingdom of Great Britain and Ireland. My Dad, born in 1906, had family in Sligo and happy memories of spending time with them – before and after 1921. It hurt him when tensions between north and south in the late 1960s/early 1970s slowed his regular cross-border visits down to a trickle, and then a full stop.

I remember some of those visits to Sligo and further afield trips to Cavan, Meath, Monaghan, Leitrim, Galway and on down to Cork and Waterford. Farms and beaches were my favorite places, but I have lingering memories of how laid back everyone and everything seemed to be. But, as I said, the visits stopped.

Long after my Dad died I asked Mum what had happened. She told me it was because he was an Orangeman and member of the Ulster Unionist Party and just felt increasingly uncomfortable with what he described as the 'border mentality' of those he once regarded as friends and boyhood neighbours. As she put it, he had a growing sense he was now regarded as an outsider, an enemy of those who wanted to unite Ireland again.

He wasn't. He was fascinated by 'Irish' culture and even spoke the language reasonably well. He read *The Irish Times* until his final illness made it too difficult for him to read. He was an expert on the drawing of the 'line of separation' – as he described the border – and often told me of the damage it had done to communities where Protestants, Catholics, nationalists and what eventually became 'Ulster' unionists had lived reasonably peaceably before 1921. He was born in a united Ireland and had no difficulty in recognising the Irish dimension of his identity.

But never once have I felt Irish. I never describe myself as Irish, or even Northern Irish. That said, I have no hatred, or even dislike, of Irish culture, language, history or people. I may not have liked some of the decisions taken by Irish governments on Northern Ireland, and I always had difficulty with the seeming reluctance to extradite suspected members of the IRA; yet those personal dislikes and difficulties have never embraced the Irish people or Irish society and culture as a whole.

But as I've got older and as demographics and political circumstances have changed (particularly post-Brexit), I've found myself wondering how I would cope if Ireland were united again. I think it's fairly likely a border poll will be held within the next decade or so and that will force me to think about what a 'new' Ireland would look like. It would also force me to think about what advice to give my children.

I'll tell them what my Dad told me when, in 1973, at the age of 18 and casting my first vote, I told him I supported Brian Faulkner's willingness to cut a power-sharing deal with the SDLP (then regarded by many unionists as a front for the IRA). I wondered if he'd mind. His answer was, as ever, honest and straight to the point: 'Don't carry my political baggage with you. You'll have enough baggage of your own when you get to my age.'

The Ireland he stopped visiting in 1972/73 no longer exists. The Ireland I've heard unionists and loyalists talk about for most of my life doesn't exist anymore. The Ireland of bumpy roads taking over from the solid northern roads when you crossed the border has gone. The Ireland of Rome rule and crushingly inhibitive social conservatism has gone. Dublin often feels more British than Belfast. The poor-looking-over-its-shoulder-in-envy-at-its-cross-border-neighbour Ireland has gone.

Could I imagine my children living in and being comfortable in a 'new' united Ireland? Yes, but only if they don't carry my baggage and my memories. And that's because the 'new' Ireland would be as new to them as it would be to everyone else living in it.

Hopefully most of them wouldn't insist on carrying someone else's baggage either, for that's the only way to bring both parts together and create an entirely new whole that will be something that can grow and build its own history and story.

And me? My sense of identity is deep and entrenched. Too many of my memories are nudged by the shadow of the pain and grief that touched too many lives for far too long. My personal baggage fills too much of my hallway to embrace something entirely new, and I don't think I could just leave it behind me at this point.

But if Ireland is united again I hope we'll collectively learn from all of our mistakes since 1921 and achieve genuine reconciliation and common purpose.

Sinead Kane

Dr. Sinead Kane is an international keynote speaker, double PhD doctorate, double Guinness World Record holder, visually impaired athlete, qualified lawyer and lecturer. She is the holder of a Guinness World Record for being the first blind female to complete a marathon on each of the seven continents, which she completed in less than seven days. Sinead proves how those who persist in spite of a disability can develop determination, motivation and creativity.

Irish identity is not finite or permanent. It is a social construction, and as such it is subject to circumstance and therefore can be reconstructed. Personally, for me being Irish today makes me feel proud. I love this little island. I am proud to hang the Irish flag out the window on St. Patrick's Day. I enjoy seeing Irish athletes do well at international competition and holding the flag up in the air upon winning. Being Irish makes me think of the warmth and nosiness of people all in one. The Irish feel the need to know everything about you and everyone knows everyone in Ireland. A common expression heard throughout Ireland is, 'What's the craic?' Indeed, the art of conversation and storytelling is an important value for many Irish and a common way to build rapport.

When I think of what it means to be Irish in 2021, I think of an Ireland which has transformed from a homogenous white, English-speaking, Catholic society to a society with a mix of race, ethnicities and religions. Irish identity is socially constructed within an era of fluid modernity and is positioned between the diametrically opposed ideals of the traditional and the global. What makes Ireland unique is the cultural traditions that we still hold on to such as *The Late Late Toy Show*, making of St. Brigid's Crosses, making sure to bless ourselves when we pass a church, our talents within music and dance such as *Riverdance*. In terms of attitudes, I think Irish people complain a lot about many issues but if we compare our small country to other countries Ireland is caring in how it treats the poor and hungry. This is not to say that there aren't issues and flaws because there are many, but compared to other countries Ireland does quite well. I think people worldwide embrace their Irish heritage because genealogical lineage and wider family ties produce a sense of 'home'. It encapsulates closeness amongst members of the wider family both spatially and emotionally. This sense of belonging, of being at home, is strongly associated with family and community. I think Irish people are proud of their identity and their perseverance through struggles such as the potato Famine (1845), the Irish War for Independence (1919-1921) and ongoing tensions with Northern Ireland.

There are stunning locations all over the world but we also have plenty of our own, including the Wild Atlantic Way, the craggy rocks of the Burren, the remote beauty of Connemara, Glendalough etc. The rain in Ireland can be annoying at times but it gives all of us something to talk about. You wouldn't be Irish if you didn't talk about the weather. Thankfully, we don't suffer from weather extremes like some countries. The rain helps with our beautiful green environment.

Despite my love for Ireland I realise that many people with disabilities like myself can be left behind, left rejected, excluded, isolated and lonely. Being a disabled woman in Ireland is hard. Little attention has been paid to the specific experiences and needs of women with disabilities in Ireland. There is a lack of understanding of the ways in which gender and disability issues interact.

In our economic and political systems, women with disabilities are only beginning to become visible and their needs only starting to be addressed within the policy-making process. The struggle for women's equality has not concentrated to any significant degree on the particular needs of disabled women or on the specific strategies required to address their concerns.

I will continue to advocate for greater equality and empowerment for disabled women. I hope to see an Ireland where there will be increased participation and representation of disabled women at all levels of Irish society, more resourcing of support systems for issues such as housing, education, employment, family to address and improve the economic and social situation of women with disabilities.

Women with disabilities are not a homogenous group. Differences exist based on type of disability encompassing physical, sensory, and learning disabilities and mental health illnesses.

They also exist depending on whether a woman has been disabled since birth, or whether she has an acquired disability, and on characteristics including her age, ethnicity, socio-economic status, cultural background and sexual orientation. These differences must therefore be acknowledged in the design and implementation of responses to meet the needs of women with disabilities.

Brendan Kelly

Brendan Kelly is Professor of Psychiatry at Trinity College Dublin and Consultant Psychiatrist at Tallaght University Hospital. He is author of *Hearing Voices: The History of Psychiatry in Ireland*, *Mental Health in Ireland* and *The Science of Happiness: The Six Principles of a Happy Life and the Seven Strategies for Achieving It.*

What does being Irish mean to me?

I cannot remember the first time I realised that I am Irish. Born in Galway, I grew up surrounded by Irishness but, like the fish that never heard of water, I could not see it. Forty-eight years on, I still do not fully know what it means to be Irish and – at this stage – I probably never will. Maybe that is what it means to be Irish?

I gradually became aware of aspects of my Irishness. I learned the Irish language at school. One day, a new student joined our class: Claudine, from France. We were told that Claudine did not speak Irish and would not have to learn it. This was a revelation. Who would have thought such a thing was possible? I wondered what life would be like if I did not have to learn Irish. One of my classmates said there was 'no point learning Irish'. This concept blew my mind. I learned Irish the same way I slept at night and ate breakfast in the morning. I never questioned it. In secondary school, I came to enjoy Irish, thanks to a teacher who taught Irish poetry with visible enthusiasm. I am forever grateful to him.

> *As a student, I was acutely aware of my Irishness when I travelled. Visiting Venice in the 1990s, a group in a youth hostel called me 'Irish'. 'Hey, Irish! Get a move on!' I liked this. I was Ireland. 'I'm on my way, Dutch', I answered.*

In France, an intense Japanese teenager asked me to 'explain Ireland'. She took notes.

On medical elective in the United States in 1995, an earnest cardiologist wondered: 'Do you live near the fighting?'

'What fighting?' I asked, baffled.

At a scientific meeting in Switzerland in 1999, I was introduced as 'Ireland's representative'. *Me?* I was not certain that Ireland would have chosen me, had Ireland been asked. Still, I did my best (for Ireland).

Today, I live and work in Dublin, as a psychiatrist. My views on Irishness are shaped by aspects of my work.

Ireland's history in the field of psychiatry is chequered at best. In the 1960s, Ireland had more 'asylum' beds than any other country in the world. While there were increased rates of admission to psychiatric hospitals during the nineteenth and twentieth centuries in many countries, including England, France and the United States, Ireland's rates were especially high at their peak and especially slow to decline. Why? Was it something to do with Irishness?

Ireland did not have a particularly high rate of mental illness, so what set Ireland apart was our tendency to reach for institutional solutions more readily than other countries did. This reflects our broader tendency to create and expand all kinds of institutions to address all types of 'problems': industrial schools, laundries, mother and baby homes. Virtually all countries have analogous establishments, but Ireland's institutions were especially embedded in our communities and social life. They were part of who we were, part of what we did to each other and part of our national identity for several generations.

Today, things have changed. Ireland's rate of psychiatric admission is low by international standards. Our rate of involuntary admission ('sectioning') is half of that in England. This comes at a price: mentally ill people are visibly homeless on our streets and languish in our prisons. Maybe that is part of what Irishness means today: neglect of the vulnerable?

In recent times, the Covid-19 pandemic impacted on our Irishness. Vital public health restrictions helped re-shape identity at local, national and international levels.

Travel restrictions focused us on our local communities as never before. Confined within five kilometres of my home, I walked the streets. I met cats. I saw an owl.

At national level, I was proud of the public health doctors and scientists who adjusted so quickly to their new roles. They were uniformly strong and clear, even when the news was bad. We had no doubt that they would speak truth to power, telling the government the unvarnished truth even when the government wanted good news for a worried public. I was proud that a country as small as Ireland could produce these minds and voices, especially in a time of crisis and loss for so many.

At European level, the travel restrictions that accompanied the pandemic delayed some of the emotional impact of Brexit. With travel free flowing, the European dimension of our Irishness will flourish again. For me, Brexit heightened feelings of connection with European countries where I have friends, especially Italy.

What does being Irish mean to me? All of this – and more. And less. And everything in between. In the end, there is no limit to this thing we call 'Irishness'. That is part of it, too. Perhaps that is its essence.

Kevin Kilbane

Kevin Kilbane is a former professional footballer born in Preston in England to Irish parents. Kevin has won 110 caps for the Republic of Ireland, making him the fourth most capped player of all time. Kevin now lives in Canada with his wife Brianne. He is a proud father to Elsie, Isla, Gracie and Olivia.

Starting something so personal is always the hardest part, but although born and raised in Preston, England at no stage in my life did I ever feel like England is home and absolutely never felt English. Home was always Ireland, even though I didn't get the chance to visit much growing up as money was extremely tight. I was immersed in an Irish community where every person I met as an infant was from Galway, Roscommon, Donegal or Tyrone. I feel lucky that I was surrounded by people across the 32 counties and was able to get an understanding of what Ireland was like both North and South of the border during the 1980s and 90s, through a difficult time in Irish history.

Preston at the time had so many Irish immigrants. Most of my school friends had both Irish parents and felt exactly the same way as I did. We weren't Preston-Irish as I'd heard other Irish kids in cities around England describe themselves (for example, Manchester-Irish or London-Irish). We were just Irish. At no point in my life have I felt like I have mixed nationality, although many have judged and categorised me in a certain way. In England I was Irish and in Ireland I was English to some. In some people's mind my accent defined me.

I have always had a hunger to learn Irish history. I hated the fact that my history lessons had little or no mention of Ireland across my years in school, so my friends and I always felt that we had to stand up for our own people, rightly or wrongly. I felt compelled to learn of the suppression and exclusion many of our family members felt over the years and talked about it to friends and family. Much of this I feel is at times lost. I've heard the words uttered many times that 'we have to move on'.

Growing up in England there was absolutely no sense of the suffering in Ireland amongst English people. I felt a total disregard throughout my schooling for Ireland. Looking back, maybe we did have to move on but I just felt differently. I felt there was always a negative and very prejudicial stance towards Irish people from within England. We were always defined as 'thick Paddies'. Stereotyping Irish people has been widespread over the centuries and none more so than 1980s England. I hated it.

Of course, I've grown and I've learnt to brush it off but I've had my own identity questioned many times by Irish people who don't necessarily see me as Irish. There is a reason why mine and many other second, third and beyond generations of Irish people will always make it clear who they are because of the fight our mothers, fathers or grandparents have had when they originally left their homeland, and that mindset was strong around that time. I believe this to be true. It has been said to me that many Irish who've left Ireland feel more Irish and will always have more of a romantic or nostalgic view of Ireland which may be right or wrong, but I suppose it's only how a person is brought up and the pride they feel in being Irish.

I have always confidently declared that I'm Irish and I'm extremely proud of that. I've never wavered which I'm sure many of my school friends would testify to. I was in St Gregory's school choir and was chosen to sing at the town's harvest festival along with many other schools in Preston. Of the 100 or so children singing, everyone had to open with 'God Save the Queen' to start the festival. I told my mother what was planned but I knew what her feelings would be. I told her that I wouldn't be joining the rest in singing. I was only 10 or 11 at the time and I'd heard it played enough to realise that I couldn't sing along with the rest. I just couldn't utter a word of that anthem and chose to move my lips without saying a word. Rightly or wrongly in some people's eyes I just couldn't sing it. When I was called up for England as a young footballer I just had to decline. I hadn't had any contact with the FAI (Football Association of Ireland) and had never come onto their radar for selection.

It may well have hindered my career (Sam Allardyce, my coach at the time, let it be known to me in no uncertain words that I was letting him, and my club Preston North End, down) but I just couldn't wear the three lions and I could never stand for 'God Save the Queen' with pride.

Playing for Ireland to me meant standing for the anthem and playing for my people, and as cheesy as that sounds it meant everything to me. I'll never forget my first call up for Ireland under 21s and the first time I stood for our anthem in Drogheda. I feel honoured and privileged to have represented my country over a hundred times in international football.

Playing once would have been enough for me before pulling on the green jersey the first time, but to be part of a small group of players to have represented Ireland over 100 times, and the only non-Irish born player to do so, fills me with enormous pride.

We have a beautiful country but as I've moved to Canada over the last couple of years it's definitely hit home that it's our people that make our country beautiful. Being in Canada is a bit like growing up in Preston. I regularly meet Irish people from Down, Cork, Dublin or Limerick. We all have a pride in our nation that grows the more we're away and our children will always be reminded of who they are without a doubt.

Although I've moved away and lived a vast majority of my life away from Ireland (I lived in Dublin for five years before moving to Canada) I would love to see a United Ireland. Sport has brought our country together so if our boxers, rugby players or athletes can compete internationally as Ireland I would love for our people North and South of the border, whatever their religion or beliefs, to come together as one nation. Maybe I am a dreamer.

I, maybe naively, believe it is achievable. Many would say I have no right to have a say now I am away (which may be true), but our country has been hurt badly by religion and narrow-minded beliefs. Over the last 10 years we've had our constitution rewritten in ways that I'd never have imagined possible as a child. I believe that anything is possible.

Haven't I already said that maybe I'm a dreamer?!

Peadar King

Peadar King is a documentary film-maker and nonfiction writer. For almost two decades, he has presented and produced the RTÉ global affairs series What in the World?, filmed in over 50 countries across Africa, Asia and The Americas. His latest book is *War, Suffering and the Struggle for Human Rights* (2020).

A Farm Boy's Story

As a child, my parents took the very practical precaution against what they regarded as the nefarious influence of television by not having one in the house. That was until 1968, six years after RTÉ television first broadcast. But, as in any blanket ban, there were chinks in the prohibition. Every Sunday night my father, but not my mother, and up to six of my sisters and brothers decamped to Monica and Dickie Linnane's house next door – well nearly half a mile away – to watch *The Riordans*. There we were joined by Teresa Russell and her equally large brood who lived about half a mile on the other side of our television hosts. Often as many as twenty people, mostly children, were crammed into the Linnane kitchen for a half an hour every Sunday evening. Apart from some out-of-sync presences like the Church of Ireland minister (the Church of Ireland seemed a complete misnomer as there was only one church in Ireland), this rural drama was a seamless if not entirely non-contentious representation of rural life in 1960s and 1970s Ireland.

And yet.

Even as a child, I could not see myself or find myself in that rural world. A world from which I felt excluded. A world that left me cold. If this was rural life, I wanted out. The gauche, gormless Benjy. The perennial gossip that was Minnie Brennan irked long before I heard the word misogyny. The urbane (if ever a word drives me nuts, it is this) and always better dressed brother Michael found a life for himself far away from the farm. And so too, would I.

Meanwhile, amidst growing pressure from their children and perhaps to ease the pressure on their neighbour's kitchen, my parents partially succumbed to the lure of television. But, in a rural solution to a rural problem, they only agreed to get a television set for the autumn and winter months. And so, on 1 October 1968, Michael Gleeson from the nearby town of Kilrush brought the first black and white set into the house. Frank Hall was the first television presenter to break through. He would later make a name for himself lampooning rural life – from the comfort of the city.

And there it was.

The lampooning of rural life. The crude caricatures. The cute hoors. The small mindedness. The Ballymagash Urban District Council. Ha Ha Ha. As if cute hoorism vanished with the birth of 'modern Ireland'. Rural life 'a symbol of Éire passé' to borrow a phrase from Ken Whitaker, author of the now-famous 1958 plan, *Economic Development*, which was to become synonymous with his name and which was to usher in an Ireland of mohair-suited politicians, tax-avoiding transnational companies and speculative property developers aided and abetted by the unscrupulous machinations of global financial institutions underpinned by an avaricious neoliberal ideology that eschewed regulation in favour of rampant individualism. A revered world. A world beyond lampooning. A world that has cost us dearly.

It wasn't, of course, just *The Riordans* that caused me to want to rush to 'the city' (well initially Ennis to be honest), to abandon life on the farm. As one of four boys and five girls, staying on the farm wasn't an option for all nine of us, but I made my parent's choice (read my father's) somewhat easier by making it plain that I did not want to remain on the farm. That left the choice down to the other three boys. In 1960s Ireland girls did not inherit farms. Unconsciously, I had internalised the 1960s/1970s rural bias that was such a feature of the drive for modernisation that gripped not just Ireland but Western Europe too, most notably expressed in the famous Mansholt plan named after the first European Commissioner for Agriculture that resulted in the evisceration of small land holdings and mass rural decline. Even John Lennon (in normal circumstances, I wouldn't countenance a word against John Lennon) got in on the anti-rural act in 'Working Class Hero'.

> And you think you're so clever and classless and free
> But you're still fucking peasants as far as I can see.

Like, what was that all about John?

An anti-rural bias that found expression in a culture of snobbishness that infected all levels of Irish society. Born in the West of Ireland, Albert Reynolds was elected Taoiseach with the active support of the disparagingly constructed 'country and western brigade', despite the burden of the nomenclature of 'the Roscommon Slasher', while David Andrews, the Dún Laoghaire TD whom he appointed as Minister for Foreign Affairs, was routinely referred to as 'urbane'. Brian Cowen was another burdened rural Taoiseach, this time with the nomenclature BIFFO (big ignorant fucker from Offaly). Along with John Bruton, a farmer from Meath, all three are the shortest serving Taoisigh in the history of the state. Two other Taoisigh, Charlie Haughey and Bertie Ahern, the latter the second longest serving Taoiseach, were both Dubliners. Both had tribunal of inquiry findings made against them. Both unencumbered by the kind of nomenclatures that Reynolds and Cowen had to live with.

It was hard not to internalise such sentiments growing up in West Clare in the 1960s and the 1970s. Growing up anywhere in rural Ireland. And then.

Years later, I found myself filming among *campesinos/campesinas* of Latin America, initially in Nicaragua and later across South America. In Latin America there is pride in being a *campesino/campesina*. The peasants of Latin America. Rural people. People of the land. 'Our ancestors, our family are lying under our lands.' Atilo Curinanco, who along with his wife Rosa Rua Nahuelquir, both members of the Mapuche people of the High Andes on the border of Chile and Argentina, gave up urban living to return to the lands of his ancestors told me: 'Their spirit is calling us somehow.'

I don't believe in spirits but somehow now that I'm in my seventh decade, I feel the place of my birth. The place I grew up. The land. The trees. The soil. The fields. Páirc na Staellaigh field. The Cottage Field. The Burrow Field. The Quarry Field. The Fort Field. The Well Field. The Meadow Over. John Clancy's Field. The Corner Field. The Bottom Field. The people with whom I grew up.

And now I can say not with pride but with a deep sense of belonging that defies my own understanding, I too am a farm boy. That I too come from peasant stock. Come from a peasant community. The *campesinos/campesinas* of West Clare.

And it feels good to say that.

Teresa Lambe

Teresa Lambe is an Associate Professor and Principal Investigator in the Medical Sciences Division at the University of Oxford. She is one of the Principal Investigators overseeing the University's Covid-19 vaccine programme. The vaccine has now been delivered to nearly half a billion people worldwide and has played a pivotal role in the fight against the virus. Professor Lambe was awarded an honorary OBE in the Queen's Birthday Honours in 2021.

I'm from Ireland, but have spent most of my adult life living in the UK. The dreaming spires of Oxford, that were so intimidating at first, are now my home, feeling both familiar and welcoming. When I first emigrated, I didn't expect there to be such a difference between the UK and Ireland. Of course, I had heard of Twiglets, Marmite and 'real ale', but it was more than that. Historically, and culturally, the two countries see the same events through very different lenses – with the truth often somewhere in between.

Coming from a small country town with more pubs than shops – full of cousins, neighbours and friends – I was used to the hum of banter, built on everyone knowing everyone else's business. I was certainly not used to the temperament of a small British city. I did not recognise the pulse, the flow, the character. It seemed alien; agnostic of its inhabitants, regal in its indifference. Being Irish did open some doors; in my experience, we're seen as generous and gregarious, a nation full of life and laughs. Eventually, Oxford welcomed me in, or maybe I just accepted her indifference and realised it didn't really matter! If you're open to people and places then they can become as much a part of you as where you were born.

What I do defines me as much as where I am from. I'm a mother. I'm a scientist. While not mutually exclusive, they are two very different roles. I never really planned a 'career in STEM' – I just followed what I enjoyed doing. My parents always encouraged me to treat the 'world as your oyster'. I was always inquisitive (some would say nosey); always asking questions, trying to figure things out. Science allowed me to do that. I never thought about being a 'woman in science'. I'm a scientist. That is it. There are no qualifiers.

But I think there is a naivety in youth, that you can 'have it all'. The idea breeds discontent and disillusionment. I believe that you need to make informed and deliberate choices – weighing up benefits and also, more importantly, the drawbacks. I worked part-time when my children were young; this did impact my career, but it was a conscious decision – one that I'd happily make again.

During the pandemic, I have worked a lot (and I mean *a lot*) and again, it was a decision that I made – I needed to do what I did. I needed to develop, test and progress a vaccine against Covid-19. I missed my kids, my family, my friends. I missed my life, but it was a decision I'd happily make again.

For me that's part of my 'Irishness' – a ferocity, a tenacity, a determination (mixed with a good sense of humour). An ability to make mistakes – to get knocked down – but also a fire to get back up and go again.

None of this is possible without support, without family, be that through blood or through friendship. The people who support you, shape and mould you. Any career, but perhaps more so in academia, is fraught with highs and lows. It makes for strong friendships and a willingness to go the extra mile when needed. Again, this to me is being Irish, a trait firmly inherited from my family – a dogged determination to protect your own, to go 'above and beyond' for the ones you love.

Oxford is as much in my blood as my Irish roots; it's where my children were born, where I choose to live. My friends, my family, my job, my home – all these things shape me into who I am. I'm a mom. I'm a scientist. I'm Irish. I'm an OBE. I'm a mix of all these things and more.

If I could tell my early self anything it would be, 'not everyone will like you and that's okay; you do you and be proud of everything that means.'

Robbie Lawlor

Robbie became active within the HIV community after his diagnosis in 2012. He is a member of European AIDS Treatment Group and is a co-founder of Access to Medicines Ireland. He has provided sexual health/HIV workshops to over 100 schools and universities throughout Ireland, UK and the US. He is co-host of The PozVibe Podcast which provides a platform for the voices of other people living with HIV in Ireland.

It was 10 o'clock at night. I was in my mam's house, sitting at the kitchen table, staring at a giant pink pill. I knew little about what I was medicating against, but I knew that once I took this pill, I had to take it every day for the rest of my life. Worst of all, once I took this pill, I couldn't deny my diagnosis anymore.

In 2012, I went for my very first sexual health check and three weeks later I received the news that I was HIV positive. I was just 21 years old and it felt like the world collapsed in and around me.

How had this happened? I didn't even know that HIV existed in Ireland. I never discussed HIV with friends or previous sexual partners. I would later realise that this ignorance was a symptom of poor sexual health education I had received growing up gay in a country where sex and shame go hand in hand.

The unknown reality that escaped me was that there were thousands of people living with HIV in Ireland, yet I didn't know one person living with HIV who was out about their status.

When I was diagnosed, I was quickly reassured that medication will stop the virus from replicating and it will allow my immune system to work as normal. This giant pink pill would mean that I can live a long healthy life and that I will never develop AIDS. This should have felt like good news, however, I remember thinking, where was the pill for the sense of shame I was feeling? Living with HIV in Ireland was like living in a deafening silence, where fear and stigma created a vow of secrecy.

'Be careful who you tell because once it is out, you can't take it back.' These were some of the first words I heard from my social worker after I received my diagnosis. Although well-intentioned, these words were emblematic of Ireland's attitude towards HIV. I heard these words for what they truly meant. It meant that I now embodied the shame that my country attributed towards sex.

I was told that I was salacious gossip. I was told to be careful of who I trust. I was told that openness would lead to hurt. That I was a dirty secret.

Over the years, stigma became more apparent when I started to make friends with many people living with HIV. Regardless of our community's diversity – male, female, trans or non-binary; straight or queer; black, brown or white – the majority of stigma and discrimination was born out of fear and ignorance. An ignorance perpetuated by Ireland's shame around sex and drug use.

Is it any wonder that so few of us are out about our HIV status? Forty years after the first cases of AIDS were reported, people still think that we can pass on HIV from kissing, and from sharing a glass of water or even a toilet seat in Ireland.

Once Ireland got access to effective treatment and people living with HIV stopped dying of AIDS, we as a nation stopped talking about it. This is where the deafening silence ensued. Ireland never truly grieved, we failed to educate or remember, and as a result, the legacy of AIDS still affects the lived experience of those living with HIV today.

Trauma grows where silence reigns. Thankfully, change is happening thanks to a mobilising HIV grassroots movement and advancements in HIV treatment. In 2015, ACT UP Dublin was re-established. It was formed out of anger at governmental and societal inaction over Ireland's rising HIV rates. ACT UP Dublin effectively used direct action, social media and outreach work to ensure that HIV was once again prioritised. Their work included fighting for access to the HIV prevention drug, PrEP, and after many years of protesting, PrEP became available for free for those who have a higher likelihood of acquiring HIV.

Finally, and most importantly, the science became conclusive; the safest people to have sex with, in which not to get HIV, are those who know their HIV status, who are on effective treatment and who have an undetectable viral load. In addition, we can have children without fear of passing on HIV. The risk is ZERO. This science created a paradox. A seismic shift in how society sees us, but also, in how we see ourselves.

Today, when I take that big pink pill, I know that I am enabling myself to not only survive, but to thrive. By being healthy and refusing to stay in the viral closet that society forced upon me, I fought back against Ireland's culture of shame around sex. This act of transgression, my openness, never led to hurt. It instead led to a life of being my true, authentic self. By living shame-free of HIV and by whole-heartedly placing my trust in Irish society, I have embodied resilience and power, not shame.

The growing number of people living with HIV who are now coming out about their status is an indicator of Ireland's slow, but progressive, shift in attitudes towards sex and STIs.

To accelerate this progression, Ireland needs to treat *all* people with respect and dignity. Only then can we overcome the silence and shame around sex and HIV.

I believe that by providing comprehensive sexual health education we can enable everyone to lead a healthy and happy life. A life that moves away from silence and towards the sound of wisdom and shared experience. Only then can Ireland become a place where we are no longer as sick as our secrets.

Ola Majekodunmi

Ola was born in Lagos, Nigeria and raised in Dublin, Ireland. She is an Irish language broadcaster, freelance journalist, Gaelgeoir, creator, co-founder of Beyond Representation and Board of Directors member on both Foras na Gaeilge & Mother Tongues Ireland.

It took me a while to accept my Irishness. I did not even know at first if I was 'Irish' enough, especially when I thought I did not look it. I remember being a child who answered an innocent 'Nigeria' whenever someone asked where I was from. All they saw was a supposedly poor, black child who ended up in Ireland somehow.

It was only as I grew up and tried to understand the nuances of identity that I realised Irishness is something from within; I did not need any documentation to prove that. I had always been Irish because my everyday experiences were Irish. Your identity need not to be fixed, it is very much shaped around experiences. My dark skin and coily hair should not take away from my Irishness, that is all of who I am.

The idea of being 'Irish-American' is so yearned after internationally, yet we are still trying to get our heads around 'Afro-Irish' here, even though a lot of us from that community had grown up here. Irishness is so synonymous with whiteness that it seems so challenging for people to open their eyes to what the real Ireland looks like today. The country has changed whether people like it or not, and the homogenous Ireland many grew up in is no longer.

You would laugh at the number of times people have asked me how I have Irish or why I even do. I struggle to understand at times what is it that is so surprising about a person of immigrant background speaking the first official language? Not only that, but why is it threatening to some that I do? There are complexities within Irishness. We are not proud of who we are as a nation, yet we have this beautiful, cultural heritage. I fear it may all slip from our hands one day without us realising that now's the time to cherish what we have.

I will never forget that moment when I got news that I had been granted Irish naturalisation. I was at my local library studying for my Leaving Cert and suddenly I felt like I was one of you, one of the team, one of the nation's people. I looked around me and I thought inwards, 'yes finally, this is it! I'm accepted now!' How wrong teenage me was. You might cry at the number of times I have been trolled online with phrases like 'you'll never be Irish,' but I laugh and roll my eyes.

I tear up sometimes appreciating how much *Gaeilge* means to me. I seriously cannot imagine my life without her. *Gaeilge* is what moulded me into who I am today, yet people who make fun of the language with contempt, fail to recognise this unless they open themselves up to her. You certainly do not need to speak Irish to be Irish, but I do not think any of us can deny how much a part of us she is.

It is funny how the likes of me are accepted as Irish abroad more so than at home. I wear my Irishness like a badge abroad, I am so proud of this little island; how far we have come, and how much we have yet to go. I let my Irish lilt speak for itself at the top of my lungs. If some traditional music broke out in a bar, I tell you I would be dancing those *haon, dó, trí's*.

Please do not get it wrong, I am proud of my Nigerian heritage just as much as I am proud of my Irish experiences, this duality can be a struggle, but it is quite a beauty. I have had the two cultures carry me through my life and I really would not have it any other way. I am Nigerian just as much as I am Irish. Dublin is my home and so is my birthplace, Lagos.

When you are of immigrant background engaging with Irish culture, you can sometimes be accused of 'trying too hard' or assimilating. It somehow seems you can never win, trying to be loyal to each of your identities.

It is clear to me now that the Ireland I grew up in is miles away from the Ireland of today. We are now a nation that cherishes our uniqueness, beauty and future. I intend to spend most of my life on this isle with excitement for what is to come. *Is Éireannach mé* and I am glad I can now confidently say so.

Martin Mansergh

Martin Mansergh, former diplomat, Taoiseach's advisor, and Tipperary Fianna Fáil TD, was actively involved in the peace process, taking part in the negotiation and early implementation of the Downing Street Declaration and Good Friday Agreement. He is a member of the Royal Irish Academy. Martin is a member of the Church of Ireland, a monthly contributor to the *Irish Catholic* newspaper and on the Governing Board of Carlow College, St. Patrick's.

Being Irish is both a personal story, and also about belonging to an independent state, but in a divided island, both parts of which are commemorating their centenary. The development of independence is one part of that experience. The other part, manifest over half a century, is the inextricable interdependence of Ireland and Northern Ireland both in conflict and in peace.

In early decades in separate jurisdictions, which both sought to prove themselves in difficult conditions, conformity was sought in church and state, with critical challenge discouraged. Majority rule was pervasive, until it began to be softened by ecumenism and pluralism, more easily accommodated in the Republic, which had only a small minority.

Long-simmering tensions in Northern Ireland eventually erupted into a progressive civil rights movement, which tragically was overtaken by escalating violence, followed by a long and unwinnable war. This was only brought to an end with difficulty by a still precarious peace process. Constitutional differences became raw again following Brexit, and preventing conflict from re-erupting will require statesmanship and forbearance. The challenge is to hold on to the gains of peace, especially the absence of a physical border.

Issues of identity, from an Irish perspective, have been largely defused. Cultural nationalism no longer excludes and sits comfortably alongside civic nationalism. Beyond obligations of citizenship, people, whether new Irish or of mixed background, are free to determine their own identity.

The Good Friday Agreement had a liberating effect, when it recognised 'the birthright of all the people of Northern Ireland to identify themselves as Irish or British, or both, as they may so choose'. Even some unionist leaders can contemplate the last option.

Being Irish today means being European, by belonging to the European Union, comprising 27 countries and 450 million people, which creates new horizons and opportunities for the entire island. That exists alongside a unique relationship and Common Travel Area with Britain, reflecting innumerable cross-border and cross-channel family, social, economic, sporting and cultural links.

The constitutional accommodation that was a key part of the Good Friday Agreement gave recognition to the diaspora in the reformulated Article 2, in which 'the Irish nation cherishes its special affinity with people of Irish ancestry living abroad who share its cultural identity and heritage'. The United States, from the President down, is in many respects Ireland's most important single partner. Several other countries have a significant Irish population, and there are also many places round the world where Irish people have contributed to development.

Any society needs to be capable of integrating or assimilating minorities, while respecting different identities. Since independence, the Republic achieved this over time through gradual mutual adjustment. Albert Reynolds as Taoiseach in the Downing Street Declaration accepted 'that the lessons of Irish history, and especially of Northern

Ireland, show that stability and well-being will not be found under any political system which is refused allegiance or rejected on grounds of identity by a significant minority of those governed by it'. An island unity involving an enduring majority/minority divide would not be a good future model. Apart from myriad practical issues, can a way be found to blend together in one national community the values of a culturally Irish, republican separatist identity with a much more British-oriented outlook, history and tradition, given that the substantive economic and religious gulfs are now much less?

In the early 1950s, the Republic remained relatively poor and, though free of old oppressive political links, suffered isolation. Then the country shifted to a different path, which from the first stirrings of prosperity in the 1960s allowed it to open up, unlock much potential, catch up with others, enjoying today a modern and respected global profile.

Though mainly brought up in Britain, in early adulthood I returned with my wife to Ireland, long home of my forebears on my father's side, eager to contribute. I never regretted that choice and, happily, all our family, son and four daughters, spouses and partner, eleven grandchildren and a brother, are at present living in Ireland.

Archbishop Eamon Martin

Eamon Columba Martin was born in Derry in 1961. He was ordained a priest in St Eugene's Cathedral, Derry, on 28 June 1987. In 1990 he went to teach Mathematics and Religion at his old school, St Columb's College. He became Head of Religious Education in 1997 and eventually President (Principal) of the College, a post he held for eight years. He was appointed Archbishop of Armagh by His Holiness Pope Benedict XVI on 8 September 2014.

I grew up in Derry close to the border with Donegal where both my parents were born. As a child, every Sunday was a trip to Granny's home on the farm in Ture and holidays were spent on the wonderful sandy beaches of Inishowen or, in my teenage years, travelling with my parents to different parts of Ireland.

My mother was a fluent Irish speaker – the Master in her local school was from Kilcar and taught everything through Irish. My father also grew up on a small farm on the Northern side of the border and enjoyed telling us tales about cows being helped over the border and reciting lines from Mummers' plays. He had a strong connection to the land and the seasons; he loved gardening and liked to forecast the weather by the moon.

I am one of twelve children, most of whom still live in different parts of Ireland, as do my many cousins and relations. We are quite a clan and keep in touch with one another.

My parents both had a strong Catholic faith which shaped our family life. My father led the Rosary every evening. My mother's faith gave her a deep sense of fairness and charity. She told us about her father giving milk from the farm to poor neighbours when she was a child. In turn, she often invited Traveller women into our home for a cup of tea – money was tight for us but she could always offer a kindly welcome with some of her home-made bread and jam.

Growing up we 'discovered' Ireland – the beauty of its landscape and the richness of its history told in the round towers of Monasterboice to Clonmacnoise; painted in the green Glens of Antrim and the lush vales of Avoca and Glendalough; sketched in the enchanting lakes of Fermanagh and Killarney; written in legends from the Causeway coast to Connemara and the Burren.

Feis Dhoire Cholmcille was a big event every year. As a young boy I had learned 'mo chéad cúpla focal' at a local community centre. We enjoyed competing in the various music, drama and poetry events. It seemed that everyone in Derry loved to sing. Music also introduced me to friends from other Christian traditions whom I joined in various ensembles.

With this background it is hardly surprising that I have always had a strong sense of my Irish identity. I am proud to call myself Irish. Being Irish has helped me to value faith, family and tradition, hospitality and love of the land, language, music and culture.

The Bible invites us to remember 'the rock from which you were hewn (Isaiah 51:1)'. Growing up in Derry during the difficult years of the Troubles, the political landscape did little to make me question my identity and roots. However it did awaken in me a sense that Ireland holds a 'terrible beauty' and that 'being Irish' is a delicate and complicated matter.

I realised that, while people from different backgrounds shared some common ground, there are other identities and cultures with their own stories and traditions and strongly held views on how things should be – and be put aright.

Ministering as a priest brought me face to face with the devastating aftermath of conflict and violence. I have witnessed the heartrending pain and grief which has torn lives, families, neighbourhoods and communities apart. I have found myself searching much deeper than my Irish identity for answers to the reality of difference and division, suffering, evil and inhumanity. I discover those answers in the message and sacrifice of Christ. There I find the love which reaches out to all, a reminder of the inherent dignity of every human person, and a constant call to healing, reconciliation and peace. It is the same message that St Patrick and the early Christian evangelists brought to this island many centuries ago and which generations of Irish missionaries have in turn shared with peoples in the farthest corners of the world.

Recently, reflecting together as Church leaders on the complex questions surrounding the 'centenaries', and the challenge of ensuring that Ireland is a place of belonging and welcome for all, we remarked that 'Christ's teaching, ministry and sacrifice were offered in the context of a society that was politically divided, and wounded by conflict and injustice' (Statement of Ireland's Church Leaders, St Patrick's Day 2021).

We acknowledged and lamented that as Christian churches 'we have often been captive churches; not captive to the Word of God, but to the idols of state and nation.'

Therein lies the challenge, not just of 'being Irish', but of 'being human' today – to discover the 'deeper connection that binds us, despite our different identities, as children of God, made in His image and likeness'.

Micheál Martin

Micheál Martin was born in Turners Cross, Cork and attended University College Cork where he qualified with a Bachelor of Arts degree. He was elected to Dáil Éireann in 1989 and served as Lord Mayor of Cork 1992–1993. He has served in previous Governments as Minister for Education, Minister for Health, Minister for Enterprise Trade and Employment as Minister for Foreign Affairs. He became Leader of the Fianna Fáil party in 2011 and was elected Taoiseach on 27 June 2020.

This edition of *Being Irish* is very timely. The twin traumas of Brexit and the Covid-19 pandemic have required us to confront the question of what national identity means more directly than at any time since the Good Friday Agreement, when the first edition of the work was published.

The effect of Brexit has been complex – the changed relationship with Britain will take time to fully understand, but the experience has had two primary effects on my sense of Irishness.

The first is a much more distinct feeling of being European. The process and now the fact of Britain's departure from the EU has required unprecedented engagement with our fellow member states. The solidarity that they have shown has had a lasting impact on me.

It has also highlighted the truly global footprint that we as a nation and a culture have achieved, after many generations of effort.

The second impact has been in terms of the North. Brexit has brought the Good Friday Agreement centre stage again and while its success in delivering peace is widely understood and accepted, the debates and tensions around Brexit have reminded us of the extent to which its promise as a tool of reconciliation has not been realised.

For my part, Brexit has inspired me to recommit to the open and generous spirit of Irishness so memorably expressed by John Hume, ironically in a speech to the European Parliament, when he said that the Agreement proposes 'accommodation and respect for the identities of both sections of our people and creates the circumstances in which both sections of our people can work together in their common interests and by doing so we can break down the barriers of the past'.

Of course, the Ireland, and indeed the Northern Ireland, of 2021 has many more component parts and an ever richer tapestry of backgrounds and perspectives than it had in 1998, but the generosity and self-confidence at the heart of John's approach remains an inspiration for me.

The pandemic, and our response to it, have confirmed for me many of the qualities that I have long associated with my Irishness. The centrality of family and community, and loyalty to our sense of place, has long manifested itself in our sporting and cultural activities.

During the most difficult periods of the pandemic it manifested itself in the overwhelming sense of solidarity across the country. We accepted and adhered to previously unimagined restrictions on our lives, understanding at a very deep level the importance and value of looking out for our neighbours.

At a time of such grief, when deeply embedded rituals and traditions were not available to us, our communities still found safe ways to be with the bereaved and put our arms around them.

As we have emerged from the shadow of Covid, that sense of community and place is as strong as ever. In fact, all across the country we see evidence of families reconnecting with their place, as they have reappraised their lives and are now ready to 'move home'.

We will all take time to reflect on our experience of the pandemic, but I know that I will never again take for granted the freedom and joy of a walk in West Cork.

Like so many others across the country, I rediscovered the physical beauty of our natural environment and the emotional beauty of our literature, our art and our music. In that time of relative quiet I achieved a new level of understanding of the absolute imperative to protect our native biodiversity and its role in our national identity.

I missed the communal experience and celebration of our sporting endeavours in a very profound way.

The experience of the pandemic did not change these fundamental ingredients of my Irishness, which have been with me since my youth.

But it distilled them and gave me an appreciation of them that I am quite certain will never leave me again.

Sinéad McArdle

Dr Sinéad McArdle is a Consultant in Emergency Medicine in the Mater hospital, Dublin. Originally from Waterford, she is married to DJ and has two young children.

I'm not a very deep or philosophical person. I would describe myself as logical and I just take things as they come. My mother often wonders 'who do I talk to about things' and I usually tell her I'm fine or I'm grand (definitely two phrases used more in the Irish culture than any other). Therefore, I know growing up I never thought too much about my identity or how Ireland shaped me into the person I am today. It wasn't until I started to travel in college that I realised there was something unique about being Irish.

I studied Medicine in University College Cork. Every summer I went abroad. Year one was Paris, where I worked in a fast-food restaurant, 'Quick'. I stood out like a sore thumb. If someone was short a centime I would let them off. My boss would be furious at me for being generous; she would throw her hands up in the air and give out about the Irish giving things out for free. At the end of the week my till was always out by a franc or two which I paid up from my purse, always happier that someone had maybe gotten a drink or an ice-cream for the sake of a hundredth of a franc.

The next two summers I waitressed in America on J1 visas. I never questioned it for being anything but normal, the thing to do when in college. But looking back it resonates with what we Irish take for granted. I never thought twice about arriving at a new country with no accommodation, no connections, no phone, no job and being only 20 years of age. I just relished the prospect of experiencing something new, getting a stamp in my passport and having a summer of fun with friends, albeit amidst work as I needed to return home with money for college.

In 2006, following completion of my internship, I moved to Australia to work in Emergency Medicine. Even at my junior level the Irish doctors were hugely respected; we were known for working hard, being conscientious and adaptable. I was proud to be Irish. There is a pedestrian bridge in Melbourne city centre, Sandridge Bridge, which I used to cross regularly. It depicts the immigrant arrivals to Australia by country of origin since 1788. Initially most Irish immigrants were convicts sent by the British to serve time. By 2006 most of the immigrants were professionals, all adding value to the growth and prosperity of the country. I realise I was very lucky to have worked and visited Australia on my terms, whereas only two to three years later I had friends move out of necessity in the post-boom recession era and stay for much longer than desired.

On my return home in July 2008, I started on my career path to become a Consultant in Emergency Medicine. In 2016 I was appointed in the Mater University Hospital in Dublin. There are many days the job is tough and demanding, requiring long hours and dedication. Patients often share not only their medical history with you but their stories, their passions, their fears, and I view this as an honour to have met and been privy to so many interesting stories throughout my career to date. GAA is often at the cornerstone of these stories. There is such a unique passion and joy for the sport that even in the bleakest of moments, when someone has been given bad news, the most important question is will they see their team win the All Ireland or the county championship.

> *As a young female consultant there are extra challenges. First and foremost, you are regularly presumed to be the nurse until, and sometimes even after, you introduce yourself as the doctor. A male doctor has never been mistaken as a nurse in Ireland.*

My class in college was 75 per cent female and I still recall sitting through a lecture from a male surgeon where he spent most of it lamenting the future of his speciality. What would happen when all these female doctors had babies and wanted family-friendly working conditions? The suggestion is never that the husbands of female doctors should take up family responsibilities, freeing their spouses for their professional work? Instead, the HPAT exam was introduced to even the playing field and increase the number of males being offered medicine. When the balance was in reverse, what special tests were implemented to engineer equality of numbers for women?

Unfortunately, as much as we are progressive here in Ireland, coming out in droves to vote for same sex marriage and to repeal the eighth, we are not at the stage that being a stay-at-home dad is commonplace or socially acceptable. Ireland has a way to go to support women working full time, to challenge attitudes about the responsibility of parenting and carrying the mental load of all the things that need to be done to ensure your children are getting the best opportunities and your house stays standing.

My story wouldn't be complete without touching on working on the frontline in a global pandemic. I'd like to thank people for the supportive texts they sent when I went to work every day, especially in the beginning when so much was unknown about the virus, its virulence, its long-term effects. It made it all worthwhile. I'd like to acknowledge the exceptional work, courage, compassion and generosity of the hospital staff that went above and beyond for patients. Staff had to be so much more for patients outside of their normal roles, as patients were isolated from family and friends and all the social supports that usually get them through. We survived it together and everyone had a role to play.

Andrew McCammon

Andrew is a born-again Christian from Whitehead, County Antrim, now living in Belfast. He works as a dentist and spent six years in the British Army, where he gained the rank of Major. He is passionate about the Irish language and is heavily involved with the Turas Irish language project in East Belfast, along with East Belfast GAA.

The first time I thought about the identity question was during a history lesson in third year at Carrickfergus Grammar School. One day, the teacher decreed that the four corners of the room were to represent Irish, British, Scottish and Northern Irish identities and that we had to position ourselves somewhere in the room according to how we felt. It was a big question for 14-15 year olds, and I think few of us understood the significance of it (us being members of the post-Good Friday Agreement generation). I remember the majority going towards the Northern Irish corner, with some going to the Scottish corner if they felt their surname was particularly Scottish. I was one of the few who ended up closer to the Irish corner than any of the other corners.

I grew up in Whitehead which was different to other towns in that area in that it was a fairly mixed community. At the time, it was more or less devoid of flags, even during the marching season. My friends and I would travel by train to school in Carrickfergus, which would be full of British and Paramilitary flags at certain times of the year. The walk from the station also took us past a huge bonfire site in the summer. I remember feeling proud that Whitehead wasn't like this. To me, it felt like my town was defiant and unoccupied by those who seek to oppress the community and enforce their way of thinking. Since the 2012 flag protests more emblems and larger bonfires have started to appear in Whitehead, but the presence of these just makes me want to express my Irish identity more.

As a person who grew up within a community where people would be more likely to consider themselves British or Northern Irish than Irish, I often got into discussions about the identity question (most recently when the 2021 Census was circulated). When challenged, I used to maintain that I was putting something as central as identity into a geographic entity rather than a political, man-made one. A few years after the classroom experiment, I would choose to be baptised and put my identity first and foremost in Jesus Christ. Nevertheless, I still thank God that I was born in Ireland, a perfectly sized piece of land perched on the outskirts of Europe, covered in green grass, rolling hills, and possessing a culture that to me represents resistance against the odds, community spirit, light heartedness and a unique respect for those who are humble. He definitely chose the right place to put me.

I love that there's so much variety in this world. For me, it would be an awful shame if we all looked the same, spoke the same language and enjoyed the same activities. The world would be poorer for it. In my early thirties, I made the decision to become fluent in the Irish language and to try hurling for the first time. Ironically, I actually made this decision during my time in the army when I was posted to Fort George in Scotland – a fortress that was built next to the highlands and oversaw the demise of the clan system and Gaelic culture following the battle of Culloden in 1746.

I initially joined the army because it would give me the chance to see the world, meet new people, and allow me to test myself in the face of rigorous training. I actually applied to both militaries on the Island, as well as every service, but only the British Army were accepting dentists at the time. Like the experience of many Irish people who work in Great Britain, I discovered the special connection you have when you come across other people from here. I also found myself making friends most easily with people from Commonwealth countries (a phenomenon that others have written about in the 2000 version of this book). There's so much I value from my six years working overseas, but one of the things I cherish most (and is of particular relevance to this book) is the appreciation I developed for the culture we have here.

How special is it that we have sports developed right here on this island, or a language shaped over thousands of years by the very environment that is still around us until this day. It is sometimes not until you leave somewhere and look back you realise the value of what you have left behind.

I'm lucky in that I had the chance to do that, to make the decision to come back, to settle here and maybe raise a family someday with children who speak the way we speak, who might experience the island and culture the way we do, and who continue the story of this island that is still in progress.

Larry McCarthy

Larry McCarthy Ph.D., became the 40th President of the GAA in February 2021, the first from an international GAA unit (Sligo New York). He started his GAA administrative career at Thomond College, Limerick before moving to the US and holding numerous roles promoting Gaelic games with the New York GAA. He is an Associate Professor in the Department of Management at Seton Hall University in New Jersey.

As I was born and reared in the independent Republic of Cork, what it meant to be Irish is a query I never considered!

All joking aside, I never really contemplated the question. Growing up in Cork in the sixties was not a time when you met a lot of people who were not Irish. Yes, the Cork-Le Havre ferry started in 1968, the *Innisfallen* had been sailing from Cork to Fishguard for generations, and the airport was a connection to the continent, but there was not a broad swathe of people that you came into contact with who were not Irish, which might trigger contemplation of the query.

It was only when I traveled abroad that I had reason to begin to think of what it meant to be Irish. I was very lucky in that I was a member of the CBSI so I travelled abroad on a few occasions as a child and as a young man participated in a number of international scouting events where one was identified as Irish. That is when I began to contemplate the question.

Being Irish to me meant we were happy go lucky, taking life as it comes, hesitant to be confident about ourselves, but highly competent in whatever we engaged in. We were hard working, but always capable of enjoying ourselves.

When I moved to the US in 1986 to begin post-graduate studies at New York University, I found that perception had not altered significantly. We were highly competent, shy about putting ourselves forward, and thoroughly capable of enjoying, not only ourselves, but making life a lot easier for many others with our happy go lucky attitude.

As a result of being competent in so many areas we had, and still have, a very low tolerance for those who speak too much and do less. To coin a phrase, we have a very low propensity for what might be termed balderdash! We tended to cut to the chase professionally whilst being strategic, and successful, in our approach to issues.

Being Irish and working in the construction industry (to fund my graduate studies) in NY in the 1980s meant that one was the butt of racist observations on occasion. Thankfully, it did not happen frequently, but being addressed in derogatory, collective, terms was not unheard of. Mind you, the response might have been no less disparaging. In a small way it helped to frame an understanding of the hurt felt by other ethnic groups who were constantly derided.

What was different from my earlier experiences of being abroad was the connection – the connection with other Irish in a major metropolitan area, the connection with Irish culture, the connection with home through a constant search for news.

For me, the NY GAA and Gaelic Park became a hugely important element of being Irish. It meant I was constantly engaged, through Gaelic Games, in Irish culture, it meant I had a community of support, and it meant I had a source of Irish news.

As the late John Keane from Sligo said about Gaelic Park in the 1970s and 80s, it was the internet, before the internet, you found out everything there.

It took me a long time to appreciate some manifestations of Irishness. The importance of the St. Patrick's Day Parade in NY for instance. Not the importance of the day, but the importance of the parade. As a child I had marched in St. Patrick's Day parades with CBSI in Cork, so a parade was no big deal. Indeed, I viewed the NY parade with its strict rules and regulations, and decidely pro-catholic ethos, as totally anachronistic. It took me a while to recognise that marching up 'The Avenue', 5th Avenue, was an important statement of identity in a huge multicultural city.

When I moved from the NY metropolitan area, first to Ohio and then to Georgia, being Irish made me unique. In both of the communities where I lived, I was one of the very few Irish people who were born in Ireland, although many of those I worked with, studied with and met socially would all claim 'I am Irish as well'. When queried about their family tree there was usually a lack of knowledge of where their ancestors originated. The claims of affiliation with Ireland amused me initially, but the longer I was away, the more I began to understand the search for links in a multiethnic society.

Being Irish, and living abroad, was a very positive experience. While I was looked upon as different, perhaps due to a rabid Cork accent which has not lost any of its intensity from being abroad for 36 years, being Irish was a huge help, personally and professionally. My experience was that one was respected and appreciated for who and what you were.

Gareth McCay

Gareth is the founder and Managing Director of McCay Solicitors which has branches in Derry, Strabane and Omagh. Having suffered a catastrophic spinal injury in 2010, Gareth has spoken at events in Europe and America about life after spinal injury, positivity and disability rights. Gareth lives in Derry with his wife Colleen and three children Annie, Alexandra and Ryan.

Identity is a difficult topic when it comes to people from Ulster and, unfortunately, nationality is intertwined with religion.

As 1980's Ulster went, I had something of a sheltered upbringing as I spent the first 10 years of my life living in the County Tyrone village of Sion Mills. The village emanated from the Herdman flax mill and they made a concerted effort to build a village which was inclusive and devoid of sectarian divide. The village school was integrated, both religions lived side by side, so much so that fans of both teams would watch old firm games side by side in the local social club. Growing up we played cricket and football and religion never came into it. It was an idyllic environment which really should have been the blueprint for tackling divided societies in the North. Against that backdrop, I would be lying if I said that I felt a real sense of Irishness from an early age.

In 1993 my family moved to Derry and perhaps naively my parents moved to the predominantly Protestant Waterside and I was catapulted into a very different environment. I took a few kickings shortly after having moved and had to quickly adapt. I began to pay more attention to events going on at the time and I vividly recall the newsflash of the Rising Sun massacre at Halloween just a few miles outside Derry and feeling it was chillingly close. Events such as this made me inquisitive as to what the conflict was all about.

My grandmother, Annie Burke, lived in Bishop Street in Derry close to the Bogside and Brandywell. I would often stay with her and she would educate us at the kitchen table. She had been heavily involved in Civil Rights and the labour movement and, seeing injustice all around her, she became involved in the Republican movement. She was a proud Irish woman and always advocated equality and respect rather than superiority or hate. Between that schooling and the education at St Columb's College I had a real thirst for Irish history and politics which I studied at university.

I excelled at sports at school and in particular soccer and Gaelic football; I had also joined Brigade Cricket Club. That created the strangest of Saturday schedules in the summer months of Gaelic training with Doire Colmcille on Saturday morning, before dashing to Brigade Cricket Club quite often with my GAA kit still on. Although the only Catholic at the club, I was made very welcome and I captained the underage team right to the point where I chose to concentrate on soccer as I had begun to travel regularly to English clubs. I spent five years with English clubs and was always struck by how keen people were to tell me of their Irish heritage and how many identified as Irish, despite only having one Irish grandparent. My own great granny was a Geordie but I don't recall ever proffering that information when meeting an English person. It gave me the feeling that being Irish was something special and to be proud of.

By the age of 14, I knew who I was. I was selected for Northern Ireland at youth level but it wasn't something I was particularly enthused with. In truth, young players from Derry were treated very poorly at the time and I opted not to continue travelling to Belfast for training sessions after a game against the Republic of Ireland where I felt I was on the wrong team.

I lived in England for a number of years and we were all Irish regardless of creed as that is how we looked and sounded. In my twenties I got a job in the Irish Heritage Centre in Manchester, solely on the basis that I was Irish.

I encountered the huge Irish diaspora in the Northwest of England. In many respects they were more Irish than us, particularly the second/third generation who didn't have the accent so it meant more to them to submerge themselves in Irish culture. I loved my time in England and it is probably the period when I felt a heightened sense of Irishness or when identity mattered the most.

Being Irish wasn't always positive, and in my early legal career I encountered some racism being referred to as a 'pikey' on a regular basis by a Senior Partner. The more I was denigrated, the taller I stood as it harked back to Annie Burke's kitchen and a struggle to prevail.

Over the past 10 years I have been lucky enough to follow the Irish football team around Europe. Everywhere we have gone we have been fondly welcomed and Irish fans have been lauded for how they behave. I am a firm believer that sport unites and that an all-Ireland football team will over time bring the people on this island together. Ireland has changed hugely in the last 20 years and now with Brexit, the United Kingdom has changed too, and for the worse both culturally and economically. It would now seem that we are on the cusp of building a new, inclusive Ireland where there is a place for everyone. If a united Ireland does transpire it is of the upmost importance that we learn from the past and ensure that Irish, British and Northern Irish identities are all respected and religion plays no role. Perhaps they should go back and look at the Sion Mills blueprint . . .

Oisín McConville

Oisín McConville is a former Gaelic footballer who played for Armagh in the 1990s and 2000s. He won an All-Ireland Senior Football Championship medal, seven Ulster Championships and a National League title with the county. Despite his success, Oisín developed a serious gambling addiction and spent time in a rehabilitation centre. He has since helped hundred of athletes as a trained addiction counsellor and much sought-after public speaker.

Growing up in Crossmaglen, County Armagh, gave me a strange sense of identity. Crossmaglen was an area known as 'bandit country' – so it wasn't exactly something you'd be jumping up and down about. When we travelled North, and were ever asked where we were from originally, we were always advised to say Newry. As a result, there was no major pride instilled in me about where I was from; it was the self-preservation that was more important – we were seen as 'Fenians' from 'bandit country'.

There were a lot of negative connotations with my area. I attended the Abbey Grammar School in Newry, and a memory that sticks out in my head from that time was a teacher telling me not to worry too much about my studies, as I would probably end up smuggling anyway. I felt as I grew up and matured, I had more of an appreciation and understanding of the resilience and the fight shown by the community of which I was from and started to take pride and ownership in it. We were also starting to achieve big things on the GAA pitch. At last, our identity was something to be proud of! Now I love to say I'm from Crossmaglen. It is an area known for its sporting greatness, and something the whole area can take huge pride in.

When I think back to growing up in the middle of the Troubles, I think back to living as normal a life as possible at the time. You would always see the discrete facial expression of someone when you told them where you were from, and it was difficult constantly hearing your home getting ridiculed. Upon hearing this, I would begin to circle the wagons, defend, and try to accentuate the positives of my hometown – of which they were many, especially the GAA club. The GAA gave us something we could be proud of and it helped that we had the people to facilitate that. We wore our colours with pride and we began to realise that this was our road away from the negativity and the success we were achieving backed that up. We were at last the benchmark for sporting success.

Later in my career I had the opportunity to travel to all corners of the world promoting GAA. I travelled to the Middle East and Australia, and it was then that I could see the esteem with which people held me personally and the success at club and county level. It made me realise that perhaps, in my own journey through life, I had taken my Irish identity for granted. This was reinforced when I could see how those who were forced to emigrate clung onto their Irishness through the GAA. This realisation made me appreciate my club and my home a lot more.

There are many challenges in today's society, including the pressures to conform to what people want. In the country we live in there is still a hesitancy to express our beliefs and that is regardless of what community you come from: you're either seen as an extremist or you're someone who is afraid to express who they are.

As much as we've travelled an amazing journey to peace and reconciliation, we still lack the freedom to express our identity without fear of repercussions. The challenges are also for us all to be cognisant of the fact we don't all have the same identity or beliefs and to be comfortable enough to live life taking that into consideration.

I'm very proud to be Irish. Ireland is a much different place than it once was. Some of the crap that goes on from day to day wouldn't exactly fill you with pride. We have been let down by our leaders, we still hold on to the baggage of old. I'm from an area where the Troubles have left an indelible mark and for a lot of families the hurt is still as raw as ever; our daily challenge is to try and remember loved ones but also move on and help the next generation live in harmony.

Being Irish is still a great source of pride, we are still held in very high regard across the world. We are seen as friendly, welcoming and very importantly a nation that doesn't take itself too seriously. Being Irish abroad is thankfully still seen as a positive.

The standout qualities of the Irish include kindness, and a welcome like no other. Self-deprecating, we undersell ourselves all the time yet we are capable of being anything we want to be. Think of the people who have left Ireland and have become worldwide successes in business and sport.

Sharon McCooey

Sharon McCooey is Head of LinkedIn Ireland and Senior Director of International operations. She has helped the company grow from a staff of three people in Dublin ten years ago to over 2,000 today. With a passion for inclusivity and development of people, Sharon is a key support of LinkedIn's Women's Initiative (WiN) to help mentor the next generation of female leaders in business.

Being Irish by choice – it's a state of mind

I consider myself lucky to be born on the Island of Ireland to parents who were inter-generational Irish. I grew up, went to a school and lived in a town where everyone was Irish. I never thought about being Irish, looking Irish or any other element of my identity.

This changed when I went to New York as a first-year college student in 1988. New York was a completely different place to anything I had experienced before – a land filled with people from countries all over the world; some in New York by choice, others from necessity.

After my first night in a YMCA, I walked onto the streets of New York to calls from builders on overhead scaffolding, 'Hi Irish!' or 'What's the rush, Irish!?' It took a few moments to dawn on me that they were Irish immigrant builders working in New York who could recognise a fellow Irish person (pale skin from a lack of sunshine!)

This simple encounter gave a sense of identity to me for the first time and made me wonder what being Irish was. In the thirty years since, I've met people from around the world, and have come to realise that many have multiple identities and places they call home. I have heard people tell me they are Japanese-American and don't feel they belong in either place. In Japan they are American and in America they are Japanese. They are part of a tribe of people who do not belong anywhere.

> *To me, being Irish is a state of mind. It's not a place and it's not being born here to Irish parents. It's a sense of community, where people feel they can belong. You can find yourself in any part of the globe and be able to strike up a conversation with a stranger over this shared bond.*

This is one of our unique attributes and one of the reasons why people all over the world consider themselves Irish. In parallel, the Island of Ireland increasingly feels open to all, with a growing number of people integrating into Irish society and helping it evolve.

This evolution has picked up over the last ten years and one I have been particularly observant of as someone who works for a tech multinational and as a mother. Wearing both hats, I have met, worked with and become friends and neighbours with a growing number of people who have chosen to call Ireland home. The majority of whom have settled here, taken up citizenship and had Irish children. Similarly, some are here for an adventure like I was that summer in New York City. While they may only be passing through, I hope when we part ways that they leave with some of that Irish state of mind to take with them.

My ambition for my future grandchildren and for everyone who calls themselves Irish, or considers themselves to be partly Irish, is that we become a collective, with a shared identity and state of mind. We will continue to show the world that Ireland is a wonderful place to live, a place to stay and to be part of a community. We are all Irish, whether born here or choosing to become so.

Thanks to our open nature and evolving society, being Irish will become a much richer experience as our community becomes more diverse, even more lively and with an enriched state of mind.

AP McCoy

Sir Anthony McCoy, known as 'AP', is a former Northern Irish National Hunt jockey. McCoy recorded a phenomenal 4,358 winners during his career and was crowned Champion Jockey for 20 consecutive years, every year that he was a professional. He lives in England with his wife and two children.

I grew up in the small Catholic village of Moneyglass in County Antrim, one of two counties in Ireland with a Protestant majority. In Moneyglass we thought of ourselves as Irish. Our culture was self-contained. I went to mass; I attended a Catholic school and I played Gaelic football for the local GAA club. I considered myself Irish then, still do and always will.

That is not to say that we were sectarian or hostile to the Unionists of the surrounding area. In fact, one of the most influential people in my young life and career as a jockey was a local Protestant horse trainer, Billy Rock. He bought a horse from my father, and the two became close friends. It was through Billy that my love of horses began and was nourished. I was so obsessed with horses that Billy's religion didn't matter to me at all. What Billy told me about horses was more important to me at that time than what I heard at mass on Sundays. Billy was someone who had a huge impact on me and moulded me as a person. He used to wind my parents up that he was going to dress me like an Orangeman and bring me to the Twelfth of July march.

Years later, I went to work for Jim Bolger, horse trainer, in Kilkenny. It was New Year 1990, and I invited my two workmates to come home with me to Moneyglass for New Year. They were 17 years old, and one came from Kildare and the other from Mayo. 'No f**king way I'm going up there,' was the colourful reply. They were talking about the North of Ireland as if it was on the other side of the world. At that time, it may as well have been.

Northern Ireland's history has been sad, in so many ways, yet now most visitors that come to the North don't think twice about it with the buzz of Belfast city, beautiful scenery, our coastline and world class golf courses in places such as Portrush. We have a lot to be proud of, and yet we could do better in promoting it, and retaining our talented young people rather than them having to move away.

During my career, I had the privilege of being invited to Stormont, in which I had a long chat with Martin McGuinness about the past, future and even about his meeting with the Queen. I believe that the arrangement and interaction between himself and Ian Paisley changed the North of Ireland for the better, and it would be a better place today if they had a longer time working together in power.

Recently, the North has undergone a period of great change, especially with Brexit. Yet perhaps this could be a time for creating a plan to bring all the people together. A plan that would create optimism and a new energy for everyone, and make the North a place where more people would want to live and work and invest in.

I've lived in England since 1994, have cemented roots and have raised my family here, yet there is no place in the world like Ireland. Our friendliness makes us unique. I've been used to people saying hello as you walk down a street all my life, even strangers, which is something you don't see in other places. My children hold Irish passports, yet my daughter show jumps for Great Britain, with the Union Jack flag on her jacket. I would never have imagined that being a possibility when I was growing up.

In 2002, I passed Gordon Richards' total of race wins and afterwards I received an invitation from the Home Office to receive an MBE at Buckingham Palace. I rang my mother and talked it over with her. She was a woman who had strong Republican views, and she understood the complexities of the invitation. Having thought it over, she eventually advised me to accept it, saying that I had lived in England a long time, was rearing my family there and that it was the right thing to do. But on every invitation date that was sent to me for going to Buckingham Palace I was busy racing. So, after many rearranged invitations, the Mayor of Oxford had to hand deliver it to me at home. I'm sure he wasn't too pleased!

Then in 2010 I won the Grand National and received another letter from the Home Office to award me an OBE. So, I said to myself, I had better attend this time. I went up and stood in front of the Queen and my jaw dropped when she said, 'it's nice of you to show up this time.' I made an apology about my racing schedule, and she smiled and said, 'You don't have to apologise to me. I read the Racing Post every day, I knew exactly where you were.'

When I retired in 2015, I got the news that I had been awarded a Knighthood. I rang my mother who, upon hearing this, said: 'I'm going to have to go into hiding around here now!'

Mary-Lou McDonald

Mary-Lou McDonald is Sinn Féin President and TD for Dublin Central.

To me, being Irish means so many different things. There is no one way to be Irish or to feel Irish, any more than there is one way to be human.

The Irish have many qualities which make us unique. When you live in Ireland, it can feel hard to put your finger on exactly what Irishness is. Often, it's only when you leave these shores and have some distance from it that those characteristics come into clear view.

I'm very proud of our people; our sense of fun, of fairness and of community. Undoubtedly there is a closeness and a friendliness which I think comes from being a small island nation. This can be both a blessing and a curse. At the best of times, this creates a cosiness and an intimacy. But the flip side of that can mean an intensity and propensity to overstep the mark into people's lives.

For me, what it has meant to be Irish has changed over time. My experience of being an Irish woman began as an Irish girl born into a very different Ireland. In many ways Ireland at that time could be quite an austere and judgmental place to live if you were seen as being 'other'.

Ireland overstepped into peoples' lives and choices in too many ways particularly when it came to peoples' families, their sexuality or how they chose to live their lives.

My parents separated in 1979 as the Pope was preparing to come to Ireland. There was an ugly social stigma at that time, a certain harshness towards families which were 'othered' or seen as different. I'm relieved that Ireland has collectively owned up to that past now and that we have shown how we can make room for what we might have previously seen as 'otherness'.

Throughout my lifetime, Ireland has embraced many changes which have improved our society for the better. I am so proud of our country legalising marriage equality and the huge progress we have made on women's rights in recent years. Such changes would have been unthinkable and perhaps impossible at a certain point in time, but these changes became unstoppable.

I have no doubt that greater change is still to come for Ireland. This year marks the centenary of the partition of our country. What happened a hundred years ago was a collective trauma for the island. In the north, a discriminatory, theocratic state was imposed while in the south too often Home Rule really did mean Rome Rule.

It has taken generations, but we are now on the cusp of finding our way back and healing from this trauma. The prospect of Irish unity is a necessary, normalising change which needs to happen for all of the island. This change is happening, and I believe that all of us need to begin preparing for Irish unity and to prepare ourselves for the changes ahead.

Our society has shown a capacity to be inclusive and to make room for 'otherness' and differences in identity. The unionist tradition and identity have a home here and will continue to do so within a united Ireland.

When I look to the future, I am full of optimism and hope. The younger generation are remarkable and will continue to shape Ireland with a sense of fun and fairness. The Ireland that my children are growing up in is so different to the one I knew as a child myself. The opportunities that they have and the paths they can choose to take are so different.

When I was younger, my older brother graduated on a Thursday and emigrated to Boston the next Monday. For many young people of that generation, the option to stay and build a life in Ireland simply wasn't there because there weren't enough jobs or opportunities.

I worry that the same situation could arise for our young people now, as the housing crisis continues to spiral and many people feel they can't build the life here that they want. Young people should be able to emigrate and explore the world with optimism, excitement and choice, rather than leaving because they feel forced to do so. They should always feel that they have the option to come back if they wish and to know that they have a home here.

Undoubtedly, the experience of Irishness has for centuries been intertwined with that of emigration. I was so moved when I visited the Irish Memorial in Philadelphia. The sculpture tells the story of the countless Irish people who fled Ireland for a better life, with passengers getting on a coffin ship and then bravely embarking into a new world. I found it devastating to look at the vast sculpture with this all too familiar agony wrought in bronze. But I was also so moved at the sense of community among the Irish Americans who came together to erect it a century later. They were many generations away from Ireland but had not forgotten the struggles and pain their ancestors endured.

It reminded me that in many ways, to be Irish is to remember and to survive but also to move on with determination and hope. The Irish are an incredibly resilient people. When immigrants come to Ireland, we must show them the same compassion and we must also know that they bring those same reservoirs of resilience.

The experience of colonialism has had a profound impact on the Irish mindset. This state of mind – of rebels, rogues, saints and scholars – is fundamentally about freedom. I believe we all have a responsibility to stand against imperialism and colonialism around the world. The experiences of the people of Palestine speak so directly to me as an Irish person. They are a people who are destitute, dislocated and who too often see the world turn its back on the profound injustices they endure.

Undoubtedly, the pandemic has also brought huge change to Ireland since Covid-19 first came to our shores in 2020. In many ways the upending of our lives has brought everything back to basics. Our famous sense of community has shone through in these dark times, our compassion and our desire to look after our neighbours and come together in solidarity. The expression *Ní neart go cur le chéile* – there is no strength without unity – has been embodied in how people were united together to protect all our communities at a time of profound loss and sorrow.

As we face into the future, I have no doubt that Ireland and what it means to be Irish will continue to evolve and change. I am optimistic about that change and believe we can look forward to that future with confidence and hope.

Archbishop John McDowell

The Most Rev'd Francis John McDowell, Archbishop of Armagh, was born in 1956 in Belfast. He was educated at Annadale Grammar School, Queen's University Belfast (History) the London School of Economics (Business Studies) and Trinity College Dublin (Theology). He worked in business for a number of years before ordination formation. He is married with one daughter.

You might think that being literally a lifelong member of a body which proudly calls itself 'The Ancient Catholic and Apostolic Church of Ireland', and holding office in that body as the '106th Archbishop of Armagh in succession to St Patrick' would make writing about being Irish straightforward for me. Probably my main dilemma should be what to include and what to leave out.

But nationality and identity are now recognised as complex and tumbling concepts, not least for those of us who live on this island but who can trace many tributaries that flow into the river of what we are now: what we add up to. Yet I'm by no means certain still what they will add up to when the river meets the eternal sea.

In my particular circumstances it's not that I wake up every morning wondering if I'm Irish in a British sort of way, or British in an Irish sort of way. I made up my mind a long time ago (in my late teens) what is at the core of my national identity, even though it didn't correspond to an exact geographical unit. So, in my case being Irish is something of a mixture of conscious choices and their interplay with the contingencies of ordinary existence at a particular time in history. Or should that be the other way round?

The conscious choices are easy enough to identify. For instance that late teenage and rather visceral psychological jolt brought on by reading Cecil Woodham Smith's book on the Famine, *The Great Hunger*. Or listening to a politician justify the ugly murder of Patsy Gillespie and thinking that the sort of clever inhumanity that can turn guilt of that sort into justification should have no part in this country.

Ernest Renan, a nineteenth century French historian of religion (he wrote a very famous *Life of Jesus* which Oscar Wilde called '...that gracious fifth Gospel...') said that the nation was 'a daily plebiscite'. In that sense it is a bit like the Church or even the Kingdom of God, with some people gradually and imperceptibly slipping out of membership and others moving into membership.

Often these realignments can be seen only on retrospect, although they can be gathered up and marked by a gesture.

> *In one small example from my own recent history, conscious of the great privilege and responsibility of being Primate of All Ireland, I changed the designation of nationality on my Wikipedia page to signify that I was both British and Irish.*

But there are some more uncomfortable or even turbulent elements also flowing into this river of identity. For instance, there is nothing more uncomfortable and sometimes humiliating than being in a house where one clearly isn't welcome. Of course it's possible to stand on one's legal entitlements and say, 'I've as much right to be in this house and take my equal share from the table as anyone else'. Possible, but not exactly making for cohesion or integrity, much less identifying with another of Renan's definition of the nation 'having done great things together and wishing to do more...'

Of course, how welcome I'd be in someone else's house might also be open to question, so being Irish carries the risk of new kind of homelessness.

Maybe that new form of homelessness shouldn't worry me too much when I add that being Irish, or being anything else for that matter, is not my foundational identity. That lies in being human and being 'in Christ'. All other forms of identity – given or chosen, or a mixture of both – must be seen in relation to these. Unfortunately, the Reformation of the sixteenth century gave a special place to 'national churches' and very often allegiance to the nation led to the undermining of the Churches' true foundation – being disciples of Jesus Christ. Here's how a very early Christian writer describes the relationship between church and nation:

> For the Christians are distinguished from other men neither by country, nor language, nor the customs which they observe. For they neither inhabit cities of their own, nor employ a peculiar form of speech, nor lead a life which is marked out by any singularity... They dwell in their own countries, but simply as sojourners. As citizens, they share in all things with others, and yet endure all things as if foreigners. Every foreign land is to them as their native country, and every land of their birth as a land of strangers (Epistle to Diognetus c.130 CE).

So, although I love its landscape and its coast, its literature and its music, its myths and its history, this is how I hope to be Irish.

Fiona McEntee

Fiona McEntee is the Founding and Managing Attorney of McEntee Law Group. Fiona first moved to Chicago from Dublin in 2002 as an international exchange student at DePaul University's College of Law. Fiona has published her first book, *Our American Dream,* an award-winning children's book on immigration, which helps to explain the importance of a diverse and welcoming America.

I was born in November 1981 in Dublin. Growing up, I'm confident I never really thought about being Irish and what that meant to me.

All that was about to change though in 2002 as I embarked on a one-year exchange program through UCD to DePaul College of Law in Chicago, Illinois. That move became permanent in 2005 when I returned to the United States to study and qualify as an attorney. Chicago has been my adopted home ever since and I've been practicing as an immigration lawyer since I was sworn into the Illinois bar in 2007.

Living in America, I'm constantly aware of my 'Irishness'. And while I am an immigrant to the U.S., due to the sacrifice, hard work and opportunity given to previous generations of Irish immigrants, I am now the beneficiary of true privilege – the Irish immigrant privilege. Nowhere is that more apparent than in the city of Chicago. Being Irish in Chicago certainly has its perks. Being Irish means warm American welcomes, stories of ancestors, tales of immigration, generations of pride. Questions about Dublin, County Galway, Tourmakeady. It means invites to judicial receptions, top tables at Celtic Lawyers Luncheons, and St. Patrick's Day zooms with President Biden.

With the acknowledgement of this privilege comes the recognition that it was not always this way. The Irish were not always as welcome to the U.S. as they are today.

It was not so long ago that Irish immigrants were desperately fleeing religious persecution and economic deprivation. They arrived not to open doors, but as immigrants that many considered unnecessary, unwanted, uncouth. Some feared they would take jobs away from Americans and would strain welfare budgets, rhetoric often still used against other immigrants today.

Nonetheless, these brave immigrants made the treacherous journey across the Atlantic to this land of hope and dreams. Today, their ancestors embrace being Irish with a tremendous sense of pride, and I witnessed first-hand how they bestowed *céad míle fáilte* to me, a newly arrived Irish immigrant.

I believe that with these welcomes and my Irish immigrant privilege – coupled with an added security of now being a naturalised U.S. citizen – comes responsibility. For me this responsibility translates to advocating for a more humane and accessible immigration system for all immigrants. This includes the millions of undocumented immigrants (Irish included) in the U.S. today, a subset of whom are the Dreamers (those brought to the U.S. as children). My advocacy also includes lobbying for the long overdue updates U.S. immigration desperately needs for future immigrants, including speaking to Congress about a potential startup visa, a personal mission of mine for many years.

I am not alone in this work. I'm constantly inspired by my team in McEntee Law, colleagues in the American Immigration Lawyers Association, and by grassroots activists, including my friend and mentor former Irish Senator Billy Lawless, who have been advocating for the rights of immigrants for decades.

Being Irish to me means remembering – and, when necessary, mentioning – that the Irish story has long been one of emigration. *The Irish Times'* Fintan O'Toole summed it up perfectly in his *New York Times* opinion piece, 'Green Beer and Rank Hypocrisy'. This piece was penned as the Trump Administration prepared to celebrate St. Patrick's Day in 2017 with a mid-Muslim/Refugee ban in what many felt was the personification of hypocrisy. 'Does green beer taste better laced with hypocrisy? Does shamrock smell sweeter perfumed with historical amnesia?'

Being Irish to me means highlighting to some, a small few – as Fintan so accurately said – this historical amnesia. Reminding them that it was not so long ago that the Irish did not meet the warmest of welcomes. As an immigration lawyer who works with clients from all backgrounds and from all over the world, I'm profoundly aware of the difficulties many face on their quest to live their American Dream today. You don't have to look that closely to see the parallels between some of the present day migrants, especially those at the southern border, and those who made that long, uncertain journey from my homeland all the way to America.

In my children's book on immigration, *Our American Dream*, I explained that:

Families travel far, by day and night.
Fleeing terror and violence, it's a dangerous plight.
They seek shelter and refuge at America's door,
like generations of immigrants who have come before.

While writing this passage, Annie Moore came to my mind. Annie was the first immigrant to come through Ellis Island in 1892. She came to the U.S. from Cobh in County Cork as a teenager, and she brought her two younger brothers with her. Annie's story is not that different to the children – 'unaccompanied minors' – we see seeking shelter and refuge at the border today. Being Irish means advocating to ensure those children, and all arriving immigrants and refugees, receive the same *céad míle fáilte* I receive daily in my life as an Irish immigrant to the U.S.

Eamon McGee

Eamon McGee is a GAA footballer, father of three beautiful kids and partner of Joanne.

'I'm a fan of man' - Satan from the movie *The Devil's Advocate.*

I've had this question posed to me quite a few times in the last few years and to be honest it's something I've always struggled to answer. Is there even an answer to that? In a world of climate change, pandemics and globalisation is being Irish even a relevant question?

Is there something tangible about me or something deep in my character that you can put your finger on and say, yeah, he's Irish? I'm a Gaelic footballer who speaks Irish, I come from a place in Ireland called Gaoth Dobhair, a place where a picture of it could be posted beside the word rural in the dictionary. I've won an all-Ireland with Donegal, an actual all-Ireland, surely this should give me extra credits in the bid to reach the quota of Irishness? On the negatives I don't actually know our own national anthem, I hum along to it before games and sometimes sing it when I see the words on the big screen in Croke Park. I've had it levelled at me that I'm no Irishman because of some of my more liberal views. I live in a border county on this island and literally, as the crow flies, 15 miles away from my home there are people who consider it a personal insult to be called Irish, or try telling my good friend Stephen, who has lived in Australia for 15 years and is likely to stay there, that he isn't Irish. Expect a clip round the ear if you do.

Consider all that and you can perhaps understand why the question what it means to be Irish doesn't have a simple answer.

At the end of the day. I'm Eamon, that's what I identify as. Everything else after that is a layer, a footballer, a father, a partner or even Irish. At the core of it all I'm Eamon.

I'm a man of limited life experience, I can only give my own insight and I can no more tell anyone what Irishness should mean to anyone else than I can try to explain quantum physics to a few of my teammates. What I can tell you is what I'd like being Irish to represent. This tribe we have built in an island in the west of Europe and how it branched off in to the every corner of the world. I think it should mean something more than an imaginary boundary society creates.

The values I'd like us to share, the feelings that I'd like it to give each of us. I think the idea of being Irish is something we can pass freely to everyone.

When we talk about Irishness we need to be careful because we've seen more and more glimpses of it in Ireland and other countries around the world. That's the narrow lanes that nationalism or some misunderstanding of patriotism creates. The more I learn about human nature, our place in the universe and the vastness of it all the more I've struggled to understand how anyone could be attracted to something so boring and unimaginative as nationalism. If that's where the conversation leads when we talk about being Irish I want nothing to do with it. What a banal journey we would travel if it we narrowed our vision of society to that.

What I'd like us to do is be the best we can be. Be a shining example to every country around and lead the way like we did in 2016 when we decided that Ireland would vote Yes to allow our LGBT brothers and sisters to have the same rights as us; other countries looked to us. In 2018 we decided we had enough of exporting a problem overseas and turning a blind eye to women; Irish people made the compassionate decision to do away with the eighth amendment of the Irish constitution. I've been involved in both campaigns and I can't understate the feeling of pride it gives you to see a letter from a young gay man's father saying his son was helped by the support shown, or a women who's had to travel to England walk up to you and say, 'thanks for helping, make sure no one else has to travel'.

Everyone involved in both campaigns worked their arses off to make it a better country. Ireland is a great country but it can be so much better and it doesn't mean we should be happy to park all that energy from those campaigns. There are so many things we have the power to fix now. Homelessness and a housing crisis? A mental health crisis (that was here long before the Covid pandemic)? Offer something better than direct provision to our brothers and sisters?

When someone says they are Irish I want them to represent a positive ideal. I want us to be an example to everyone else around the world. In order to do that we have to work for it and as we've seen in recent referendums, when we work together there isn't much we can't do.

Lisa McGee

Lisa McGee is an award-winning screenwriter and playwright from Derry and the creator, writer and executive producer of the acclaimed *Derry Girls*. She co-created, co-wrote and was executive producer on *The Deceived* with her husband Tobias Beer. Her other TV credits include *London Irish*, *Raw*, *Being Human*, *The White Queen* and *Indian Summers*.

Article adapted from an interview with the Editor.

It's our way of moving from light to dark that makes us unique.

My sense of identity is bound up with Derry. I was conscious of being a Derry person before I was aware that I was Irish. Events in Northern Ireland shaped us. Growing up we saw flags on lampposts, soldiers on the streets. We had to be forceful about what we were and what we were not. Derry not Londonderry. Irish not British. We had to defend who we were. In a sense Derry is misplaced. We are not so much Irish as a type of being Irish. We are different from our neighbours in Donegal. But we are different from Belfast also.

Moving from Northern Ireland to England, there was suddenly no point trying to explain to the English the type of Irish person I was. It seemed that people I knew who had moved over from a unionist background even gave up trying to differentiate their identity and eventually answered to Irish. To the English we were all Irish, pure and simple. But one thing we all did was to react to being or becoming English. I noticed my accent getting stronger. In my work in the TV industry, I became aware of the class differences too. There were so many people working in it from a privileged background. By contrast Derry is working class. You have to work hard for what you have or want to have.

There is a huge lack of female writers in the British TV industry. I found myself the only woman in the writing team. I was also the only working-class person. I wondered how people got into this industry. To me the barrier was class more than gender. I went to Thornhill College in Derry, an all-girls grammar school. We were pushed very hard. I never thought gender was a barrier to me as I had a lot of female mentors.

I often reflect on the differences between my generation and that of my parents and grandparents. The major difference was the lack of opportunity. My parents left school at 15 and their parents even earlier. Their world was also dangerous, surrounded by violence. This was in the seventies and eighties. I grew up in the nineties when the violent conflict was easing off. I admire them so much for doing what they did and for not giving up. And I am in awe of their positivity and sense of humour. All around them there was an epidemic of post-traumatic stress disorder which still hasn't been dealt with. They held firm to their aim of getting their children educated. I went to university and all the opportunities I have had are due to my education.

I lived in London for ten years and my husband lived there for twenty. We now live in Belfast. We always wanted to come home and our children's education and identity were the deciding factors. My son is losing his English accent for a South Belfast one. When I was living in England, I missed Ireland and Derry. It's the sense of humour. In England, when picking up the children at nursery, the parents wouldn't talk much. In Ireland the parents can't wait to tell you just how bad their own children are! And we can hardly wait to start slagging each other!

Humour, honesty, a sense of community and generosity are features of the Irish. In Derry people would give you their last pound. In London everyone is anonymous.

Living away from 'home', there was so much I missed, and I suppose that is why I write about it so much. I missed Bridies' fish and chips. I missed the quintessential glamour that is getting dressed up for a Derry night out, and the pre-drinks with the gang before even leaving the house, which is where all the craic was.

As a Derry woman I am proud to be Irish – but there has to be space for those who are not Irish. In NI one half of the population is pushing something on the other half. If we could only identify the words and terms that we could all agree on.

Maybe in the next twenty years we might just find the terminology that we are all comfortable with. I am optimistic for NI if we can concentrate on integrated education. For example, NI has the best TV crews in the world. Why can't we be proud of that instead of whatever flag you are waving? I speak to our young people. They are intelligent and understanding but loud voices drown them out.

Some events that influenced my identity. I remember the 1998 Good Friday Agreement and the optimism and energy that it released. I also remember the Omagh bomb from the same year that caused 29 deaths and hundreds of injured. I was at an age when I was questioning everything. No other country in the world has events like these.

I remember Hallowe'en in Derry. It's the time of the year when the souls of the dead return home seeking hospitality. It's not a big deal anywhere else but it is huge in Derry – perhaps because we have so many people telling us that we can't say this or we can't do that, so we dress up and wear a mask, go mad and frighten each other. Hallowe'en is almost part of my identity.

Are the Irish unique? I cannot speak for the country, but I think Derry is unique. It's the way we can move from light to dark, from life to death. We deal with trauma by framing it in ways that make it work. We use storytelling. Our sense of humour tells you everything about us. Derry has been pushed down by economic depression and by violent conflict. Yet we always have hope. Not just the hope of surviving but of achieving something worthwhile. If not unique, we are certainly special.

Tom McKnight

Rev. Tom McKnight is a Texas lawyer who went into the pastoral ministry, came to Ireland in 1981 to work for a year, met his wife there, and stayed. From June 2020–2021 he was President of the Methodist Church in Ireland.

In my home state of Texas, becoming a Texan is easy. All you need do is to move to Texas and call yourself a Texan. (In fact, twelve of the heroic Texans who died at the Battle of the Alamo were born in Ireland.) Becoming Irish seems not quite as simple. When I reflect on what 'Being Irish' means to me, several disparate aspects come to mind.

My Northern Irish Heritage. While growing up in Oklahoma and Texas, I was often remined by my dad that our ancestors were *Northern* Irish. My dad had served in Europe during the Second World War, and I thought he had spent almost the entire time in Northern Ireland since that was the only place he ever mentioned. Much later I learned that he had served equally long in England and France; he had simply *loved* Northern Ireland. I also remember him saying once that our family could wear *orange* (!) on St Patrick's Day, rather than the traditional green, because to him the colour orange was associated with Northern Ireland. So I was already aware of my Northern Irish heritage when in

1981 I came to work for a year with the Methodist Church in Ireland. I am still here.

Belonging. When I got to Ireland, I felt I belonged. My dry sense of humour finally found a home. My theology seemed to fit well within Irish Methodism. My height, at 5' 7', somehow didn't feel as short as it did in Texas. And less than two months after I arrived, I met the young woman who was soon to become my wife.

Feeling Irish. As the years have passed, I have felt more and more Irish. Although I have only ministered in churches in Northern Ireland, the Methodist Church in Ireland has always been an all-island Church. The first time I realised how much more in common I had with Ireland than with Great Britain was in January 2001. That month several of us from Irish Methodism attended a conference in England with Methodists from around the world. At some point we were broken into national groups. Because Northern Ireland is in the United Kingdom, Irish Methodists coming from there were, despite our protests, put into the national group with Methodists from Great Britain, while those from the Republic of Ireland were put in the European group. That misplaced grouping caused me to realise how much our identity as *Irish* Methodists trumped our identity as Methodists who just happened to live in the United Kingdom part of the island of Ireland.

Becoming British. In 2005, I was naturalised as a British citizen. This was not a difficult decision, since I had by then lived in the United Kingdom for more than two decades. My wife, who was born in Belfast, had never held an Irish passport, despite being entitled to one. To me, British citizenship was sufficient since this also made me a citizen of the European Union. However, because of the United Kingdom's exit from the EU, my wife now intends to get an Irish passport and I have begun to study the requirements for Irish citizenship by naturalisation.

In conclusion. I am an American. I have an American passport. I speak like an American. I file an American tax return every year, as required by US law. In common with most Americans, I use the Oxford comma before 'and' in a series. In common with most Americans and most linguists, I am prepared to often split infinitives. And in common with many Americans, I have Irish ancestry.

I am a Texan. I was born in Dallas. I have worked for an oil company. I inherited 0.00046293 of a small oil well. My birth certificate has 'Native Texan' emblazoned over the Texas flag.

I am British. I now also have a British passport. I have memorised both verses of 'God save the Queen'. I use the British spelling for 'colour' and 'centre'. I drink tea with my breakfast – and when I say 'tea' I mean what in Texas would be called 'hot tea'.

I am Northern Irish. I have now lived in Northern Ireland for most of my life. I know how to pronounce 'Ahoghill' and 'Donaghadee', and where to put the accents in 'Newtownards' and 'Ballinamallard'. I have even worn orange socks on the Twelfth of July.

And I am Irish – and not least because every Saturday I buy *The Irish Times*.

Fiona McLaughlin

Fiona McLaughlin is a secondary school teacher from Donegal. She is married and has two young daughters.

I've never really thought about my Irishness, isn't that a privileged thing? In fact, I've never even thought about 'privilege' until recently. I suppose I've never had to think about it much because I've mostly felt accepted. My Irishness has always felt a bit like an advantage, my 'oh wow-wee', my trump card. I'm much more likely to cross examine my identity as a woman and as a mother – maybe that's because I'm more defensive and protective of these titles. Or perhaps it's because I haven't always been as accepted. Maybe the 'mother' in me isn't seen to be as good craic as the 'Irish' version of me. I'm also aware that being Irish has given me a romanticised view of Ireland. Having lived away for so many years, I'm reluctant to let the rose-tinted glasses slip too far.

Born in the mid-1980s, and the youngest of five, I grew up in Inishowen, Donegal. My childhood memories are filled with recollections that were mostly based in our home – cartoons on Saturday mornings, hotter summers, colder winters and being outside until late eaten alive by midges. On Sundays we went to Granny's and visited our cousins before falling asleep in the car and being carried inside. Sundays also meant that Dad left. He went back to Scotland to work for the week and the nightly rotation of who got to sleep beside Mammy began. Of course, being the baby of the house, it was nearly always my turn. I think this might be one of my first memories of the 'Sunday night fear', the 'I haven't done my homework' feeling because that's when my uncle arrived to collect Dad. It signalled an end to the weekend, to the runs in the car, to the treat of a 'Football Special' drink and eating biscuits usually kept for visitors. My eldest brother left for work too, so did some cousins, and then years later my brother-in-law and even my husband. Is this an Irish thing? Or a construction industry thing? It's something that has been so familiar to me that I don't even think about it – you just follow the work.

So, when the opportunity arose for me to leave Inishowen and go to university, I did. Without question. I didn't go too far, Queen's University in Belfast. Here, I became aware of my Donegal identity. I was one of three students on part of my course from the Republic and I noticed it. We were the culchies from the 'Free State', the ones who did the Leaving Cert instead of A levels in exotic subjects like Drama, the ones who were slightly younger than our classmates and changed over our money to sterling on a Sunday evening. My best friend happened to be one of those three culchies too. We had the same surname, Doherty, so everyone assumed we were sisters. They were wrong. We were just from a peninsula where if your name wasn't Doherty, it was likely to be McLaughlin.

Despite being attached to home, I left again to complete my teacher training. This time to Newcastle Upon Tyne. Within one day of being in this beautiful city, I knew I could live there and I knew the exact reason why – it reminded me of Ireland. I saw so much 'Irishness' in the Geordies. Their warmth, their sense of fun, the way women older than me seemed to have that 'mother-hen' instinct; during my time there I was taken under the wing of many women who looked on me as either a little sister or a daughter. That's a lot of what being Irish means to me.

Feeling that warmth, that compassion, that sense of welcome coupled with a quick wit and an ability to slag you off, cut you to the bone and run with a joke until you've completely exhausted it, all in the same conversation.

Part of being Irish is also the way we seek each other out – perhaps it's a version of, 'like finding like'. We gravitate towards one another in strange surroundings, foreign countries and even in all-inclusive resorts. Our ears prick up at the sound of a familiar lilt or the sight of an Irish name. During an intense teacher training year, an Irish colleague sought me out. A toothache had reduced me to tears between lessons and I was taking refuge in an empty classroom. She found me, provided tissues, made a dental appointment and consoled me with stories of the first few years of her training. She recognised that behind the guise of a toothache, there was some homesickness too.

Years later, I didn't escape the homesickness in Australia either. Newly qualified and full of optimism, I returned to Ireland having completed my teacher training, but the recession was having none of it. Being Irish, I followed the work, this time to Sydney.

A one year stay snowballed into over three years and homesickness hit an all-time high. I pined for Ireland. I missed the Inishowen air, the way it reached out and slapped you alive, filling your lungs with the icy Atlantic. I even missed the rain.

The very things that had annoyed me about home became the things I yearned for. I wanted to go into a shop and meet the locals again – people who often seemed to know more about me than I think I knew about myself.

I hated the anonymity of city life; it was lonely. I'd also become a beach snob. I was underwhelmed by Bondi Beach and couldn't quite see what all the fuss was about. Maybe that's a Donegal thing, though? We're spoiled rotten with our landscape.

Eventually, I settled. A nanny position with an Irish household became a surrogate family, my (now) husband and I moved in with my cousin, friends lived opposite us, and we waved excitedly to each other from our sunny balconies and our accents thickened in each other's presence. We had found our familiar, our safety net. Before long, I secured a teaching position. It was no coincidence that the school was deeply rooted in Irish heritage and the *cailín* in me smiled a smug little grin when I was asked to pronounce Gaelic names on the register.

However, behind the alfresco breakfasts, flat whites, park runs, barbeques and stubby holders Ireland beckoned and it's where I find myself now, a stone's throw from my family and the sea. My two daughters have Irish names – 'inner cailín' smiles at this too. Three maps hang in our kitchen – Newcastle Upon Tyne, Donegal and Sydney. Donegal hangs in the middle, at the centre of everything. I hope my daughters will feel like this about their home and their Irishness too. I hope that the Ireland they grow up in will be one devoid of the judgement and tutting of past eras. They say it takes a village to raise a child so I'm glad we chose a good one.

JP McMahon

JP McMahon is a chef, restaurateur and author. He is culinary director of the EatGalway Restaurant Group, which comprises Michelin-starred Aniar Restaurant, award-winning Spanish restaurant Cava Bodega, and Tartare Café & Wine Bar (Bib Gourmand). He runs the Aniar Boutique Cookery School and plays host to one of most talked about international food events in Europe, Food on the Edge.

While researching *The Irish Cook Book* (Phaidon, 2020), I searched in vain for a stable identity for Irishness. At the outset of the research, I thought I understood what Irish food, and thus Irish people, was, or at least were. But the more I probed into our tangled 10,000 year food history and the many ways of migration that populated our island, the more unsure I became of what Irishness was. Indeed, it was difficult to even find a point when we suddenly became 'the Irish'.

For almost 8,000 years, we lived without any sort of national identity. Who were we then? What did we call ourselves? But at what point does a tradition begin? At what point can we say the people on this island became Irish? Since the beginning, since the first farmers, since the Celts, since the Vikings, since the Normans, since the British? In the second century AD, Claudius Ptolemy's (roughly AD 90–168) *Geographia* provides the earliest known map of Ireland. Ptolemy called the island Iouerníā from which eventually arose the Irish/Gaelic names Ériu and Éire. He also provides a reference to habitation in the Dublin area, referring to a settlement in the area as Eblana Civitas. However, it was Roman historian Tacitus, in his book *Agricola* (c. 98 AD), that used the name Hibernia to refer to Ireland. So nearly 2,000 years ago, the process began of creating and crafting an Irish identity, an identity that to this day continues to evolve and transform itself anew.

Identity is a fluid thing and the more we understand its history the more we can know about ourselves. The fact that our identity emerges from outside ourselves, from the distant past or from our family or the place we are born, should give us hope to know that even though it's something beyond our control, it's not something that is fixed forever. We can learn to shape it.

Growing up in Ireland in the 1980s, there was a lack of diversity, or at least it seemed that way. We appeared distant from Europe and the world. Visiting my great grandparents' farm in Armagh, I still felt connected to that world. I remember vividly the day a boy from Ghana joined our school. The whole school seemed to stop and look at someone that seemed so different from them. It seems common place now to talk of Irishness in terms of different coloured people and a multiplicity of gender identities, but back then that wasn't the case. Irishness meant something different, something other: something more akin to the men and women that had made Ireland their home from the nineteenth century onwards. A simple, poor, modest people who never looked beyond themselves.

I don't know what changed things. Was it our sudden affluence as a country? The digital revolution that showed us the rest of the world and brought it into our bedrooms? That showed us new ways of living, new ways of being? Or was it cheaper airfares, which brought me to Paris and Barcelona, that showed me different ways of living, ways that I would bring back home and eventually open up a Spanish restaurant to showcase that beautiful communal way of eating? All that happened was not inevitable and my own personal journey is mixed up with the public history that we all acknowledge. But it seemed for a period that all was truly moving forward, towards some manifest destiny.

The crash of 2008 and the subsequent bailout in 2010 brought us all back down to earth. Not in a particularly bad way, though for some, for many friends, all was lost. It seemed after this point we became Irish again, though it doesn't seem to make sense. Many us of returned to food, to the land. Maybe national identity gyrates, turning in circles across historical time, a time that we cannot stop, merely watch it as it goes.

I'm glad we're more open now as a society, more inclusive. We still have a long way to go but I feel we're on the right track. Irishness now is more an idea as opposed to something rooted in material reality. There are 15 million Irish passports in the world. The diaspora, so tragic at the time, has yield untold worldly benefits.

Irishness now is not Irishness then but elements remain, weaving themselves into future moments for others to catch or grab. Perhaps those first settlers, who made their home at Mount Sandel, County Derry can still teach us something: that community is perhaps the most important thing, even if you do know your place in the world.

Being Irish is a state of mind wrapped up in a particular way of being. It's a fluid identity that has many coloured faces and many hyphenated ethnicities. I look forward to the next fifty years, to the next five hundred, to see, and imagine, how Irish identity will transform itself into the future.

Annie MacManus

Annie MacManus, popularly known as Annie Mac, is a renowned DJ, broadcaster, events curator and author. Annie presented a varietiy of shows on BBC Radio 1 and can be seen at music festivals around the UK and abroad. She also produces her own podcast, 'Changes with Annie Mac', where she chats to artists, writers, musicians and others about change. She grew up in Ireland, but now lives in London. *Mother Mother* is her debut novel.

When you are an Irish emigrant, you have the privilege of being selectively Irish, to call on it only when you need it. It's a line cast into a conversation, looking for a bite. It's a crutch to lean on to explain and justify questionable personality traits, an easy way to remind people that you belong somewhere. I've been doing this for over twenty years. I realised recently that I have lived longer in England than I have lived in Ireland, and I worry if my Irishness is depleted somehow with this new reality. I think of the millions of us who have spread away from Ireland, populating new countries exponentially like some sort of friendly virus, and I wonder what Ireland did and did not do for us, that made us take our Irishness away to the safe confines of other countries and cultures?

I have just read Sinead O'Connor's book *Rememberings* and the Galway poet Elaine Feeney's award winning debut novel *As You Were*. The two books are stories of women, real and fictional, who each, for horrific reasons of childhood abuse, carry profound shame. In *As You Were*, the main character is unable to confront what happened to her, her shame manifests in her memories, compelling her to resist love and to repeatedly try and destruct any place of safety she exists in. In Sinead's case she fights shame like a warrior, relentlessly seeking to expose the ugliness of it for the world to see. It conspired to be a brutal and lonely battle to fight, resulting in mental health crises and long spells in hospital.

It struck me reading about these brilliant women, corrupted by their childhoods, that despite the extreme nature of the experiences they went through, I recognised their behaviour. I have seen it reflected in much smaller ways in my own, and in the Irish people around me.

If you live in Ireland, abuse or no abuse, you inherit shame. It is passed down from generation to generation, silent and insidious, to live with and to measure everything against, every thought of self-expression, every notion of turning the other way from the rules of religion and societal norms.

Women have been disproportionately lumped with it of course, for the dangerous capabilities of our bodies. We carry shame around like a purse in our handbags, always there, banging at the side of our hips as we walk. And when it's occasionally exposed to the public consciousness, from the unspeakable hell of septic tanks under playgrounds in Tuam, to the tearful confessions of middle aged men, men who once were vulnerable children in the system, I wonder what will Ireland *do* with it all? How to deal with the infinite matter of a country steeped in shame?

Us stragglers watch Ireland closely from across the oceans. Faces right up to the screens. We cried when the people of Ireland voted for same sex marriage. And we cried again when three years later, Irish women realised their collective power and led the referendum to repeal the 8th amendment. There would be no more of women travelling to England for abortions. No more of the journeys Feeney describes in *As You Were,* 'Irish women, rollie cases, taxis, coffees, airport toilets, sobbing, solitude, trauma, travel, Solpadeines, secrets'.

We see from the outside, Irish people trying to wrestle with shame, trying to own it, trying to bury it all over again. We know that a lot of us are running from that shame. We are escaping forwards, but we can't stop looking behind us.

It feels more and more that there has to be a way for the diaspora to stand in solidarity with Irish residents when it comes to confronting and prevailing upon the shame in our psyches. We have some of the worst voting rights in the world for emigrants and I hope this can change. But for now we must come together to share and compare the burden of Irish shame collectively, through art, through talks, through film and song. I am so inspired by the Irish music I'm hearing. There is a new generation of young principled Irish creatives who grew up in an Ireland with a floundering church and excellent internet connection, who care about speaking out against abortion, racism, gentrification and gender identity. These are artists who pride themselves in singing and rapping about the rejection of shame.

In our new chosen homes, we are Irish ambassadors whether we like it or not. Maybe it's time to stop being selective about our Irishness and embrace every part. Let's tell the world that the Irish are people who are trying to fly and not be caught in the crosswinds of shame. Let's tell the world that for all of its trauma and baggage, Ireland is a country moving forwards, and regardless of how far we've travelled, and for how long, we are moving with it.

Ryan McMullan

Ryan is a singer songwriter from County Down. He has played all over the world, performing on some of the most prestigious stages. He has toured with Ed Sheeran, Snow Patrol, Kodaline and the Coronas. Ryan is known for his ability to communicate story and emotion in his singing.

I'm not one hundred per cent sure on the truth of this statement, but I once heard that when St Patrick drove all the snakes out of Ireland, he replaced them with shitty broken guitars and sent them to everyone's nanny's house. Don't quote me on that. But I could believe it. That's how I came to be a musician. I was too shy to tell a joke and I sure as hell couldn't dance, so whenever it was my turn to 'do a trick at nanny's house' that beaten up guitar was my only way out. The storyteller in me wants to romanticise about that guitar. To tell you how I still have it now and still write songs on it to this day. But the Irish in me won't let me. I'd break it twice if I could. But what I am certain it did do, was give me an identity.

Identity to me is recognition. It carries favour, instils pride, evokes passion and offers hope. It becomes more apparent and less obvious, like the badge on a jersey or the style of a song. An Irish musician. That's me. I am sure there is more to me than that, but at first glance, that's how I'm identified. The musician identity has afforded me to travel the world playing shows and the Irish identity has given me company along the way.

Again, don't quote me on this, although it definitely has more merit than the last statement, but I heard recently that there are more Irish people off the island of Ireland than there are on it. I can't prove it to be true, but I've yet to play a show as the only Irishman in the room. Admittedly, that in itself tells a lot about us. We love to travel, but we don't travel well. I think that's why we congregate wherever we go. To keep home close to us.

Something I have always found funny is when I get the chance to meet some of the Irish people after a show, or whenever it may be, they always tell me that for an hour or so, I was a little bit of home to them, but get surprised when I return the sentiment.

Truth be told, at every show that I hear an Irish accent, I immediately relax. It is like an invisible comfort blanket. And then the show itself becomes this unspoken conversation of home.

History has always told us to get out of Ireland. How there is nothing for us there, and we have found that hard to move past. But there has been a shift in that tide. Time has moved on and our generation is now starting to reap what was sown by the generations before us. Ireland now has become as much of a paradise as anywhere we were leaving for. And the grass is most certainly greener.

Dominic MacSorley

Dominic MacSorley is the CEO of Concern Worldwide, Ireland's largest international humanitarian and development organisation that operates in 24 of the world's poorest countries. He was awarded an OBE in 2009 in recognition of his services to international humanitarian aid and, two years later, was honored by the Northern Ireland All Party Group on International Development for his outstanding contribution to international humanitarianism.

Being Irish – Defying Indifference

In the last year of her life, my mother asked that her collection of clothes – the good suits and coats that she had gathered over the years – be donated to the Concern charity shop in the small seaside town of Newcastle, County Down. As a child she had been evacuated there during the war, away from the bombs that struck Belfast, and for her it always symbolised a place of refuge and safety.

Started as a one-day jumble sale to help children in Somalia caught up in war and famine, the 'Harrods of charity shops', as it is known, had provided a steady stream of funds to support Concern's work in multiple countries over two decades. My mother's donation of her good clothes was simply a small gesture of support to an extraordinary network of volunteers that comes together across the country, organically and energetically, to make a difference in the lives of people they have never met.

For almost my entire working life, I have had the privilege of seeing first-hand the difference Concern makes. Leaving a much-troubled Belfast in 1982, I ended up right back in the heart of conflict – in places such as Darfur, Rwanda, Iraq, and Kosovo – where I saw how public support was critical, enabling organisations like Concern to respond rapidly and effectively to people caught up in horrendous crisis.

People like Lydia, the mother of four who I met in the Democratic Republic of the Congo. A local militia had killed her husband and burned her village to the ground, forcing her and her children to hide in the forest for six months. Médecins Sans Frontières – the only other organisation working in this remote, insecure region – was treating her, but she was struggling to find the strength to start over again. When I asked if there was even one good thing that she could focus on, she said it was the day Concern provided her family with some plastic sheeting and blankets, along with cooking pots and pans. This, she said, was enough to get her started again.

Humanitarian assistance is not just about the things people need to survive, it is so much more. It is about dignity, justice, a new start – in a word: hope. In the raw immediacy of suffering and despair, it is the generosity of public support that enables first responders to be there, to bring light into the darkest, most inhumane, situations.

In December 2016, a few months after my own mother died, Kay O'Loughlin Kennedy passed away. Kay was not a household name in Ireland, but in 1968 she founded Concern along with her husband John, to raise funds to support relief efforts on the ground in Biafra. Neither wealthy nor politically influential, Kay and John were driven by a determination to do something, and succeeded in mounting the largest humanitarian response ever to come out of Ireland.

The horrific images of starvation from the world's first 'televised' famine in Biafra that played out nightly on television screens had a profound impact on the Irish public, whose own memory of suffering and death was awakened. Everyone took part. Businesses north and south of the border raised money. Newspapers gave free advertising space; editors and reporters kept stories of Biafra on the radio and nightly news for nine months.

Each county was allocated a fundraising target based on population and every county, driven by compassion and competition, exceeded their target. Cork was insulted that they had been set such a low target and so went on to prove the point by raising six times more than they were asked. *The Kerryman* carried seven news items related to Biafra in one issue and, by the end of September, Kerry had reached over 800 per cent of its target.

Within 30 months, the people of Ireland had raised the equivalent of €65 million, dispatching five large ships of vitally needed supplies to Biafra. At a time in Ireland when only church or state managed anything of scale, Kay and John managed to tap into the conscience of a nation, channelling the compassion of the Irish people directly to those who needed it most. More than 50 years on that compassion is undiminished.

It is the individual stories of the often unseen and unsung heroes, those who devote their time and energy to others, that are the hallmark of who we are as a nation. It is the totality of their acts that has such a powerful force, one that matters more than we could ever imagine.

At Kay's funeral, 20 men and women from Ireland's Biafran community had one message: 'She was our mother too and without her we would not be standing here today.' It was an incredibly powerful moment to reflect on how Kay's actions, supported by the strength of Irish empathy and compassion, have resonated thousands of miles overseas, and for generations afterwards.

George Bernard Shaw described the essence of inhumanity not as hatred, but indifference. Being Irish, in its purest sense, is actively defying indifference to prevent the suffering of others – suffering that we know and understand – and in doing so, we not only are restoring humanity for others, we are strengthening our own.

Bulelani Mfaco

Growing up in the apartheid ghetto of Khayelitsha in Cape Town, Bulelani Mfaco became involved at an early age in protests for adequate housing and access to land. In 2017, he claimed asylum, seeking protection from violence and targeted killings of LGBT+ people. Bulelani campaigns for the right to work for asylum seekers, and to end Direct Provision. He is on the board of the Irish Council for Civil Liberties, and is part of Equinox, a coalition of anti-racist campaigners.

'Native education should be controlled in such a way that it should be in accord with the policy of the state... If the native of South Africa today in any kind of school in existence is being taught to expect that he will live his adult life under a policy of equal rights, he is making a big mistake... There is no place for him in the European community above the level of certain forms of labour...' – *Hendrik Verwoerd, addressing the Senate in 1954.*

Verwoerd was the Minister of Native Affairs and later became the Prime Minister of Apartheid South Africa and was stabbed to death in the chambers of the South African parliament. He is regarded as one of the architects of Apartheid South Africa, although he did not invent racial segregation and white supremacy. He merely articulated it and ensured that it was official State policy.

Other parts of the world had their own ways. I use Verwoerd because he is the most familiar example when discussing race relations. You see, Verwoerdian is found anywhere in the world where there are racialised people. Race in Apartheid South Africa determined how far you can go in life. The colour bar ensured that a Coloured person or Indian person working with a Black person and a White person in the same post was paid less than their White colleague but more than the Black person.

It might be difficult for an Irish person today to accept it, but ethnicity in Ireland is shaping access to opportunities for certain racialised people and it is deliberate. Members of the Traveller community who have had to change names in their CV for a chance at getting a job would have no trouble understanding that.

Similarly, an asylum seeker who spent years in the abhorrent system of Direct Provision, passed their leaving cert and could not further their education due to the imposition of extortionate fees when their parents were legally barred from working, would have no trouble understanding that identity has an influence in their experience of life.

Last year, the Catherine Day Advisory Group, which was established by the government, published a report calling for asylum seekers to be treated no differently to the way the State treats Irish nationals in terms of providing accommodation, welfare, all levels of education and make it easier for asylum seekers to work and contribute towards their upkeep. This was shown to be more humane and cheaper than the system of Direct Provision. It can only be beneficial for the Irish State as one in every two asylum seekers will be an Irish citizen someday. Unsurprisingly, the response from the government maintains the status quo, allowing only a small number of asylum seekers to have access to financial support towards their third level education. Asylum seekers who do not meet the exclusionary criteria have to stop dreaming about pursuing third level education. They've done no wrong to deserve to have the state deliberately imposing barriers on them reaching their full potential. And even when they kiss their academic dreams goodbye and try to get a job to earn a living, the Economic and Social Research

Institute tells us that racialised people experience discrimination in recruitment and selection. Such experiences engineer a class of racialised people whose poor outcomes in life are shaped not by lack of effort on their part, but by the deliberate structural barriers imposed on them due to their ethnicity.

While the civil servants and Ministers who make policy decisions such as creating and maintaining the institutionalisation and segregation that is Direct Provision, restricting access to education and the labour market for asylum seekers are not Verwoerd, they do appear to be flirting with Verwoerdian ideas. The only major difference is that Verwoerd owned his racism. He did not pretend to like Black people while implementing Apartheid. This is something the Irish bureaucracy needs to learn. To make policy decisions and own them.

Making speeches about integrating asylum seekers into all manner of Irish life from day one while imposing and maintaining barriers that make it hard for asylum seekers to get on with their lives is a cruel joke. Moving towards an Ireland of equals requires that each of us feels a sense of belonging. It is difficult to cultivate that sense of belonging when identity has a profound impact on how far a person can go in life.

Irish women should have some understanding of that. They have had to negotiate their existence in a patriarchal society. Racialised people around the world must negotiate their existence by constantly proclaiming their humanity. This is exhausting. The path towards the 'good society' cannot be carved with Verwoerd-era policies that prioritise one group over another, while ensuring that the undesirable other spends their lifetime surviving and recovering from trauma. At minimum, the Irish state must cherish all our lives.

Paddy Monahan

Paddy Monahan is a dad from Raheny in Dublin. He continues to campaign for an end to religious discrimination in the Irish education system as policy officer at Education Equality.

It was in 2015 that I realised how much Ireland has changed and how far it still has to go. I had spent the early months of the year campaigning a few hours a week for Yes Equality – the movement to legalise same-sex marriage. The reception on the doorsteps of north Dublin was unbelievably positive. But I also realised how very late to the show I was. I met people who had fought for gay rights for decades, who had held public demos around Ireland since the early 1980s when there might be a dozen or so supporters and little but incomprehension, fear and hostility in response from the public. The marriage equality referendum passed resoundingly.

My abiding memory of early 2015 is of bright, crisp Saturday mornings knocking on doors canvassing around Coolock, coming home and feeling our first child kicking in my wife's belly. That may sound hokey but it happens to be true – good vibes were in the air.

Shortly before Cormac was born in March that year, almost as one might browse absentmindedly through a catalogue of paint colours, I looked up our local primary school online. I started scrolling through its admissions policy and something jumped out at me – it prioritised Catholic children in admissions on the basis of their religion. That couldn't be legal, right?

I called the school and spoke to a really lovely secretary. She was very reassuring and told me the religious admissions policy only applied if the school was oversubscribed – if it wasn't they'd take everyone who applied. I said thanks a lot and hung up. I was happy to hear this. And then I wasn't.

Was the school usually oversubscribed? Was it oversubscribed last year? If a Catholic kid showed up the day before school started would my child be shunted out? When would he be 100 per cent assured of his place at the school? How can parents have certainty in this situation? Also, *is this legal*?

I called back. Yes, the school was usually oversubscribed, but children not in the priority enrolment category (that is, unbaptised children) may be offered a place closer to the start of school as Catholic families turned down the offer of a place and took places elsewhere. I was dumbstruck – frozen somewhere between disbelief and rage. I didn't have it out with the very nice school secretary.

A bit of research taught me a few things. First, yes it was legal – thanks to an exemption in the bedrock of Irish anti-discrimination legislation, the Equal Status Act, which said that religious discrimination by schools in admissions is not discrimination. It literally said that. I also learned that around 96 per cent of taxpayer-funded primary schools in Ireland are controlled by religious patrons (90 per cent being the Catholic Church). I looked up the enrolment policies of every school I came across on Google maps, searching a wider and wider area. I learned something else – the 'Catholics first' provision was a standard clause in virtually every enrolment policy in the country. My mind was swimming a bit at this stage.

Here, in short, is how the next few months went. I contacted a few local politicians – shrugs and tumbleweeds in response. I started a petition to end religious discrimination in school enrolment. The petition grew legs, picked up thousands of signatures and I met many like-minded parents who had been on the sharp-end of what would come to be known as the 'baptism barrier'.

Parents like Nikki Murphy and Roopesh Panicker had already been actively protesting against the baptism barrier. Their children were denied places by school after school in their local areas and they were forced to apply to (and be turned away from) schools further and further from their homes and their children's friends. During a busy summer myself, Nikki and Roopesh were kept going addressing the national and international media on an issue that really shocked people.

And then the law changed, right? Well, no. I handed in my petition to the Dáil later in 2015 with 20,000 signatures, but I was learning politics is a funny business. However much attention an issue gets, ultimately it is down to politicians to change laws and that process is quite a slog – to say most politicians are averse to rocking the boat is an understatement.

It helps to have a well-organised group to push for social change. Education Equality was formed in December 2015 to campaign for an end to religious discrimination in Irish schools and I was honoured when they asked me to come on board as policy officer – a position I hold to this day.

It took years more campaigning by Education Equality to finally see the end of the baptism barrier in the 90 per cent of taxpayer-funded Irish primary schools controlled by the Catholic Church. It should be stressed that this change was bitterly opposed at all stages by the Catholic hierarchy and their representative organisations.

Ireland has a real blind spot when it comes to religious discrimination (particularly when it serves the purposes of the dominant faith). Equal access to school was only half the battle. Education Equality continues to fight today for equal respect and an end to the daily religious discrimination faced by children within our schools.

It is amazing what people can pass off as 'nice', 'harmless' or 'tradition' when it is in support of their own particular world view. Despite the baptism barrier victory, religious discrimination remains a daily fact of life in most Irish schools. Under the national school curriculum almost as much time is spent per week in primary schools on religious faith formation (two and a half hours) as is spent on history, geography and science *combined* (three hours in total). This does not include numerous daily prayers, trips to church, unannounced visits by priests and the massive time commitment involved in the communion and confirmation years. To be clear, this is not a question of learning *about* religion – it is about indoctrination in a particular faith.

The Irish Constitution explicitly sets out the 'the right of any child to attend a school receiving public money without attending religious instruction at that school'. The way in which most schools 'uphold' this right is by first requiring families to declare their desire to opt out of religious instruction. Once this is done the child will sit alone in the classroom during religious indoctrination every single day of their school going lives, segregated from their peers, marked out as different from their friends as they sing songs and interact. Without even referring to the Constitution it is obvious that this is deeply morally wrong.

Education Equality says that, in order to uphold the rights of all children in our schools, any faith formation or indoctrination must take place *outside* school hours on an opt-in basis. As the US Supreme Court noted on the issue of requiring families to actively opt out, a 'reluctance to be stigmatised' can see children and parents 'avoid claiming their right'. Besides, since when are basic human rights something that need to be requested?

My reflection on Irish identity? So much has changed for the better in recent years. But these changes did not happen merely by the passing of time. They happened because people made them happen – people fought for years to shape the country into what it is today. The religious discrimination at the heart our education system has no place in a twenty-first century democracy and we will not stop fighting until it ends.

Daniel Mulhall

Daniel Mulhall has been Ireland's Ambassador to the US since September 2017. During his forty-year diplomatic career, he has served as Ambassador to Malaysia, Germany and the UK, and as Consul General in Scotland. He is the author of *A New Day Dawning: A Portrait of Ireland in 1900* and co-editor of *The Shaping of Modern Ireland: A Centenary Assessment*. His book on James Joyce's *Ulysses* is due in January 2022. He was awarded the Freedom of Waterford, his place of birth.

We are all shaped by the things we see and hear around us as we grow into being who we are.

It was within a happy family in Waterford during the late 1950s and 1960s, presided over by dutiful parents, Tom and Alice, that I learned to be who I am. The Ireland I experienced as a child was composed of the city streets and country roads of Waterford concertinaed with fleeting impressions of other parts of the country visited during family holidays and while accompanying my father to support the Waterford soccer team for which we shared an avid enthusiasm.

Being Irish meant watching hopefully as Irish athletes competed in the Olympics, hanging on to the words of radio commentaries as our soccer team struggled to qualify for the World Cup, yearning to see our rugby players capture an elusive Triple Crown and, yes, I admit it, urging on the Irish entry in the annual Eurovision Song Contest.

But, despite those periodic national passions, for the most part my boyhood sense of identity was a matter of county rather than country, more Waterfordian than Hibernian!

As a student in Cork, I began to put some learned flesh on those bare bones of identity. This occurred through the study of Irish history and the writings of Yeats, Joyce, and others who pinned Ireland down on the printed page. There were also student debates and late-night conversations during which we tested our apprentice notions of the country and the world around us.

I still remember the eye-opening experience of encountering more advanced societies – in Kansas City in the summer of 1974 and on rail journeys through Europe two years later. Ireland appeared to be an eternal outlier, never quite able to keep pace with our more worldly-wise neighbours.

By the time I joined the Department of Foreign Affairs as a trainee diplomat in 1978, I had come to see Ireland as an underperforming society that had much work to do if we were to shed the disappointments of the past and play catch-up. One of the joys of my life has been to see Ireland mature into an advanced country with a developed economy and an open, tolerant society, comfortable in its skin as a member of the European Union. I say this without any hint of complacency and with an awareness that there is a road still to be travelled for Ireland to realise its full potential.

For most of my life, I have seen Ireland from afar through a lens both telescopic and wide-angled. My sense of Irishness stems from that fairly unique perspective. Since I first departed our shores in 1980, I have spent almost 30 years outside of Ireland, but in a series of obsessively Irish environments: our diplomatic missions in New Delhi, Vienna, Brussels, Edinburgh, Kuala Lumpur, Berlin, London and Washington.

Seamus Heaney once described himself as:

An inner émigré, grown long-haired
And thoughtful ...

After spending so much time overseas, I have the opposite feeling, that of being an external insider poring over my country from a distance. That is because every day of my life outside of Ireland I have trawled the Irish media, worked with other Irish people in buildings carrying our country's name and flying its flag. I continually talk about Ireland, think about its interests, represent its government and promote its culture. As Ambassador, whether I like it or not, wherever I go I am viewed as quintessentially Irish. The upshot is that I probably muse about my homeland and its identity more often, and more intensively, than those who have spent their lives there.

There are myriad ways of being Irish, but my indomitable Irishness stems not from touching the surface of daily life, but from living in the wake of our history and arguing with it, being moved by our literature and the physical and intellectual landscape it evokes, and hearing our music chime while having something mysterious inside me sing back.

In more prosaic, anecdotal terms, it is about making a journey to Thurles for a Munster Hurling Final and having a casual conversation with someone who had seen the legendary Christy Ring play there decades before. Perhaps most of all, it's the camaraderie of Irish people, especially when we are overseas, the sense of satisfaction we derive from being together, the hum of conversation we generate, and the welcoming way we relate to others which accounts for our positive international reputation.

I am proud to represent a country that tries to be the best it can and that has in recent times embraced with equanimity the realities of a fluid, variegated society in a ruffled world. The journey continues, but our current way station as of 2021 is, I think, a spot that we can at least be modestly happy about having reached.

Anthony Murphy

Anthony Murphy is a journalist, author and photographer from Drogheda in County Louth. He has published nine books (nonfiction as well as fiction) inspired by the mythology and cosmology of the great Neolithic monuments of the Boyne Valley. In 2018, he discovered the remains of a giant late Neolithic henge close to Newgrange. He is a subeditor and graphic designer for the *Irish Farmers Journal* and curates the Mythical Ireland website. He is married to Ann and they have five children.

W hat does it mean to be Irish? I once might have naively believed that the Irish were a unique, standalone genetic race, separate from our European brethren. But to ask who the Irish really are and to search for our beginnings is to ask the impossible.

Being an island, Ireland was historically accessible only to those who could navigate. The truth is that our genetic origins lie far beyond these shores. What we should really be asking is what power this island holds over us, and in what way does it transform and transfix us upon our arrival here.

Because of our complex history, which is full of arrivals to and departures from this land (all of which is mirrored in our invasion mythology), we are a people keenly and fascinatingly aware of the wider world. Our inward migrations have made us culturally diverse; our outward migrations have made us acutely aware not only of our own wanderlust, but of the plight of fellow humans whose migrations have been made out of necessity, not desire. In one respect we are a small island nation; in another, we are a truly global people.

I am firmly rooted to this magnificent green and rocky home. The wanderer in me only wants to see deeper into the Irish landscape, a landscape of soul and spirit and marvellous otherworlds. There is enough of the world here to satisfy my own wanderlust. The poet in me wants to follow that beam of sunlight that glistens off the western ocean in the evening, only to pursue it to Tír na nÓg. I to watch in the midnight moonlight for that dancing troop of fairies around the ancient *rath*. I want to approach the door of Síd in Broga (Newgrange) to ask Oengus Óg to reveal Étaín to us, in her crystal bower.

To be Irish is to be a dreamer, and to invoke the images of the dreamer, the myth-maker. In the words of poet John Boyle O'Reilly, 'a dreamer lives forever, and a toiler dies in a day'.

Far beyond the narrow purview of the rational and quantitative mind, there is an indescribable something, a transformative and perhaps magical power to be found in the Irish landscape, a liminal threshold through which another world seems constantly on the verge of brimming through into this one. I call this the '*sidhe* power'. In myth, the *sidhe* were the portals or sacred thresholds which offered access to other realms. In seeking to approach those otherworlds, we flit and totter on the verge of an ineffable profundity.

There is something here, in the fields and trees and rivers and mountains, in the very essence of the landscape, of an altogether different world, one uncorrupted by the ceaseless scheming of humans, one, in many places, yet untainted by the frantic madness of man.

The monks may have been keenly aware of the transformative power of the Irish landscape. It has been suggested that the Irish once saved civilisation. When the world beyond these shores seemed shrouded in darkness, the men of sacred learning kept a flame burning. The idealist in me likes to think that the Irish always keep a lighted candle burning, so that in the event of darkness returning to the world there will always be a shining light.

To be Irish is, I think, to be optimistic. Even when we had nothing, we possessed an extraordinary generosity, a spirit of sharing. When we venture out into the world, we bring that generous spirit with us. We also bring the good humour for which we are rightly renowned.

Those who have stayed here and persevered against all kind of adversity are a hardy bunch. They are the cliff face against which the Atlantic smashes, the rocky outcrop among the grass that endures whatever the Irish climate throws at it, the river that flows ceaselessly from source to sea through an ever-changing landscape. And yet, despite their wild and rugged harshness, there is a wonderful softness to those who have endured the hardships of Irish climate and history.

I don't think there is another people anywhere in the world who can smile like the Irish do. Ours is a smile of stamina. We smile as if we have lived forever. Our soft days and drawn-out winter nights eventually yield to the light of the unvanquishable sun. That indomitable sun lives in all Irish people. Such is the wild swing of the sun on our horizon from winter to summer and back again, we are equally accustomed to the light and to the dark.

In searching for the root of Irishness, we should be careful not to pursue genetic or tribal origins too fervently. Ultimately, our origins lie far beyond these shores. But we can, I think, explore the notion of what it means to be Irish. It is what this island does to you, and how it beguiles and transforms you, that ultimately makes you Irish.

The raw *sídhe* power that seeps and emanates from every rock and lonely bush has spoken to me of an Irishness that cannot be defined in geographic or religious or political terms. Its source lies not in genetic imprints or tribal genealogies, but instead resides in immanent and transcendent realms of our irrepressible, dauntless, tenacious and sanguine spirit. The soul of the Irish is like a deep well, whose source is concealed in the unknowable depths of the bedrock of this marvellous and magical land which we are privileged to call home.

Eimear Noone

Eimear Noone is a conductor and composer, best known for her award-winning work on video game and film music. She has conducted numerous national orchestras including the RTÉ National Symphony Orchestra. In 2020, Eimear made history by becoming the first woman to conduct at the Oscars, leading the orchestra in excerpts from the five nominated film scores.

'Haven't you got an arm and a leg yourself?'

That was the question my mother posed to us when we dared to complain. She brought us up to be fiercely independent. No whining, no self-pity. There's no entitlement. Just get out there and do it. That's why Irish women are very capable. They exude tenacity. It is the core of my Irish identity.

It's part of being raised in a small village in a rural place, Kilconnel in East Galway. Everywhere I go, the west of Ireland is in my mind. The Atlantic is in my blood. I am of this place. Growing up, I spent a lot of time on my own surrounded by natural beauty. It makes me an outsider. When young I felt an outsider even in Ballinasloe, a small town a few miles away.

Ironically, it gave me a global perspective. Big cities were places I saw on TV. I felt as much of an outsider in Dublin as I did in Los Angeles. Kilconnel is my home, and the rest of the world is where I live and work.

I sometimes joke that there weren't enough people in my village to say that what I wanted to do was impossible. You could dream big dreams, because there was nothing in your way – everything was as impossible as anything else. Composing and conducting was as difficult as anything. When I was accepted by Trinity College Dublin and then the College of Music, I was so excited for the opportunity. I had no sense of entitlement. I got there because I put in the work. It was empowering. It gave me the confidence to compete. The only item I was ever charged was a sports bursary – and as a musician, I still couldn't tell you where the sports hall was!

Tenacity and confidence are part of my Irish identity. But the overriding trait in Irish identity that I am most proud of is empathy. (*Nádúr* in the Irish language means nature, innate characteristic, kindliness, empathy). At home we say, 'there's great nature in that person'. He is full of empathy. Or we say, 'there's no nature in him'. In Ireland it is not okay to be cold. 'I can't deal with that right now.' How can you choose not to care about someone's problem? You can't turn empathy on and off. Judgments are not black and white. You must leave room for humanity.

The *meitheal* (a working party in Irish) is a good example. Neighbours gather up to save the hay or cut the turf for someone in need with no expectation of having the favour returned. You would never hear, 'if I do it for you, what will I get out of it?' To expect a return would be tasteless.

Irish women can take setbacks and rejection. It hurts but we can stick with the task. It is important that we have a name for doing what we said we would do. In a small village your name is everything. You can't avoid accountability.

Our humour is global, and my Jewish American husband Craig is a devoted fan of *Father Ted*! I am proud to be Irish and I am optimistic about the future because of the confidence of Ireland's youth. That does not mean that I am uncritical of Irishness. When it fails or falters, I am disappointed because I expect better of the Irish.

And when it came to the two recent referendums, I was not disappointed. In May 2015 the same sex marriage referendum was carried by a majority of 62 per cent, making Ireland the first country in the world to approve marriage equality by popular vote. In May 2018 a referendum to repeal the Eighth Amendment was carried by 66.4 per cent. The Irish felt that the issues were not black and white, and they made room for common humanity. Our common nature.

Looking back, I believe that when the British left southern Ireland in 1922 the people did not have the confidence or opportunity to follow their true nature. The Church took over from the State, and this partnership gave us among other things the Tuam Babies scandal. We must openly acknowledge this and all the other skeletons in our cupboard to ensure that they are never repeated.

We must also acknowledge the 'famine'. I use inverted commas because it was not a naturally occurring, drought-driven famine. It was caused by human action. When the potato crop failed, London was still exporting massive amounts of corn from Ireland to England. In nearby Ballinasloe a housing development has a large green gap in the middle of it with the words *Gorta Mór* (Irish language for 'the great hunger') picked out in flowers. It marks a 'famine' mass grave. If there is one thing I could change about Irish education, I would love to erase the word 'famine' from our discourse.

Maureen O'Brien

A native of Galway city, Major General Maureen O'Brien has forty years' service as an officer in Óglaigh na hÉireann. She has had seven tours overseas, to Lebanon on two occasions, Western Sahara, Chad, East Timor, Bosnia and Syria. She is the first woman in the Irish Defence Forces to reach the rank of Major General and is now serving as the Deputy Military Advisor, Department of Peace Operations, in the UN Headquarters in New York.

The pilot instructed me to strap myself in. As there were no seats, this meant that I had to sit with my legs hanging over the side of the Bell UH-1 helicopter, carrying my rifle and helmet on. It was June 2001 and I was now embarking on the last leg of my journey to deploy with the United Nations Transitional Administration in East Timor.

In the relative comfort of commercial flights, I left Dublin two days earlier destined for Darwin, Australia, where I spent the night. Early the next day I flew in a military C-130 from Darwin to Dili, the capital of East Timor, and now I was the only passenger on a helicopter flight headed for Suai, the Sector Headquarters, where I was to take up my appointment as an Operations Officer.

As we passed over tropical forests and gained altitude, the open doors of the helicopter allowed some passage of air and some relief from the combination of extreme heat and 75 per cent humidity. Forty-five minutes later we landed in a small clearing and I was deposited there, on my own, with nobody in sight. I was never so happy to see an Irish man in my life when Captain Barry O'Riordan emerged from the trees to greet me. He was also happy to see me as my arrival as his replacement assured him that he would be returning home to Ireland soon.

The next day I attended an extraordinary meeting of the Australian General leading the UN Sector and the Indonesian General responsible for the Indonesian forces deployed along the border of West and East Timor. The meeting was convened to discuss mechanisms to repatriate East Timorese people who were in Refugee Camps along the border with East Timor. The meeting was held in an open-sided tent on a flat elevated berm separating the two sides. It was being held against the background of accusation of some Indonesian Forces being involved in alleged war crimes during their occupation of East Timor.

The Indonesians sat on the west side and the UN sat on the opposite side. The tension was palpable, fueled by mistrust on both sides. When the meeting concluded, the Indonesian General stood up, walked slowly towards the back of the tent, in my direction. He pointed to my Ireland flash on my left arm, smiled and said, 'You're from Ireland. Do you know Captain Johnny Murphy?'

It turns out that he had worked with Captain Murphy as a Military Observer with the UN Mission in Bosnia and Herzegovina (UNMIBH) in 1995 and 1996. He recounted stories of their work together and his respect for the Irish officer. You could feel the tension of the meeting dissipate instantly.

The events of that time in East Timor and other similar events and encounters will resonate with many Irish Defence Forces personnel. My social interaction with the Indonesian General on that day opened doors, created trust and mutual respect for the work we were doing. It made the mission more operationally effective.

The extraordinary work of our Irish peacekeepers is renowned in UN circles. Every single day, throughout the world, Irish military personnel are leveraging their 'neutrality', their empathy as citizens of a small country which has learned for her own past experiences and are

228

happy to listen, share and support. Let's not get carried away though, we are not without our faults, we are human after all. Importantly, we don't pretend to be perfect. In fact, I believe this makes us more relatable. The themes of empathy, partnership and independence highlighted by Ireland in our successful bid for a seat on the UN Security Council are not just empty words – they are values lived by the women and men of our Irish Defence Forces throughout the world every day.

Each of the seven times I have deployed with the UN, I have been proud to serve as an Irish Officer. Now that I am working at the highest levels in UNHQ, I am reminded every day of the service of all UN peacekeepers. Some are working in very complex and dangerous missions. Indeed, many have paid the ultimate sacrifice, including 87 Irish peacekeepers who gave their life in the service of peace.

As a seconded military officer in UNHQ, I am reminded that I am now 'an international civil servant' and not specifically serving Ireland. However, when I wear my Irish uniform with the UN flash on my right arm, I am just as aware of the Ireland flash on my left arm, recognised by the Indonesian Officer all those years ago. For the last forty years, being Irish has meant serving my country with pride. As an Irish woman, I will continue to serve with great pride for as long as I believe that I can make a difference.

Orla O'Connor

Orla O'Connor is Director of National Women's Council of Ireland, the leading national women's membership organisation in Ireland, with over 190-member groups. She was Co-Director of Together For Yes, the national Civil Society Campaign to remove the 8th Amendment in the referendum. For her role in Together for Yes, Orla was recognised as one of the 100 Most Influential People by TIME magazine in 2019.

Being Irish brings many different and at times conflictual feelings and perspectives. My experience is shaped by my personal experiences of being a woman, lone parent, settled, white and non-disabled and living in the south of Ireland. Simultaneously, my life is shaped by my role as Director of National Women's Council, my feminism and activism and my life long work campaigning with women, men and families in poverty, homelessness, with women experiencing deep racism, domestic and sexual violence and structural injustice and denial of economic, social and reproductive rights. In 2021, I recognise there is much to celebrate in the significant changes that have occurred for women, however I lament the long journey still to travel to reach a society that is built upon feminist values and an Ireland I can be fully proud of.

Consequently, being Irish in 2021 means continuing the struggle for women's rights, especially for and with women who are being left behind. The consequences of the global pandemic raise deep questions about our society, has illustrated the need to approach our recovery from an all island perspective and shone a light on the critical need for global solidarity. Our struggles are global, living in an environmental crisis means decisions we are making now must reverse already detrimental consequences for our planet.

Decades ago the Catholic Church and a patriarchal theocracy ensured women's lives were shackled. Decisions and choices were limited. This remains captured in Article 41.2 of our Constitution, which assigned 'a woman's place in the home', clearly articulating the value and worth of women's lives in a society that incarcerated and abused women who did not fit in with their prescribed role. Ireland no longer holds these values. Redefining our constitution to include values of inclusion, care, recognition of all families and non-discrimination is a prerequisite to achieving a feminist society, as is the separation of church and state in our education and health systems. A national comprehensive programme of sex education delivered across primary and secondary schools would ensure that young people have necessary knowledge and resources for the rest of their lives. Delivering public health care across the island of Ireland is a necessity for women's health. And we need full state authority, ownership and governance of our hospitals to determine medical practices and provide for the reproductive health care needs of women into the future.

Being Irish for me means living in a country that has yet to address the deep-seated racism in our society evidenced in racist discrimination against Travellers and institutionalised into state structures. Inward migration has forced some change, but we see a continuity of institutionalised racism, for example in the system of direct provision where those seeking asylum are structurally ostracised and deterred from establishing relationships with Irish society. Contemporary racism takes many forms, including harassment, discrimination, hate speech and physical racial attacks on Travellers and Roma, black people and people of colour. In addition, the growth of the far right demands a collective response not only to prevent the spread of the far-right ideology of hate, but to work towards a society that thrives in our diversity, incorporating strong feminist values of care and inclusion and treats every person with dignity and respect.

The sense of living on one island is a part of my Irishness, as is the legacy of both living in a divided country and living with hope for the future, the latter symbolised by the Good Friday Agreement and the work of the Women's Coalition. The pandemic has shown the importance of all island approaches and of working as one island to respond to the crisis.

In our debate on a shared island the challenge is not a united island based on socio-economic and gender inequality, but one based on substantive equality for all. Being Irish for me is about aspiring and mobilising for a new Ireland based on rights, equality and fairness for all. Participative processes can move dialogue forward, the revival of the Civic Forum (included in the Good Friday Agreement through the work of the Women's Coalition), a Citizens Assembly process have the potential to develop shared thinking prior to any constitutional referendums.

The repeal of the 8th amendment to remove the constitutional ban on abortion was my proudest moment to be Irish and a critical moment for women's rights in Ireland. The conversations that took place in every home in Ireland showed our collective sense of compassion and care, and our ability to act to realise women's rights. We made a broader statement on women's place in Irish society and took strides to release women from the past. Within the Citizens Assembly on Gender Equality, the people have shown once again they are far ahead of the political leadership in their desire for women's rights and the recognition of women in all our diversity. This leaves me, as a woman and feminist, optimistic for the future. I know that it will take many campaigns and struggles to achieve a feminist society across the island, but I am confident that more change is coming.

John O'Doherty

John is the Director of the Rainbow Project, an LGBTQIA+ charity. Originally from Maghera, County Derry, he now lives in Belfast with his husband Martin. John was one of the key campaigners for equal marriage in Northern Ireland and a founder of the Love Equality Campaign. He has written numerous research papers on the issues impacting on LGBTQIA+ people in Northern Ireland.

I am blessed to have travelled the length and breadth of Ireland, a blessing I have only really understood as I got older. Like so many Irish children I spent a lot of my youth with my grandparents, in particular my grandad who loved to travel. He would bundle my sister, cousins and me into the car and we would take off on some unknown journey full of travel sickness and frustration but also laughter, song and stories.

As we grew up, and my sister and cousins outgrew our trips, I as the youngest was the last remaining passenger on a guided tour of back road Ireland. A lover of ice cream he never seemed happier than when he sat at the coast eating an ice cream cone and staring out to sea. My grandad loved Ireland and particularly Irish music – and in true Irish fashion the radio was never on, we made our own music.

Whilst he taught me the words to 'the old bog road' he would regale me about family that had emigrated from home – with pride and sadness in his eyes. Without a blink he would move on to sing a few bars of some limerick I assume he learned in his youth, stopping to laugh when he got to the cheeky part. I don't remember the words and I'm not sure I ever understood them, but I remember the joy.

The further we travelled the deeper the conversations. He spoke of his parents, his sister, a nun, who was buried in Youghal and his childhood, little of which I remember now, unfortunately. He reminisced about JFK visiting Dublin and how he and my Mum looked up and waved directly at him among the huge numbers of well-wishers.

On our longest journeys he would start to talk about his time as a member of the Irish Army, serving in the Congo. He told me about how his life changed when he moved his young family, including my mum who was born in Dublin, back to a cottage in Maghera. The barracks had running water, indoor toilets and electricity – none of which were on offer in their new home.

Sometimes he would tell me about his time in the Congo, living in the jungle surrounded by danger and living in fear, while he expertly manoeuvred roads so dark I couldn't see anything, never breaking his gaze. As I write this, I am struck by the strength to manage and live with this trauma.

I never got to come out to my grandad – not actively anyway. At that time, I was working for the Rainbow Project and could often be seen on TV campaigning against the ban on gay men giving blood or in support of equal marriage. As a dedicated daily consumer of local news, I have no doubt he saw these, but if he did, he never told me and we never got to have that conversation as he sadly passed away in 2010.

My mum, however, told me of a day he visited her. Out of nowhere he proclaims, 'You know Margaret, gay people don't choose to be gay. They are born that way.' It turns out he was a huge fan of *Hollyoaks* and they had covered an LGBT storyline that had reached him in some new way and given him a moment of realisation he felt important to share.

One of my most prized possessions is my grandad's UN medal. Never a one for ceremony, he gifted it to me one typical mid-week evening when I brought him and my grandmother up their dinner. He called it his 'peacemaker' medal, and that word has lived with me ever since.

At the age of 17 I joined the SDLP. I heard the call of another peacemaker, John Hume. Growing up in a single identity community and attending a single identity school, I had little interaction with people from the PUL [Protestant, Unionist, Loyalist] community, certainly none who were political or actively involved in PUL culture.

I struggled to reconcile this childhood hatred of this 'other'. Regular fights I had had with boys from the Protestant school in the mornings as our paths crossed seemed ridiculous. There had to be a better way, a way of peace, justice, understanding and compromise.

As a member of SDLP youth my tours of Ireland began anew. Trips to Galway to attend Tom Johnston summer school with my friends in the Irish Labour Party. Attending Pride Parades in Dublin. Volunteering to raise money through Workers Beer where we pulled pints for around eight hours at Slane.

These were some of the greatest years of my life. I got to meet Irish heroes like Senator David Norris, President Mary McAleese and John Hume. I worked with giants like Denis Haughey, Mark Durkan and Brid Rogers. They inspired in me a sense of Irish belonging, akin to the belonging that I share with the LGBTQIA+ community.

A shared culture and language that is full of beauty and tradition. A people who are welcoming and generous. A shared history full of tragedy and loss, from the Irish Famine to the Omagh bomb. A politics driven by equality and human rights. A family that spans the globe.

On 22 May 2015 my two identities collided – Ireland voted to legalise same sex marriage. That evening, my now husband and I were travelling to Spain for our first holiday together, and in a first for us both we had to seek out an Irish bar while abroad to celebrate this new won freedom in our homeland. Even though I knew equal marriage would still take some time to achieve in Northern Ireland, this historic moment marked a sea change in what being Irish meant and what Ireland stood for.

Santis O'Garro

Santis is mother of two wonderful humans, a life coach and creator of the 'Budget Mindset Planner' which teaches people to build tangible habits around their budgets. Originally from the Caribbean Island of Montserrat, also known as the Emerald Isle of the Caribbean, her mission in life is to spread awareness and joy with a sprinkle of kindness.

I moved to Dublin in 1995 from the Caribbean Island of Montserrat. My name is Santis O'Garro, a name given to my ancestors, the enslaved. My blood is rich with the Celtic deities as much as the African Orishas. I am Irish. I am 37 years of age and I feel Irish.

I grew up in Donnycarney on the northside of Dublin. In Ireland, being a predominantly white country, I really felt my blackness. Most of the time I was delighted to be put in the same league as Aretha Franklin, Oprah or Moesha. They were my heroes and the ignorance of people worked in my favour a lot of the time.

Our house was like the united colours of Benneton: my stepdad Dermot being white and Irish gave us a positive insight into Irish society. He is one of the kindest people I have ever met. However, a few rotten eggs did slow down my journey to accepting my Irish roots. Let's face it, being a teenager is tough. Here you are starting to realise that the world is kind of scary and you're figuring out where do you fit in exactly. Growing up it was those awkward years that I found defined me for so long. I was given roles to play by so many people. From being more Irish than the Irish, to being told to go home, followed by a slurry of horrible insults.

It was perplexing and worst of all I chose to allow the negativity to define me. However, for every one person that berated me, I had an army of people that chose to uplift me. It is the nature of the beast to focus on the bad instead of embracing the good. In my defence abuse went from verbal, mental and physical. It stopped my normal sunny outlook and it stopped me from trusting anyone I met. The majority of times I was putting on a front as I had such a mistrust of people. It would take me to my mid-thirties to break this cycle of allowing other people's behaviour to define me and I broke it spectacularly.

Having been rocked like so many other black people following the murder of George Floyd in May 2020, I started to revaluate my Irishness. For the first time I spoke out and spoke up. I realise that I had allowed negativity to control my actions. I let the abuse build up a wall of mistrust around me. How could I be Irish if I navigated my life through a fear-filled lens? When I spoke out it felt like an outpouring of shame. When I asked for support, I received so much that I felt even more ashamed.

I learned a very important lesson in 2020. Shame is a weapon against yourself. Being Irish is not about turning up and singing ballads or wearing green on St Patrick's day. It is how we carry ourselves. What we put into this country for future generations. It's respecting and preserving the culture. It's about taking time out to listen to my grandad before he passed so that I can pass on stories with pride to my own children. Being Irish is not degrading our country but adding to it. Sometimes it's speaking about the hard topics when no one is willing to or standing up for what is right.

Being Irish is paying homage to those in the past and accepting what we have now with absolute joy. Being Irish is not saying, 'Hey, I have a passport!' 'I was born here!' In my humble opinion it is the mark I will leave when I pass. It is my integration into Irish society, revelling in the culture and adding my own spice. I'm a self-professed tourist. I will always pay money to see *Riverdance* and shush my friends when I hear an Irish ballad being sung. I do not ever really want to learn it, but I appreciate the drumming of the bodhrán. To be Irish is to be kind, to be proud of who you are but also willing to adapt and grow. This country has some of the most beautiful landscapes on earth and I am part of it.

On the surface I might not be the first thing that comes to mind when you think of an Irish woman. And that's okay. After all, I'm a proud Montserratian also. The black Irish of the Caribbean. I often say that it's no accident that Caribbean and Irish people are so similar. It's that same quick-witted sense of humour and the ability to disarm almost everyone when we are being our most honest and authentic.

In some ways I feel I'm a bridge. I'm a black Montserratian and I am very Irish in nature and attitude for the most part. I value kindness, respect and community.

I am a black single mother who cleared €15,000 in debt in one year. I now share this experience with others. I am the mother of two beautiful humans, Louis and Eliza, and I know it's my responsibility to guide them into adulthood as being the kind of people that give more than they take. Sometimes I think Irish people are almost afraid to be seen for the wonderful people they are. It is about time we all start accepting the privilege of being Irish.

Ray O'Hanlon

Ray O'Hanlon is the editor of the New York-published *Irish Echo* newspaper. A native of Dublin and graduate of UCD, O'Hanlon worked for the Irish Press newspaper group before moving to the United States in 1987. His latest book, *Unintended Consequences,* is a history of Irish immigration to the United States Ray is married to Lisa and they are the proud parents of three grown children.

It's a spring morning and I'm listening to something, missing something. I'm listening to the birds welcoming the new day, American birds, feathered New Yorkers. I'm missing those Irish birds who comprise the famed spring dawn chorus. I am always here and forever there; there being Ireland.

I have now lived in America for more than half my life. My wife is from the midwest, Illinois. Our three grown children are all New Yorkers. I alone speak with an accent that signals an origin on the other side of the Atlantic. From time to time Americans will say to me, 'you haven't lost your accent'. I will smile and make light of it. 'No, but my wits, that's another matter.' Others will remark that I haven't got much of an Irish accent at all. My rejoinder in this case is that I am from suburban Dublin and that doesn't really make the brogue grade.

I have spent the bulk of my working life as a journalist in New York, writing for and editing an Irish American newspaper. I am acutely aware of the fact that I am not Irish American. That said, I am an American citizen and have sworn to defend the United States with arms. Naturalized citizens have to do that. The native born do not. Guess I'm a regular Minute Man.

So I have two loyalties. Luckily they are not divided loyalties, Ireland and America being such good pals and all. So I am Irish and American, and sometimes American and Irish.

But most of the time I find myself looking at the world with an Irish eye. That, I reckon, is because of the age I was when I moved here permanently. I wasn't ten or twenty. I was thirty. By that age you are well set. And I was well set in my Irishness.

That is not to say that I don't sometimes cast a critical eye towards Ireland, or the Irish in America. Being away does give you an enhanced critical perspective, even as you battle the occasional wave of nostalgia. But being away does other things too. Being married to an American and being an American Dad quickly made me decide where 'home' was. It was here, in America.

Ireland is a home too of course, but unlike many, if not most, Irish-born in the United States who constantly say 'home' and mean Ireland first and foremost, I am inclined to call Ireland by its name. I know it might have been otherwise had my wife hailed from Ireland too. So I've had it easy in a way. There has been little or none of the kind of second guessing that I've seen in Irish couples living here.

Obviously, and this is partly due to my job, I sometimes have to explain Ireland and being Irish to Americans who might not be overly knowledgeable, but who are nonetheless curious. This task reached something of a peak during the Celtic Tiger years. I had a few lines of explanation that I would deliver most of the time. Occasionally I would shrug my shoulders, laugh and admit that I hadn't a clue and that it all seemed rather mad.

Thus far I have been explaining myself as someone in America looking back at Ireland. What happens when I visit Ireland? Well, I have no problem at all blending in. Nobody comes out with the 'returning Yank' jibe. They know they will be flattened with a rapid fire 'feck off'.

Obviously I notice changes, though my work tends to lessen the surprise. I have a fair idea of what is going on from day to day, though the degree of urban sprawl is a bit of a shock, especially in my native county.

But do I feel American among my fellow Irish? I do, a bit at any rate, because I find that I am treated somewhat differently. Just about every emigrant notices this. My late mother used to advise me on places to shop, or to go for a nice walk. I would shake my head and respond, 'Yes Ma, I know'.

When I am in Ireland I feel perfectly at ease and function with native certainty. But I am aware that home is over there, beyond that setting sun.

My paper has a recurring feature called Page Turner. It's for writers and such. They answer a series of set piece questions. The last one is 'You're Irish If...?' Over the years there have been many witty and pithy responses to this. I've tried to come up with one or two witty and pithy responses of my own. Ultimately, though, I just give up. I'm Irish regardless of any ands, buts or ifs.

Only now, something else besides.

Hilary O'Meara

Hilary O'Meara is a Managing Director at Accenture, joining the global professional services company in 1993 after graduating from UCD with a Computer Science degree. During her 25+ year career, Hilary has supported clients across the public and private sectors to implement major business change. Outside of work, Hilary enjoys spending time with her husband Sean and their three children, Aisling, Eoin and Katherine.

More data centres than donkeys

The first time I gave serious thought to what it means to be Irish was in my early twenties. I was travelling and meeting people from different countries who seemed to have a clearer idea than me about what Ireland was like. I was surprised to be told I was living on an island full of donkeys and carts, a pastoral idyll that bore no relationship to the place where I grew up.

What struck me at the time was that my identity was more tied up with being a 'Dub' rather than Irish. Why wouldn't it? My parents and both sets of grandparents were Dublin born and the modest but comfortable life I lived in South Dublin was all I really knew. Unlike many of my schoolfriends, I didn't have relatives in the country that I could visit in the holidays to confirm or deny an abundance of donkeys.

There's no doubt that a wild and rugged beauty still feeds the picture postcard image of our island, but there are more data centres than donkeys in modern-day Ireland. I didn't realise it at the time, as I made my way through university and into full-time work, but I was living through a major change – cultural and economic.

Culturally, I happened to be part of a generation that brought greater diversity and inclusion into the workplace. Thanks to the support and open-mindedness of my parents I had no sense of this, I was just doing what they encouraged me to do and pursued a university education that they had missed out on. My mother reared me to be independent and shoot for the stars in a way that felt pragmatic and practical.

I took a computer science degree at UCD – because I liked maths, not because I foresaw the technological revolution – one of a handful of women in a class of 40 men. At a time of high unemployment, I applied for a job at Accenture because it advertised more positions than anyone else, and I figured I had a better chance of getting one of them! The sector was a traditionally male environment – I remember getting wolf-whistled in a corridor at an external meeting one day – it didn't bother me until it did.

Some years later, a male-dominated management meeting came to a conclusion that was at odds with what I felt. I had a conversation with a female colleague, and it was amazing to realise we shared the same view – a feeling that a different perspective, a woman's perspective, was being overlooked. That meeting turned out to be a watershed moment for me as I realised the importance of diversity in decision making.

In the early 2000s, I was leading a gender equality team in Accenture. There was an ambition to do the right thing by women but no clear idea of what that meant. So we put a programme in place to better support women in their careers. Today, Accenture has a reputation as a pioneer in inclusion and diversity in Ireland and around the world and has set a target of a 50:50 gender-balanced workforce by 2025.

Economically, Ireland changed too. A steady flow of foreign direct investment, enabled by the excellent work of the IDA, made Ireland home to some of the biggest tech companies on the planet, many of them Accenture clients. With third-level education providing a pool of talent and drawing on an inherent Irish appetite for problem solving, it was no surprise when Accenture chose Ireland to be the location for The Dock, its flagship R&D and Innovation Centre.

For me now, being Irish is about the way these cultural and economic changes have forged a new national identity. I see it in the way we bounced back from the 2008 crash, which I fully expect to be replicated as we emerge from the pandemic. I see it in our sense of social justice and the inclusivity that drove Ireland to become the first country to legalise gay marriage in a referendum.

Through it all, I'm still a Dub. I married a Dub, originally a guard (now a psychologist) from three generations of guards. We share the same values and the values of a lot of Irish people. Push me to explain them and I'd talk about being open minded, inclusive, and very accepting of difference.

As other countries have faltered and embraced dangerous strands of populism, I would credit our people – and our politicians – for trying to do the right thing. We have something special here, a social conscience that we all need to work to protect.

We've come a long way from seventies and eighties Ireland, when poverty and lack of jobs drove a generation away to the US and UK. Even in my graduate year in the nineties, I was one of the few to stay and make a career at home. Now, as a parent, I'm glad it's changed. I'm also grateful to my parents that my children – two girls and a boy – will be the beneficiaries of what they stood up for, the belief that everyone should be able to pursue the life they choose, irrespective of gender or social background. That's real progress and it makes me proud to be Irish.

Alison O'Neill

Alison, known as Ally, is from Omagh, studied in Glasgow and has lived and worked in New Zealand and Mexico. She now lives in Belfast, where she is Head of Brand and Culture at an ad agency.

A curly haired rogue from the local estate and a polished country girl from a good family. Catholic meets Protestant in County Tyrone, Northern Ireland. Irish identity to me is knowing that thran, stubborn and often brave natured spirit that says – *'I know I shouldn't do this, but I'm going to do it anyway'.* That's what my mother and father did in 1984 when they eloped and hopped in the car laughing to go and get married in Donegal with their two best friends.

On paper it was a no go, but they threw caution to the wind and that spirit has carried them through to today, 37 years later. That brave spirit (or thran nature – however you see it) is that thing you can't touch that makes up Irish identity for me. As much as they laugh about it, it was hard to date cross community in the 1970s and 80s. Mum was the designated driver as the surname 'Irvine' meant a quick nod at the checkpoints whereas 'O'Neill' meant a full search or worse. Nevertheless, they both persevered taking the road less travelled and creating two children to carry on the brave, thran nature.

One being myself – Ally O'Neill. Christened as Alison but in my teenage years the nickname 'Ally' emerged and consequently so did a step change in mindset. I stepped out of my shyer nature and more into the 'I know I shouldn't do this, but I'm going to do it anyway' frame of mind. My parents stole the cross-community limelight but in my small town of Omagh, County Tyrone I took a different type of rainbow limelight. Crying and trembling with fear I'll never forget standing in the kitchen and telling my parents that I thought I might be gay. They are liberal but I was still scared that my safe haven and closest form of comfort might turn away from me.

In only the way an Irish 'mammy' could my mum hugged me tight and said, 'I always knew – you've always been quite sensitive'. My Dad, a therapist by trade, blinked back happy tears. That's where I get my sensitive trait. A happy story but not one replicated in every home. I have friends who have been cast out, shamed or worse – they are still scared to come out for fear of judgement. Although our Irish identity is unique and something to be celebrated, the shame of judgement for being different sits heavy with many people. That's something in our identity I want to continue to see changed – more acceptance and more open mindedness.

Funnily enough, I left my beloved Ireland to open my own mind. I decided to work every shift I could in Spar (are you really Irish if you haven't worked there?) to save money to travel as far and as wide as I could. That was something my mother and father couldn't have done, but they encouraged me passionately to get out of Northern Ireland and experience the world outside a place where the school you attended translated into your religion.

It was during these travels that I came to realise that being Irish was much more than a passport, it was an elusive identity in itself. Everywhere you go people proclaim, '*Ah I love the Irish!*' I often wonder what it is they see in us; maybe it's that wild spirit or thran nature that's hard to describe and harder to emulate. When I returned, I was not much wiser and definitely much poorer, but I did gain a little confidence in myself and consequently bravery. This bravery allowed me to walk around holding my girlfriend's hand without wincing from embarrassment. It also gave me enough confidence to send a letter to every ad agency in Northern Ireland asking for a job.

I have always wanted to work in advertising. The ads that always stuck out to me were the Road Safety TV ads – *'three dead in this vehicle, the guy without the seatbelt did the damage'.* The music, the words, the feeling they leave you with – advertising has a craft that I wanted to learn. Six years later and I still have plenty to learn but I have spent those years working ferociously within the advertising industry. It's a welcoming place for those who are 'deemed' different or brave, and somewhere I have grown into my skin.

*It also cemented something for me in Irish Identity –
the notion of self-deprecation. No one is quicker to put
themselves down than the Irish. God forbid you might even
tell someone about an achievement or promotion – you
would quickly be accused of 'having notions'.*

Ireland may be physically small, but our passion and spirit is titanic. As Ireland moves forward, I hope that we stop being down on ourselves or discouraging bravery. All that tends to do is quell that intangible Irish spirit, which for me is one of the most beautiful parts of our identity.

Philip Orr

Philip Orr taught English and Drama at secondary level in Northern Ireland before working as a researcher, writer and facilitator in the community sector. He is a published historian who has written about Ireland's experience of the Great War. He recently produced a short book of prose and poems which reflect on aspects of the Ulster Protestant heritage. Philip is a member of the Royal Irish Academy.

... I must in course discuss
What we mean to Ireland or Ireland to us ...
– Louis MacNeice

My sense of Irishness has always been dependent on the context in which I find myself. As I write this piece, my context is the English cathedral city where I have recently been living.

That city is St. Albans, situated several miles north of London. I am training here for a diploma in counselling skills but my other location for a good part of the year is the County Antrim home which I inherited from my parents. It's where I touch base with old friends and engage with the current state of Northern Irish politics.

Being Irish in England feels comfortable these days, despite the divisive politics of Brexit. When I last stayed in England for a sustained period, it was to study English Literature at university. An IRA bombing campaign was targeting English cities and I masked my accent in public for fear of reprisals, even though I was an Ulster Protestant who had worked in a British Army Camp as a summer job. It feels like another, darker life.

Irishness seems confident everywhere in this place where I live. A neighbour died recently, aged 101. His hearse made its way out of the close with an Irish tricolour in the window. Another neighbour has a mother who lives near the Giant's Causeway and during the Covid lockdown the family moved to the Antrim coast for three months, pursuing their working life via Wi Fi.

Being Irish in my counselling class is often irrelevant. There's an easy diversity of backgrounds that needs little explication. But I think I bring occasional and special insights to bear on human suffering, conflict and the vexed search for reconciliation from the many decades I spent living and working in Northern Ireland.

I talk sometimes about the work I did with former security force personnel who suffer from PTSD. I have opinions about how nationhood, violence, religion and colonisation map onto one another. I speak of how I have enjoyed the company of people who might once have tried to kill me. I quote from Irish poets, as we discuss grief, addiction and relationship breakdown. I feel fluent, happy with words, respected.

But I am Irish in an urbanised, landlocked part of England, where Watford, St Albans, Hatfield and Hemel Hempstead are linked to one another by busy motorway and clogged trunk roads. I think back to quiet car journeys into the Antrim Hills or the blustery seaview from my Carrickfergus windows.

And here in the south of England I experience many dry, sunny days rather than the damp, cool summers months I often spent back home, trapped under that grey cloud-cover over Ulster. Yet the unremitting heat makes me yearn for rain and wind and the sound of the waves. Being Irish is about weather.

And I have been discovering that several famous literary fellow-countrymen and women were also rooted in Hertfordshire. I've had my photograph taken at the gates of the house where G. B. Shaw lived in the tiny, tree-lined hamlet of Ayot St. Lawrence. His ashes lie scattered under the lawn.

And the next time I visit Harpenden to walk our Airedale Terrier in the park and enjoy a coffee in a café on the town's main street I aim to see the building where Elizabeth Bowen once went to school.

I've travelled to the picture postcard village of Aldbury to see the house where Louis MacNeice and his partner lived in Stocks Road, during the last few years of his life. I have revelled in visiting the Greyhound pub where he occupied a seat in the shadow of the bar-room clock.

I too was the son of an Irish Protestant clergyman. The young MacNeice grew up in Carrickfergus, and many years later I inherited a seafront house there. He was happy in Aldbury, and I am happy in St Albans. Yet, as the saying goes, 'far from it we were reared'.

As I write this piece, I think of other travels on which I have paused to connect with literary Ireland: on the way to Italy when I visited James Joyce's grave in Zurich and took time in Paris to see Oscar Wilde's tomb. In the haunted mass graveyards of the Western Front, I've searched for the exact spot where the soldier-poet Francis Ledwidge was blown up by a German shell.

I am defined by the two passports that sit in my drawer – the British one I have possessed for so many decades and the other more recent one that I acquired to assert my desire for an Irish and European identity alongside my inherited British one. The tensions of Brexit have only served to double my sense of belonging.

Camille O'Sullivan

Previously an award-winning architect and painter, Camille is a singer/actress known internationally for her interpretations of the music of Cave, Brel, Cohen, Radiohead and Bowie. Headline gigs include the Royal Festival Hall, Sydney Opera House and the Roundhouse. Voted one of the 'Top 25 Performances ever on Later with Jools Holland' by the *Daily Telegraph*, she recently released *Camille Sings Cave Live*.

So I just received my Irish citizenship, having applied a few years before with stacks of info to prove my eligibility – an unconventional zoom call ceremony seated in my back room with my cat, my computer balanced on books, the official joking with us giving a typical lovely Irish welcome, then proudly standing to sing our national anthem. I had a bit of a cry listening to those who came to our shores sharing their stories on what it meant to be Irish, the kindness they felt, enhanced by what some of them got away from, the wonderful mix of their accents with the Irish lilt reminding me of my mum. An emotional occasion for me, having arrived here from London as a baby to a French mother and an English father (second generation Irish) who decided he wanted to rear us here, lured by the innocence, wildness and beauty, for which I'm forever grateful he did.

We moved back and forth before settling in a small village outside Cork. I felt like a bit of a liquorice allsort, a mixture of Welsh, Scots, English, Basque and French and though Irish I felt I didn't quite belong. Most presumed I was French until they heard the Cork singsong babble come out of me.

> *I love the people and this island and how it shaped me – the lineage of great inspiring artists, its madness, truthfulness, self-deprecating nature, friendliness, openness to connect, deep spirituality, music everywhere, storytellers in all of us, art, theatre, laughing at ourselves before others do, wild countryside, noble cities, two-faced black humor, bonkers, shyness, brashness, the western Atlantic shores...*

I felt like an outsider always observing what the norm should be, misplaced, not Irish enough, an outsider in my village, then later in Dublin being from Cork. I didn't have parents that understood the rituals and Irish ways. I learnt Irishness from school and one channel TV diet of *Wanderly Wagon, Halls Weekly, MTUSA* and the variety lucky bag *The Late Late Show*, a weekly family must-see for Gaybo's tragedy, music, comedy and moral guidance. I feel being Irish from a small island is the same, reared on UK/US/AUS TV observing other cultures learning outside of ourselves.

It was unusual to be an O'Sullivan with no relatives here, as all our Dunmanway kin had emigrated in the 1800s. So we led a very isolated childhood, my Irish connection being minded by an old lady nearby, Mrs. H, with all her sacred hearts and Virgin Marys, dotting us with holy water to save our souls. It must have had an effect – I wanted to be a nun. It didn't help that I was baptized at 15 as a Protestant. We weren't welcomed by the priest in our quirky village, so coupled with 'Brits out' sprayed on the walls, mum reared us as Church of Ireland. I was embarrassed for many years, sometimes taking communion, mumbling my way through mass so no one would know, feeling Catholic with lots of guilt but no confession to appease it. We ran quickly up the hidden back lanes to Sunday school, six in the congregation singing happily out of tune. That was my first real love of singing. I loved those old hymns and since then I've always leaned towards austere, unadorned arrangements. I'm still drawn to Virgin Mary statues and have one or two in the house, maybe connecting to Mrs. H, and I always liked being around the best aspects of religion here, the kindness and deep spirituality that Irish people have.

Having been an architect I'm now a singer, but not of Irish music. I just continued what I'd heard growing up, Jacques Brel, Weill, Cave, Bowie etc. Mum was delighted I was Irish singing these storytelling songs not French: 'You would've been far too serious and not had the darkness or black humor of the Irish.' It was whilst touring abroad I realised how Irish I was. People were delighted to hear you were Irish commenting on our shyness, humor, recklessness, how we speak, running rings around people, possibly a poetic Irish to English translation. I started to think we were like the funny little hobbits of the world. You realise how special your country is when you are far from it. Sometimes embarrassed by talking too much I relax when I hear the mad chatty babble on return.

I feel lucky I started my singing career here, intimate enough to test yourself in a little club like the Da Club until one day you played the Olympia then the Royal Festival Hall in London or Sydney Opera House. I might have been swallowed up in London/New York had I started there. But now it's where I tour the most. I've travelled abroad touring for most of my life but am happiest here at home in this country, an outsider now home bird – I don't think I could ever leave.

Sonia O'Sullivan

Born in Cobh, County Cork, Sonia O'Sullivan is a former track and field athlete, athletics consultant, broadcaster and author. She won a gold medal in the 5000 metres at the 1995 World Championships, and a silver medal in the 5000 metres at the 2000 Olympic Games. Her 2000 metre world record of 5:25.36, set in 1994. stood until 2017.

'Wherever I went to the furthest corners of the earth, there was always at least one Irish flag in the stadium.'

When I think about my Irish identity, I think first of all about the place where I was born and reared: Cobh, in Cork harbour, one of the biggest natural harbours in the world. I have always been more comfortable living around water. In London I lived by the River Thames. In Australia I did many of my runs along the river paths. It's not something that I have really thought about until recently, but I seem to navigate to the sea wherever I am in the world. I am always most content when close to the sea.

We live in Port Melbourne in Australia and I frequently watch the ships coming and going, wondering which of them ever entered the Port of Cork and berthed in Cobh. I know that many of the cruise ships have in the past. Even so far away, there is the connection that you could always go home by boat.

During my athletic career I felt privileged to represent Ireland on tracks all over the world. It is a totally different feeling to running as an individual in a competition. I always felt I was running for all Irish people, although now, looking back, maybe I could have realised more the role model I was for Irish women when I was at my peak. To see so many women take part and compete across a myriad of different sporting disciplines today is a credit to Irish sporting bodies and the encouragement that Irish women get from Irish media and their sports bodies.

Wherever I went to the furthest corners of the earth, there was always at least one Irish flag in the stadium. I recall particularly at remote track meetings in India and Qatar seeing a few Irish flags in the packed stadiums. You begin to realise there are more Irish people living outside Ireland and, when there is a reason to connect, they are the first in line. I still experience the Irish welcome wherever I go.

I remember one particular example, when I was running 5000 metres at the Melbourne athletics Grand Prix in 1995, taking place just a few weeks before the World Fire and Police games. The Irish team in town to compete all came along to support me and filled a whole section in the stadium close to the finish line. It was a big surprise to me to have such colourful and vocal support just a few weeks after I had arrived in Australia for training and racing.

Even recently on my temporary move to the US to be close to my daughter who is at university there, I have been looked after and shown around by Irish people who want to share what they have found with a fellow Irish person. Maybe it is to show why they live in this place, but also to show that they have never lost the Irish connection.

I am currently based in Portland, Oregon, but my work still involves travelling so I am never in one place for too long. As I travel and move about, I definitely feel more Irish. I am always looking for that sense of belonging, even for a short period of time, to meet people who have settled in another country and share the common bond. Irish people will often invite you to their homes for a meal and a few drinks. I appreciate these connections the older I get, whereas when I was young I was travelling for a purpose and very focussed.

When I travel home to Ireland, I sometimes question myself: why am I putting myself out of my normal comfortable routine on a long and arduous flight? But as soon as the plane touches down in Ireland, it suddenly all makes sense. We're all on the same wavelength here.

I have never been more than a year away from Ireland. This year of Covid-19 will test that statement, but I do hope to get home later this year and for me Ireland and Cobh will always be home.

I am proud to be Irish. It is true that when you live abroad, you tend to emphasise the good things. For the people who live in Ireland, the view can be negative sometimes. And there has been negative news in recent years. I was so impressed by and proud of the Equal Marriage campaign and the numbers of (mostly young) Irish who flew home to vote. They had learned about life abroad and were making sure that Ireland should change too. Ireland was the first country in the world who took this decision by popular vote.

Are there qualities that make the Irish unique? Or special? Resilience is the one characteristic that I notice. The Irish don't give up easily. When they hit a roadblock, they don't turn around. They will try to find a way around it and overcome the problem. And very often with the help of other Irish people.

There is pressure on the Irish abroad to be successful. You want to make your parents and family proud. You can't just be out there doing nothing. You have to be purposeful.

This quality opens doors for other Irish people. It also gives the parents an opportunity to travel abroad. It makes the Irish sociable. When you bump into other Irish people, there's warmth. There is an instant bond. It makes us unique.

James Patrice

James Patrice is a TV presenter and social media influencer from Malahide in County Dublin. Along with reporting for 'RTÉ Today' and his hosting duties on 'Battle of the Food Trucks', James is also no stranger to a live audience, be it in his leading role in the Olympia Pantomime or his solo shows as his drag alter ego, 'Malahide Woman'.

Growing up in Malahide in County Dublin, I was always aware of the Irish identity, not that I ever engaged in what may be considered the stalwarts of an Irish boy's childhood. I didn't frequent the GAA grounds of Broomfield (I wasn't that enamoured by the notion of a sliotar) and was more likely to be found performing a Victoria Wood monologue dressed in a convoluted cossy. But, identity for me wasn't steeped in activity or indeed a learned practise – it was to be found in the unconscious sense of self that I was born into. Something as simple as having my father's first name, which also happened to be my mother's father's name. Something as magical as my nana singing a rebel song and falling in love with the words that left her mouth before I could even comprehend them being anything other than a kind of melodic poetry.

You could probably say that my Irish identity started from the second I knew that Sunday was a day we had corned beef and cabbage at 3.00 pm (you *couldn't* be having your dinner any later sure) followed by the sacristy of *Glenroe*. Not to mention an unhealthy obsession with where we would place in the Eurovision and what type of *gúna* Mary Kennedy would wear the year she hosted.

St. Patrick's Day wasn't just a day to go into town and have my dad whoosh me high in the air to see a giant float of a questionably bearded man, it was also a day to stand in front of our house and Irish dance with each other as my sister and I tried to remember our 1, 2, 3's.

As I grew up in Ireland and subsequently learned that our fair isle isn't just exemplified by an illustration of Oscar Wilde doing a hornpipe while drinking a perfectly poured pint of stout with Bono, I began to realise that the character of Ireland's people doesn't stem from the literary greats or *The Sunday Game*, but rather from our reactive nature and our ultimate resilience to the curve balls that life can so unkindly bestow upon us. To really understand this incomparable tenacity, one needn't look any further than their own doorstep and consult the greatest phenomenon that we may ever encounter – The Irish Mammy.

See, I've always felt an affinity with Irish Mammies. Maybe it's because they have such exceptional blow dries, or that they always know the right thing to say?

Perhaps it's a result of them somehow possessing the ability to read your mind before you've even processed your own thoughts? Or maybe it's simply because they could, quite literally, run the world. My admiration for The Irish Mammy really came to the fore during the 2015 Marriage Referendum.

As a gay man in Ireland who was aware of the atrocious trauma and ridicule that previous generations of LGBTQ+ citizens had to endure, I knew that a referendum like this wasn't just for marriage equality, but it was too an acknowledgement of the trailblazers who broke their proverbial backsides to make waves of change in Ireland. Their sense of unity and almost army-like activity was in a way mirrored, for me, in the legions of Irish mothers (and fathers) who made it their business to stand proud for their children. They swarmed Facebook pages, they flooded neighbours' front doors and made sure that by hook or by crook their loved ones would be heard and respected. My lasting memory of 2015? My mum, Veronica, clad in a full roll of TÁ stickers with accompanying tote bag, marching around Malahide wielding her vote for all and sundry to see. Like I said – Irish Mammies? They could run the world.

In my career as a presenter and in social media, I've been very lucky to work as a reporter on something almost as famous as the institution of The Irish Mammy – The Rose of Tralee. While some may criticise the festival and even find great entertainment in its millions of Twitter memes, I've witnessed first-hand the overwhelming sense of pride that everyone involved has in honouring their Irish heritage. But, this pride isn't just limited to The Dome. There's an inherent urgency in telling someone that you're Irish in any place in the world. Like an invisible badge of honour, one can't help but almost gleefully wait as the subject of identity comes up in a conversation. That is, of course, if you don't already beat your new acquaintance to the punch line and tell them not only your town of origin but its places of historical interest should they by any chance have heard about it. Then again – even in its potential obscurity – of *course* they've heard about it. It's in Ireland, after all.

Norah Patten

Dr Norah Patten is a faculty member at the International Space University. Her book *Shooting for the Stars: My Journey to Become Ireland's First Astronaut* won the An Post Children's Book of the Year, senior. Norah participated in the International Space University Space Studies Program in 2010 and holds a PhD in Aeronautical Engineering from the University of Limerick.

If you asked me this same question 20 years ago, or indeed 20 years from now, I possibly would have a varying response to what 'Being Irish' means to me. What I have recognised is that as we grow and learn and move to each next chapter in our life, our experiences shape our perspectives. But something I have come to appreciate is that there is a unity, a pride, a kind of common denominator to 'Being Irish'.

Growing up in the west of Ireland life was, well, simple. My father is from Achill, and his father (my grandfather) was the only one in that family who stayed in Ireland and had children. The other three brothers emigrated to Cleveland, Ohio and fast forward 100 years, there are fifth generation Pattens still living in Cleveland, many of whom I am in contact with. I first visited Cleveland when I was 11 years of age, and I was in primary school at the time. I remember that visit, which included my first trip to NASA, and I remember my parents remarking on the graft, hard work and success of my father's cousins in the US –

one a judge at the Court of Appeals, one a lawyer, one a vice president at a company, and the list continues. So, for me, part of 'Being Irish' is having, and knowing, my Patten family diaspora; an international family who are extraordinarily proud of their Irish heritage.

And perhaps it is only as an adult I appreciate the value and impact of the Irish diaspora on my own life, particularly when I think back to all my visits to Cleveland throughout my teenage years and my numerous visits to NASA which sparked a lifelong love of all things space-related.

One of the things that strikes me most now, as an adult looking back on that early period of my childhood, is the stark difference between what it meant to be a woman in Ireland then compared to what it means to be a woman in Ireland now. I specifically reflect on my own mother, Bridie, who is one of the kindest, warmest, loveliest, most capable Irish women I know. My mother was a stay-at-home mom, like many of the mothers at that time. I think back and realise how flawed my perception of reality was; I thought my mother didn't work because she stayed at home! How wrong was I?! She worked incredibly hard and took care of so much – cleaning, washing, baking, cooking, homework, knitting – and in addition to taking care of her own five children (of which I am the youngest), she also looked after other children to help supplement the income. I imagine there were many Irish women just like my mother, who in many ways parked their own dreams while encouraging their children to shoot for the stars. So, part of 'Being Irish' to me means recognising the many women, like my mother, who simply did not have the opportunities that I have been afforded and that I have enjoyed over the past two decades. I am reminded of this every time my mother makes a comment like, 'I wonder, what if I had an opportunity to do …'. And I am also reminded that her perspective on 'Being Irish' is likely to be very different from mine.

When I left Mayo at 19, I headed for the University of Limerick to study aeronautical engineering. I remember during one of my first days on the course, I met a fellow Mayo man, Micheál, and we immediately struck up a conversation: 'Oh you're from Mayo too, where about?' 'Being Irish' we just love finding the connection to others! There is a kind of camaraderie associated with it. I have noticed this more as I have travelled and worked outside of Ireland.

I remember when I was 21, while on an internship at the Boeing Company in Seattle, Washington, I received a call one day from reception and the lady on the other end of the phone said, 'there is a fellow Irish person here doing a course and I told him there is an Irish intern upstairs' and so immediately we were connected simply because we were Irish!

So, 'Being Irish' is sometimes a common denominator.

What does 'Being Irish' mean to me? It is certainly multifaceted. It means not forgetting about our history and where we came from, and acknowledging how far we have, thankfully, progressed as a society. It means working hard, pushing ourselves, continuously learning and growing, and networking, meeting others and striking up conversations. It means being thankful to have been born at a time when I have the choice to vote, the choice to work after getting married, the choice to study at university, the choice in many ways to set my own limits.

Marguerite Penrose

Marguerite Penrose is a proud Black and Irish woman. She was born with congenital scoliosis, and is a strong mother and baby home advocate, having spent the first three years of her life in St. Patricks, Navan Road. She is also an anti-racism advocate, and a meditation, reiki master and teacher who is passionate about humanity and our planet.

W hat being Irish means to me: My story begins in January 1974, when I was born in Dublin. Most likely, only a handful of people knew about my birth, because I was placed from the maternity hospital to what we now know as St Patrick's Mother and Baby Home. I am not just Irish. I am black (mixed race/multicultural) and Irish.

To me, being Irish is embracing my homeland and my culture, and in that sense my African heritage too. I would consider myself a proud Irish woman, and my ethnicity is a large part of my Irish heritage. I have grown up knowing only Ireland, the vast green land, steeped in history and known as 'the land of many welcomes'. Throughout my childhood, I was the 'odd one out', the child who 'looked' different because of my skin colour, and due to my congenital scoliosis (curvature of the spin). However, it was my colour that flagged the most 'interest'. But I learned to embrace my difference from a young age, with thanks to my parents, sister, family and friends. To me it was 'my Irish', who I was as an Irish woman growing up in a loving Irish family and community. In all honesty,

I found that when I was younger, being black/mixed race was one of the things that attracted people towards me. People were curious, and I was always happy to proudly state, 'yes, I am Irish', and 'yes, I am black'.

Many people ask, can you be Irish with an Irish mother and an African father? Well, yes you can, and this is the message all Irish black/mixed race/POC are continually advocating. To me, there are so many factors involved with being Irish. There are all the typical stereotypes that we know of: red hair, freckles, white skin, craic agus ceol, and of course 'the gift of the gab'. We are living in an ever-changing world and, in turn, an ever-changing country. If anything, being Irish also means embracing change, acceptance of everyone, no matter their race, sex or creed.

> *We pride ourselves that Irish people are loved throughout the world, we are embraced and welcomed, people are interested in our heritage and as we know love to claim a percentage of Irish in their blood too! Therefore as a Black and Irish person, I am advocating for the same acceptance for anyone who, because of their colour, has been told, 'you cannot be Irish and Black'.*

Being Irish also means family. The love of not just your mother, father, siblings and relatives, but also your extended family, such as friends and neighbours. I would also extend this to work colleagues, as we spend such a lengthy amount of time with our colleagues, it is inevitable that bonds are formed, that go beyond just being a 'colleague', and I think this is also an 'Irishism' in my opinion.

As we are steeped in history, and I happen to live in the most historical county in Ireland (Meath), I am constantly surrounded by Celtic reminders of my heritage and that is something very special. There are not many countries where such historic reminders are right on your doorstep without having to travel miles to find them. This is also the case in many Irish counties; Ireland is really steeped in us visually on a daily basis.

Over 70 million people worldwide embrace our Irish culture. We are the only country in the world that the rest of the world celebrates our festival, St. Patrick's Day, and this again makes me so proud of being Irish. Such a unique celebration of Irish people, our heritage and way of life. When you look at how on St. Patrick's Day 'everyone wants to be Irish' around the world, it is indeed a huge privilege to be living in Ireland as an Irish person.

Throughout the years Ireland has come on in leaps and bounds moving forward to bring the necessary changes needed to accept everyone, such as being the first country to legalise by referendum 'gay marriage', and that was an enormous move, acclaimed as a social revolution and applauded around the world. This vote was indeed a welcome move towards Ireland's liberal secular society, which to me suggests that, as Irish people, we have it within us to openly bring change and think of our fellow person. I only hope in turn that Irish people campaign against racism and other discrimination in Ireland because, whilst we have come so far, we are still a long way off for many people within our communities.

Again, there are so many other parts of what being Irish means to me. We love good Irish food such as stew, cabbage and potatoes, coddle (a famous Dublin meal), Tayto crisps, Cadbury chocolate; the list is endless, and of course a cup of Lyons/Barry's tea (tea solves everything)!! Whilst it may sound like a cliche, in most families this is true. I cannot forget to mention music, something I cannot go a day without. It has had such a big influence on me throughout the years. We have such famous Irish musicians worldwide, like Sinead O'Connor, Mary and Frances Black, Phil Lynott, The Dubliners, Damian Dempsey, Dermot Kennedy, and my all-time favourites U2 and Hozier, to name but a few. The production of music within Ireland is world renowned, from traditional to dance and trance. We are a country that gives its all.

To conclude, being Irish will always be something that means the world to me. It is the country where I was born and raised and that is something that will be forever in my heart and soul.

Richard Pine

Richard Pine was born in London and educated at Westminster School and Trinity College Dublin. He worked in Raidio Teilifís Éireann 1974-99 before establishing the Durrell School of Corfu which he continues to direct. His books include *The Thief of Reason: Oscar Wilde and Modern Ireland*, *The Diviner: The Art of Brian Friel*, **Greece Through Irish Eyes** and *The Quality of Life: Essays on Cultural Politics*.

Google tells me my nationality is 'Irish'. It's a common assumption, and a mistake.* I am British, but I left the UK in 1967 and moved to Ireland. Despite going to school a stone's throw from where Boris Johnson now smirks with impunity, I retain very little sense of 'Englishness'. On my very brief visits to England in the past fifty-four years (the last was in 1997), I can hardly recognise the country I left.

Fifty years ago, the Englishman Hilton Edwards (co-founder, with Micheál mac Liammóir, of the Dublin Gate Theatre) advised me not to change my British passport for an Irish one. 'Stay what you are. Change your passport and Irish people will accuse you of trying to "go native".' It seemed good advice at the time. Not now.

Quite apart from the fact that I don't want to be a citizen of a Britain governed by an arrogant cheat and liar, I want to be an Irish citizen, yet

---

* A version of this article appeared in *The Irish Times*, 8 June 2020.

I am, apparently, ineligible because I live abroad – in Greece, where I write a column for *The Irish Times*.

For the past forty-nine years I have been married to an Irish citizen, I am the father of two Irish citizens, the grandfather of another, and I pay Irish tax. But this is not enough. Under present regulations, an *Irish Times* correspondent living abroad who is not already an Irish citizen is ineligible to apply. If they lived in Ireland, there would be no restriction. But in that case, they wouldn't be able to do the job. It's a 'Catch-22' situation. So here I am, on the periphery of the periphery in every sense, a Brit telling the Irish about the Greeks.

How Irish must you be to be Irish? If I had had an Irish granny, it would not matter if I lived in the middle of the Gobi desert and had never even heard of Ireland. I would be eligible for Irish citizenship. It irks me deeply that a retired professor of classics at Queens University Belfast, who lives in England, achieved Irish citizenship in 2018 despite having no Irish ancestry and no residence qualification. What's he got, or done, that I haven't? It hurts, but maybe that's part of what it means to 'be Irish'.

My great-grandfather made the mistake of being an Irish bastard – abandoned by a pregnant lace-maker who fled Limerick for another lace-making centre, Coggeshall in Essex, in the 1850s. His birth was never registered so, as far as Irishness is concerned, he never existed – like me. Whatever my readers may say, I can't even become an Irish bastard.

Genealogically, I am Pyrrenean, Acquitanian and Cornish, with that bastard Irish infusion. So I am, in effect, stateless. If, however, belonging to a country is a state of mind, then I am predominantly Irish. Many of my books are exclusively about Ireland and Irishness. I spent twenty-five years in the national broadcasting service, nurturing today's National Symphony Orchestra and looking after RTÉ's corporate literature. This may not make me Irish or qualify me for an Irish passport but, like every other aspect of my life in and about Ireland – a country where I made my home for forty years and which I still carry in my heart – it has imbued me with a sense of destiny, a sense of purpose and, despite the regulations, a sense of belonging. There is something peculiarly bizarre – Beckettian even – in realising that one is not sufficiently 'Irish' to be Irish. When in 1977 I took the RTÉ Singers to give a concert in London I pointed out where I went to school. 'You mean you are English?' they asked with obvious disappointment. 'We rather hoped you were Ascendancy.' Dream on.

'Being Irish' means rather more than genetics or geography. It means having respect for imagination and independence, for the quality of life rather than the pace of life. Am I old-fashioned? Yes. One reason I forfeited my right to actually become Irish (by living abroad) is the growing commercialisation and de-personalisation of both city and country.

It is a vigorous culture: music, literature, new appreciations of traditional arts, and a better sense of history. But the international momentum of Google and Facebook is dividing society along lines of knowledge and how knowledge is used. There's a danger of a 'Starbucks' mentality rather than a 'Bewley's' or – dare I admit my age? – a 'Robert Roberts' state of mind. Issues discussed in journals like *The Crane Bag* in the late 1970s and early 1980s are still matters for concern: lack of decentralisation or cultural democracy, diminishing commitment to public service media and, despite a huge creative energy in young people, little brain in government.

Ireland has come a long way to have a taoiseach who is half-Indian and gay, and a Lord Mayor of Dublin who is ethnically Chinese. So the crux of the matter is: what makes a person 'Irish'? Is it a matter of DNA or a state of mind? A tenuous connection or a profound relationship? A granny from Crossmaglen or a deep commitment to Irish topics, emotions, sensations and ambitions?

Sorcha Pollak

Sorcha Pollak is a Dublin-based *Irish Times* journalist where she writes the weekly 'New to the Parish' series. She also co-presents *The Irish Times* 'In The News' podcast. Her first book *New to the Parish: Stories of Love, War and Adventure from Ireland's Immigrants* was published in 2018. Before joining *The Irish Times*, Sorcha lived in London where she worked for the *Guardian* newspaper and *TIME* Magazine. She has also worked in Peru, Delhi, Seville and Paris.

My sense of Irishness has always felt ever-changing and somewhat contradictory.

Linguistically, it's who I am. Irish for me is the sound of love, security and happiness. It's my Mamaí singing lullabies by my bedside, my Mam (my grandmother Neasa Ní Annracháin) joking and giggling in the back seat of our family car. It's sharing secrets with my sister on family holidays, it's summers in West Cork. It's a great-grandfather who cycled the length and breadth of this country teaching Irish as a Timire Gaeilge.

My family connections to West Cork are hugely important to me – despite being born in Dublin, I've always felt a much stronger bond to the rebel county. I've spoken Irish my whole life and owe a deep gratitude to my wonderful mother for her steadfast determination to bring up bilingual daughters in a house – and a country – where English always took precedence. My first name is the Irish term for brightness, my middle name comes from my much-missed grandmother. Yet my sense of Irishness is not straightforward.

Growing up in Dublin in the 1990s, and attending the local Gaelscoil, my surname sounded and looked different. In a class of Hogans, Higgins and Lynches, Pollak was not the norm. What's more, I wasn't Catholic. I was connected to that beautiful yet elusive Unitarian Church on Stephen's Green. Writing this now feels almost comical when I reflect on the more than 120,000 Poles living in Ireland today, or the numerous religions represented across most Irish national schools. But back then, I was different.

I grew up telling people I was only part Irish – I held a deep pride in my Czech-Jewish heritage passed on to me through my grandfather Stephen and my dad Andy. I was also acutely aware of the Northern Irish presbyterian roots I acquired from my paradoxically adventurous and mould-breaking paternal grandmother Eileen. I loved my 'foreign' blood, there was no shame in highlighting my difference.

And that's where the struggle came. As a teenager I became more interested in the part of me that came from outside this island. By the time I finished school, I felt very little love for this country. I wanted to get away from here as quickly as possible and jumped on a plane to Latin America weeks after finishing my Leaving Cert. I wanted to learn more languages and meet more people. Ireland in the early 2000s felt boring, white and homogenous. And my middle class, admittedly very privileged, life felt cut off from the real world.

When I moved back here in late 2013, after studies, work and adventures in various corners of the globe, I was reluctant to put down roots. Ireland still seemed insular and closed-minded. I reconciled my return to this country as being a temporary stop-over. I would leave again. I loved its language and music but hated so much of what our country had represented throughout history – a patriarchal society where education was dominated by the Catholic faith and women and girls had been treated horrifically. I was living in London when Savita

Halappanavar died and reported on the story for an international magazine. I was filled with rage that night I stood outside the Irish embassy interviewing young women holding candles beside Hyde Park.

But then 2015 happened, and we recognised same-sex marriage. Three years later we repealed the Eighth Amendment and I cried my eyes out with friends on a rooftop in the Liberties. Through my work, I started meeting Ireland's immigrant communities and the country's newest citizens. I also met and made friends with incredible Irish women and men who dedicate their lives to making this country a better place. Last year, the pandemic forced me to stop, take stock of my surroundings and appreciate the wonderful life this country has given me.

It's not all positive – I regularly witness anti-immigrant xenophobes employing the Irish tricolour or images of historical Irish figures to further their dangerous, closed-minded agenda.

I've been accused of being anti-Irish and an Ireland-hater because I write about diversity and multiculturalism. These moments force me to reflect on the dangers of ardent nationalism. Pride in blood and roots can very quickly evolve into a discriminatory, inhumane state of mind. Pride in one's nationality and history should not, and cannot, be used as a means of excluding others.

So, after 34 years on this earth, how Irish do I feel? Very much so and – at the same time – not at all. Some days I prefer to be European above all else. Other days I want to leave this country and never come back. But most days, I feel rooted to this small, windy western island. We get so many things wrong here, and we pat ourselves on the back far too much. *Ach, ag deireadh an lae, is Éireannach fíor-bhródúil mé* (But at the end of the day, I'm a very proud Irish woman).

Tomi Reichental

Tomi was born in Slovakia deported to Bergen Belsen concentration camp. When he was liberated, he discovered that 35 members of his extended family were murdered in the Holocaust. Tomi moved to Ireland in 1959, married the love of his life, Evanne, and has lived here ever since. For 60 years, Tomi didn't speak of his experiences 'because I couldn't'. In 2004, Tomi 'realised that as one of the last witnesses, I must speak out'. His book *I Was a Boy in Belsen* was published in 2011 and he is currently working on a second.

The first time I met an Irish person was in London in 1959. It was at an occasion when I had a meal in a restaurant with my Uncle Robert. We were served by a very pretty girl and my uncle said, 'You see the waitress, she is Irish, so you will have a lot of choices in Ireland to meet pretty girls'. I even asked him, 'How do you know?'. He replied, 'She speaks with a Dublin accent'. I did not speak English at the time, so I wouldn't have known. In my ignorance I thought that Ireland was part of England, and it only came to light when I went to post a letter in the GPO in Dublin. A woman queuing with me noticed I had an English stamp with the Queen's head on the letter! You see I had lived in England for a couple of months and had a booklet of English stamps. There was no internet or email at the time, so we still corresponded by letter. As mentioned, I did not speak English, so as I was going to drop the letter in to the letter box the lady behind me stopped me and told me: 'No Queen stamp! This is Ireland, not England!'

It took time before I realised what the woman was telling me and, finally, I understood that Ireland was an independent State therefore not part of Great Britain. Unfortunately, Ireland became famous worldwide for the wrong reason when the Troubles commenced in Northern Ireland in 1968 and this was reported all over the world.

I had been head-hunted whilst studying in Germany to set up a factory in Dublin. I arrived at the end of 1959 to set up a factory to manufacture zips. During my stay I did meet one of the pretty Irish girls, fell in love and married Evanne. I became an Irish citizen, and now am very proud to be Irish. Ireland welcomed me and gave me a new home.

I can truly say that I have noticed the biggest changes in Irish history. When I came to Ireland from Germany at the end of 1959, Central Europe after WWII was already organised and economically developing. Coming to Ireland was a big change. I noticed poverty in Ireland, dirty streets and unemployment at 23 per cent. The people were very friendly and easy going. In business there was no point in phoning before 10.00 am. The staff and management were not available as most did not come to work early.

Another phenomenon unique to Ireland was when I was travelling by bus, passengers crossed themselves each time we passed a church. I had not seen this in Europe!

The most tragic event in modern history of Ireland was when the troubles in Northern Ireland began in 1968 and lasted for 30 years. Thousands were killed and wounded. It was difficult to listen to the daily news reports listing the dead and destroyed property. Finally, this ended with the Good Friday Agreement in 1998. The killing stopped, but unfortunately the problems are still not fully resolved.

The biggest change came with Ireland joining the EEC in 1973. Major projects in roadworks began linking cities and towns throughout

Ireland, distances became shorter, and driving became faster. A trip that used to take three hours, now takes two.

Investment increased with modern industries coming to Ireland. The economy grew. When the LUAS service began on 30 June 2004 I said, 'Finally, Dublin has become a real European city!' We began to see photos of the front of the tram in Dublin in all tourist advertisements. The cranes were all over the city, building was going on everywhere. Ireland was booming. People over stretched themself financially, it couldn't go on, and we ended up with the economic crash of 2008 when the real estate bubble burst.

I must not forget the varied and beautiful landscapes of Ireland. Where in the world can you see the unique emerald, green colours of Ireland? The choice of scenery is also unique for us. Whether you want to be at a seaside, mountain, lake or forest it is a matter of a relatively short drive from anywhere in Ireland. It is never too cold and never too hot. I think it is the most beautiful place in the world.

I have seen many changes from the time I arrived in Ireland. Ireland is now a highly educated population in a modern society. Highly motivated entrepreneurs. Modern and high technology factories in pharmaceutical and engineering fields. Ireland is not the country that I encountered in 1960.

I know there are some problems we need to solve, like homelessness, but we are not unique, all of Europe is struggling with this problem. I don't think we will ever catch up.

I love the people of Ireland and the countryside. I am proud of being Irish.

Louise Richardson

Professor Louise Richardson is Vice-Chancellor of the University of Oxford, and was previously Principal and Vice-Chancellor of the University of St Andrews. A native of Ireland, she studied history in Trinity College Dublin before gaining her PhD at Harvard University where she spent twenty years on the faculty of the Harvard Government Department. She currently sits on the boards of the Carnegie Corporation of New York, the Booker Prize Foundation and numerous other charities.

Being Irish for me has always entailed the combination of deep roots with a global perspective. Deep roots derived from being related to people all around you, to growing up in the house your mother grew up in, to meeting nuns at school who had taught both your mother and your grandmother, to a very powerful sense of place. The global perspective derived from both emigration and Catholicism. We knew there was a world beyond our shores because of the occasional boxes of exotic hand-me-down clothes that would episodically arrive from rich cousins in America. We knew there was also a very different world beyond our shores because of uncles who were priests in the Missions, because of the money we saved to send to famished children in Africa.

I've lived outside Ireland for almost my entire adult life, but I've never lost my sense of being Irish. Like many Irish people of my generation and outlook, I have watched with a mixture of surprise and delight at the transformation of the social, political and economic life of Ireland in the 40 years since I left to attend graduate school in the US.

Growing up in rural Ireland I was taught that Britain was the cause of all our ills. Morning assemblies in our local convent school were held beneath a crucifix and a large framed copy of the 1916 Proclamation of Independence with the photographs of the seven signatories who were executed for their role in the rising. Their names: Pearse, Plunkett, Ceannt, Clark, Connolly, Mac Donagh, MacDiarmada were as familiar to us as modern day celebrities are to my children. Their names did, indeed, still our childhood play.

I read history in Trinity College, Dublin where I learned a very different version of Irish history from my English and Anglo-Irish professors. I went to America, studied international relations, and left it all behind me.

I later concluded that the eruption of violence in Northern Ireland was not a matter of British perfidy but rather of British indifference. Until the late 1960s, Northern Ireland, whatever its internal tensions, was broadly quiet and largely ignored by Westminster. The Troubles changed all that. After the Good Friday Agreement, with the province again quiet, British attention turned elsewhere. Ireland, both North and South, was largely absent from the Brexit debate in England, and Brexit was always an English rather than British enterprise.

It has been fascinating to live in England in the age of Brexit and observe the contrasting attitudes. Westminster has acted on the dual assumptions that the Republic of Ireland is still in some way part of the British polity and would ultimately join Britain in leaving the EU, and secondly, realpolitik dictated that in a clash between Ireland and Britain the EU would side with Britain. Both assumptions proved to be false. A minority government in Dublin never countenanced leaving and confidently played its hand as a fully autonomous member state of the EU, with EU backing. Today the Northern Ireland Protocol is a circle refusing to be squared.

> *Underlying the populist push for Brexit, and the
> contemporaneous populist movements elsewhere, has been
> a sense of loss, a sense of alienation from elites, a sense of
> resentment of change occasioned especially by migration. None
> of this has been evident in Ireland, where elites are local, where
> change has been positive, and where there has long been a sense
> of empathy with migrants, for obvious historical reasons, but
> also a sense of connectedness to a world beyond our shores.*

Those of us who are frequent flyers know that there is no better passport to hold than an Irish one. We can be friends to everyone. We have no historic imperial sins to expiate. We are allies of the powerful, having fully integrated into their societies, while being also on the side of the underdog, having for so long been underdogs ourselves.

I left Ireland all those years ago, despite deep affection for the place and people, because it lacked opportunities, because it was too priest-ridden, conservative and inward looking. Today it is none of those things and opportunities abound. It is secular, liberal and outward looking. Today it is great being Irish.

Nenad Šebek

Nenad Šebek is an International consultant for media and civil society. He served as Executive Director of the Center for Democracy and Reconciliation in Southeast Europe for 12 years and was a journalist for 27, 16 of them for the BBC World Service. He grew up in Yugoslavia, Ghana and Germany and is passionate about travel, theatre, classical and World music and reading. Prefers red wine to white.

My first Irish love affair has a name – Margaret Lynch. I was eight and she was a young English language teacher at Ridge Elementary school in Kumasi, Ghana which shows that one can come from the Balkans and get to know and love Ireland even in West Africa! Margaret had an immense authority with schoolchildren, an authority that strict disciplinarians can never achieve. She was gentle and kind but probably we, the kids, could sense the passion she had about teaching and the generous care and time she invested in us. This love affair is still an ongoing one, even though more than five decades have flown by, long live my dear Margaret! During those decades I kept adding qualities to those first ones I associated in my mind with Ireland and the Irish – caring, passionate, gentle and strong at the same time (and no, I am not talking about Jameson).

Fast forward to 1992 and a trip to Estonia which yielded an unexpected story I did for the BBC. My producer and I were surprised by the number of Irish pubs in the country's capital, Talinn, most of them even with live music. Investigating the reason for this phenomena, we stumbled upon a very active Estonian/Irish Friendship society whose chairman explained in a deep, rumbling voice, 'Estonians love potatoes, the Irish love potatoes. We have the Russian bear breathing down our neck, they have the English lion breathing down their neck. We are so much alike!'

I laughed all the way to the hotel, but this anecdote galvanised a thought, a theory which has been confirmed on all meridians because I started asking people from Thailand to California: 'What do you think about the Irish?' You can choose to believe me or not, but I have never heard a single bad word about Ireland or its people. No one is universally liked, the great powers have their natural antagonists, small countries always have one quarrel or the other with at least one neighbour and bingo, at least someone doesn't like you. Trust me, my background can be found in five of today's sovereign states and sometimes they even squabble inside me! But never, not once, have I detected a sniff of animosity towards the Irish. Anywhere, anytime.

A logical explanation could be that due to its history and geography, Ireland was never an occupying power anywhere in the world, never invaded a neighbour and is universally acknowledged to have received a lot of mauling by the lion's claws. The logic is a sound one, but I do want to add that every single Irish person I met only gave me reasons to fortify my belief that it isn't about politics or geopolitics; it is all about people and what they are like.

Strangely enough, it was only at the beginning of this century that I started to travel to Ireland, cursing the rain and marvelling at the intensity of the green. I was working for a Balkan civil society organisation dealing with reconciliation and the Irish were known to be the gold standard in this field due to the immense effort, money and ingenuity they invested into reconciliation. The conferences organised by the Irish Peace Centers were innovative, intriguing, profound and let us not hide it – FUN! There wasn't an evening without a party, there wasn't a day without laughter. The participants I met were people I could learn from – storytelling as a reconciliation tool was known to me, but it was only after listening for an hour to a loyalist paramilitary who was arrested as a minor and spent almost a decade at Her Majesty's pleasure that I fathomed the depth of feelings that storytelling can produce. It was only after a dinner that I realised that a theatre company spent the whole day at the conference, capturing our discussions in a fascinating impromptu performance which hit me like a sledgehammer.

I am a World music fanatic and Irish folk music has a prominent place in my CD collection. I know the power of percussion instruments. I've been to a number of concerts by the famous Japanese Kodo drummers. But it was only after hearing the Lambeg drum in situ that I felt every part of my body resonate and react.

I come from a part of the world which boasts of its hospitality, but it was only in Ireland that a conference organiser resolutely said that no, of course I am not going to spend my final night in Ireland alone in an airport hotel. I am coming over to his place to meet his family, share their dinner, get a bed and then he flatly refused to book me a taxi, getting up at an ungodly hour to drive me to the airport himself. We had met one another three days before.

Peter Sheridan

Peter Sheridan was a police officer in Northern Ireland for 32 years and was head of murder and organised crime investigations before retiring in 2008. For the last 12 years he has been CEO of Co-Operation Ireland, a leading peace building charity on the island of Ireland.

I hadn't previously given much thought to what was it actually meant to be Irish; I suppose I just am. Having to reflect on it for this piece, I have found it to be a difficult question to answer, perhaps that is because identity is such a complex concept.

At its core being Irish means being born on the island of Ireland, even more so than having Irish ancestry, so for that reason alone I am Irish, but I don't see myself as the same Irish as someone from Cork or Galway: culturally my Irishness is different. My father was Scottish, although I don't feel I am a hybrid. I was born in Northern Ireland, part of the UK, probably watched BBC more than RTÉ and followed soccer because of George Best more than I followed GAA, despite playing gaelic football and hurling when growing up. None of this made me less Irish.

Winston Churchill once noted: 'We've always found the Irish a bit odd. They refuse to be English.' I think there is a lot of truth in that. Relations between Ireland and the UK historically have never been simple. Even though there are close family ties between the two islands, I have rarely heard anyone describe themselves as British Irish or Irish British in the way people describe themselves as Irish American or American Irish. Why not?

For me, my Irishness does not mean being pigeon-holed into one particular description of Irishness; indeed my Irishness has changed over the years but I feel no less Irish because of that.

I joined the police (RUC) in 1976. It was a British police service but its badges and symbols included the harp and the shamrock, and the uniform colour was green whereas every other UK police service had blue uniforms. Much of my adult life has been working in the British system rather than the Irish system, but none of that has diluted my Irishness.

Being Irish also means I cannot escape the negative aspects of Irish identity; I am not a flag waving patriot but I love the place I come from, its people, its traditions and its culture. Growing up Catholicism was seen as a key part of Irish identity and to be Irish was to be Catholic.

Yet in the clerical abuse scandal, the Catholic Church abused its power to such an extent that it damaged its relationship with its people. These shocking events along with the Magdalene Laundries scandal, and the deaths of 9,000 children in institutions for unmarried mothers and their babies meant Ireland was seen as very narrow minded, parochial and uninviting to those who didn't fit its social conventions.

Irishness today means a lot of these values have disappeared and for the better. Ireland is a lot more welcoming to people of differing cultural backgrounds, religion and sexuality, which is undoubtably a change for the better and as a result has upgraded my sense of Irishness. It is therefore a good thing that Irishness isn't fixed and that traditional values change.

But as an Irish person am I much different from others, such as the Scottish, the Welsh, the English or Americans? Does being Irish make me, or us, special? Probably not. I have met good, decent, honourable people all over the world and, whilst I like to think being Irish means having an irrepressible buoyancy, a joyful spirit, a warmth and a care for others, I have also observed such character traits in many other nationalities.

Growing up I sort of learned Irish at school and like many others attended the Gaeltacht during the summer holidays, but whilst I could understand it more than I could speak it, I never reached the dizzy heights of being a fluent speaker. Language is one of the strongest expressions of culture and identity, and the fact that we don't speak our own language does dilute both. Identities are built around language and when I travel to other countries and hear people speaking their native language it is a clear form of national pride and self-expression.

So back to the question, what does it mean to be Irish? Perhaps the right answer is, I don't know, it's a hard thing to describe but, I know I AM PROUD OF IT.

My Irish identity is my own and how I choose to express it and recognise it in my own separate way has no more or less legitimacy than someone else's view of it.

Kenny Shiels

Kenny Shiels is a former Irish League player winning 14 trophies in a chequered career in football. He is currently the Northern Ireland Ladies Football Manager. In management he has taken three different provincial clubs and two international teams into European qualification.

I live in a town in South Derry called Maghera, a town that had been massively segregated into two sections with 95 per cent Catholic at the top end of the town, and 98 per cent Protestant residing at the bottom. When I (a Protestant) from 'downtown Maghera' was growing up I faced many challenges. My father was a local Councillor, the father of eight boys and one girl (the youngest) who was very well known and renowned for being supportive to all communities in the town in a unique sort of way. He could drink everywhere in the town and was so well received, mostly I expect, because he showed great appreciation to hardships of both sides and never made differences in his commitments to help people. He practically mapped out my life for me and my attitude to help others.

At the height of the Troubles my father in the late sixties, early seventies, came up with an idea to bring communities together by starting up a football team. It also had something to do with the fact that I was classed as being in the 'exceptionally good' bracket. My newfound friends and teammates came from a different part of town and my father's chicken farm, located in his small farm outside the town, was where the town players came out to the country to savour my mother's homemade cooking and of course play football. This made the town a much better place to grow up. We travelled all over Northern Ireland playing in tournaments and the bonding that created as a result was insurmountable. We felt so much better in each other's company.

As the Troubles got worse, we got stronger. However, when I reflect back now, it was only natural that total trust was never going to be reached. That early period was slaughter after slaughter and our wee town got hit hard. Friends and relations were being blown up or shot, but we stood steadfast and maintained friendships throughout. We had our own terminology of course. You could still hear each other's tribalism coming out. Catholics would talk about being from the 'North' or the 'North of Ireland', whilst the Protestants would say Northern Ireland, even more so now I would think. Then there was 'Londonderry' from the Prods, the Catholics' term would be 'Derry'. This is our different powers of language.

With strong religious backgrounds, we used to wind each other up to make it seem funny rather than serious. When we got home from school, we would go to each other's houses to play football for hours upon hours. We would 'scheme' our respective schools and sneak into the forest for a day's craic. I can vividly remember my father taking us to matches in a cattle trailer and some in the car boot. We still talk about this, but the younger generation don't believe us. The camaraderie that we developed was powerful.

There came a period in our life when the police cordoned off the town by putting gates at the town's edges so that nobody could drive into town and leave a bomb in a stolen car. Rather than this segregating us, it inadvertently gave us a massive array of streets to play football in. As soon as it became dark, we played quite literally 'street football'. It was an amazing change for our freedom to play, with the streetlights and shop doors for goalposts.

Being Northern Irish in my early days was something I was and still am very proud of. I have great relationships in my life and from what my father has handed me down I feel a great sense of having so many good friends from both communities. I would never, and never will, have bad feelings towards someone who has different beliefs or a different religion to myself. That is really important to me.

I love people and love being in company. My life has always been about friends and people. Northern Ireland is my home, and I am proud to say we have the friendliest and kindest people you would ever meet. Whilst I know we have had bad people who were ferocious and murdering during the Troubles, and who have hurt me and my family immensely, it doesn't mean I will ever stop building relationships with others.

On December 3, 1990, my younger brother Dave was saving up and had put in plans for building permission. Meanwhile he was staying in a mobile home next to my father's house. He had been married to Gladys, a lovely girl from Tyrone. She had given birth to a beautiful baby boy called Steven who was four weeks old exactly (born on November 5, 1990).

At 10.30 pm Dave went out to feed the dog as normal and the IRA opened up and shot over twenty bullets into him. A stray bullet ricocheted into Gladys' eyebrow and left a permanent scar. Steven thankfully was unharmed. Talk about the wrong family to do this too. My father gave his life to bringing people together, and he felt so hurt by that action. He died of grief just over a year later.

I still meander my thoughts back to what it was like to live in the North of Ireland or, in my background, Northern Ireland. Doesn't really matter to me what one wants to call it, and despite what we have had to deal with, it's where I feel connected to. God Bless.

Juan Lopez Tiboni*

Juan is an Argentinian-born, Canadian-raised doctor with an interest in humanitarian medicine. In his youth, he had dreadlocks and played drums in a reggae band, until life got in the way and he turned to more mature pastimes like writing nonsense words for other people. Juan spent the best years of his life in Ireland, and someday he'll be back. He has no doubt.

I always knew it would be hard to leave Ireland. From the moment I got here four years ago, I've felt at home. I can't yet fully understand what it was about Ireland that charmed me so furiously. Like any other place it has its flaws – and quite a few.

I moved here as a 23-year-old medical student. Born in Argentina, my parents moved us to Canada when I was six, and I grew up there, went to school there for my first degree until I got into medical school as a graduate-entry student here in Ireland. From the get-go, I got stuck in. I took the Luas every day. Three times a week I went on the piss. I started playing GAA. I discovered Irish trad, between classes humming the Wolfe Tones or Christy Moore; I even formed a duo and we played some shows in Dublin.

The Irish understood my sense of humour, that soft-spoken sarcasm and easy-going temperament, nobody seemed to take any of my barbs personally. Quickly enough, I found myself asking what's the craic, calling

---

* An extract of this article originally appeared in *The Irish Times* on 3 August 2021

French fries chips, and taking on a subtle lilt in my speech prompting a slagging when I returned home to Canada every Christmas.

Ireland sucked me in, in that sad subtle way like a few too many pints, and before I knew it, I wanted to make a life here. My sister came to visit at the end of my first year. We went to the Teeling distillery just outside my gaffe in the Liberties, and after she came home, I showed her a bit of Christy. I remember she sat on my bed as I faced the computer. I spoke with my head turned away, feeling too vulnerable to look her in the eye. 'I really like Ireland,' I said. 'It's going to be hard for me to leave.' The conversation stopped there because I started choking up. I don't think she noticed.

Before things could go any further, I buried the subject and moved on – another habit borrowed from the locals. The only thing I could have done more Irish was pour myself a drink. This dependence on alcohol to dull the pains of life is something I never understood until I moved here.

Alcohol is not just for the pint men either, its role in Irish courtship I find equally baffling. 'Meeting' people behind the smokescreen of liquor in compensation for fear was new to me as well. I told a story once to an Irish female friend about how I met a girl in the queue to renew my Leap card at Trinity. We just started talking about nothing in particular and got on well. She seemed really cool. I asked her if she'd fancy maybe getting a coffee.

'Oh no,' my friend said, interrupting the story. 'That's weird. Irish guys would never do that. We're all much too uncomfortable. You're meant to get them drunk and shift, then ignore each other in public for a while.' I guess I didn't get the memo.

Why don't I hate you more, Ireland? This is what I ask myself. I still don't have an answer. I don't think I ever will, because as a newly graduated doctor I had to leave. The country that I love doesn't seem to want me here. For medical school graduates in Ireland, finding employment as a doctor involves applying to enter a training pathway. The first phase of this training pathway is the so-called intern year, where intern doctors rotate through several teams getting exposure to the job and finding their feet. Every year hundreds of graduates apply for a finite number of intern posts that are given based on graduation rank.

But there's a caveat: preference is given based on nationality. Irish doctors get their first pick above all others, followed by non-Irish EU doctors, followed by everyone else. As a Canadian citizen, I found myself at the bottom of the barrel.

While I was here, I did my best to leave my mark. I founded a conference, I won a national public speaking award, I finished as a national finalist in a case competition and won an academic medal at the college, I even represented RCSI in the GAA Division III All-Ireland championship (I sat on the bench, still finding it quite difficult to scoop the ball up off the ground, but I was there in uniform nonetheless). None of it really mattered to the HSE, and this was made clear to me from day one.

My relationship with identity is complicated. I grew up speaking Spanish at home and eating Argentinean foods. All my friends ate dinner at 6.00 pm and I at 8.30 pm. I never played hockey.

Maybe somewhere in my lineage there is Celtic blood, from one of the defectors who stormed the shores of the Rio Plata on English ships and turned on their captains. Admiral William Brown, one of Argentina's greatest heroes, was an Irishman after all.

There's a song by Ringo Starr, called 'Liverpool 8'. It's a beautiful tune about how he left his home, although he carried Liverpool in his heart forever. I had listened to it hundreds of times, and I listen to his words now and they hit me so much harder. I think leaving Ireland has helped me to understand my parents' own struggle, leaving their home in Argentina. I don't pretend to know their pain, but I recognise it.

This is life. It hurt me to go, Ireland my love. Things weren't meant to be, this time. I chose my career first and I'm sorry. A new adventure awaits me across the pond. Someday I'll be back with a gang of wee ones to show them where their daddy fell in love. Thanks for everything.

Ireland, I left you, but I'll never let you down.

Mary Toomey

Dr Mary Valarasan-Toomey trained as a biologist, botanist, entomologist and an ecologist. She has worked as a university and technical college lecturer and is an author of books on various topics.

Breathes there the man with soul so dead,
Who never to himself hath said,
'This is my own, my native land!'

– from 'Patriotism' by Sir Walter Scott

I have never felt that I could call myself Irish. I was born in Jaffna, Sri Lanka, formerly called Ceylon; a lush land of spices, tea, coconut palms, orchids and the majestic Bo tree under which Lord Buddha attained nirvana. An island that was colonised and ruled for 443 years by the Portuguese, Dutch and British. Ethnic conflicts and discrimination against my community after independence from Britain in 1948 led to many of us emigrating in search of better lives. I arrived in Ireland in 1967 to continue with my postgraduate studies at Trinity College via Nigeria, where I had worked as a biology teacher in a high school run by Holy Rosary nuns from Killeshandra, County Cavan. I settled down quickly to my life in a Christian-Catholic country. Neither my nationality nor my skin colour seemed to make a difference to the people I met in the streets, at the bus stops or on the buses of Dublin. Despite the weather, or maybe because of it, I found the Irish people warm and welcoming. And I was very fortunate to be mentored by two very caring, kind and helpful professors.

My scientific qualifications offered me valuable professional opportunities and I elected to stay, a decision that was cemented when I met and married an Irishman. But when I was invited to contribute to a collection of personal reflections on *Being Irish*, I had to ask myself, am I Irish by marriage or as a naturalised Irish citizen in my own right? As I pondered this question, I was reminded of the lines I quoted at the beginning of this essay, a sonnet I learned from the Holy Family nuns.

That I find myself asking this is a result of what I have witnessed only since the late 1990s, when the Celtic Tiger roared to life and Ireland became a country of wealth, attracting economic migrants, refugees, and asylum seekers from far-flung places. Suddenly the island of a thousand welcomes did not know how to cope with the influx of newcomers. And I, a naturalised Irish citizen married to a Dubliner and with a heretofore deep sense of belonging in my adopted land, was surprised. Black people and other people of colour, children of interracial marriages in Ireland – themselves Irish citizens – were now being subjected to racial abuse. For the first time I became conscious of my colour and was deeply concerned for my own daughter, born and bred in Dublin, but aware of her otherness. This disturbing shift culminated in the June 2004 citizenship referendum, which limited the constitutional right to Irish citizenship of individuals born on the island of Ireland to the children of Irish citizens. As it was signed into law two weeks later, I was left deeply saddened and disappointed. The intervening years have done little to appease those feelings as racism appears to be alive and well in Ireland. I have not travelled by intercity trains since the dreadful incident involving an elderly Indian couple just a couple of years ago and I would be very worried about going into the city of Dublin alone.

And yet, I continue to be a loyal and committed citizen of Ireland, caring deeply about what happens in this country. Therein lies my 'Irishness'. While I have been retired from teaching and lecturing for many years now, I continue to be passionate about our education system and mindful of how it serves – or fails – our young people and the future trajectory of this nation.

My own personal and recent experience dealing with private and public hospitals has been most unsatisfactory, with prolonged waiting times to see medical/surgical consultants. It appears to me that the HSE is taking care of the 'system' instead of the people in need of health care.

Has the time arrived to courageously dismantle the HSE as it stands and restructure it so that we, the public, can be served efficiently with a fit-for-purpose health care system? And has the time also arrived for us to rethink our current education system, who it serves, and to what end?

During the past twenty years I have witnessed a great deal of much-needed change in Ireland with regard to our economy, employment, standard of living and lifestyle. Yet in pursuit of secularisation, we have simply abandoned tried and tested Christian traditions and values. Never one for unthinking adherence to dogma, I had hoped for a pluralistic society where we respect and tolerate each other's race, culture, religion and sexual orientation. Consider the words of our former Taoiseach, Mr Leo Varadkar, that in 'a participatory democracy there is need for regular dialogue with churches, faith communities and non-confessional organisations' – he was obviously thinking about promoting a pluralistic democratic society as opposed to one built on 'absolute secularism'. Unfortunately, that has not happened. But love does not come without disappointments, and whatever mine may be, it is my earnest hope that I continue to live and die peacefully in this beautiful country – the place I have called home for 54 years.

Leo Varadkar

Leo Varadkar TD is Tánaiste and Minister for Enterprise, Trade and Employment. Born and raised in Dublin, he is a graduate of Trinity College and a qualified medical doctor. Varadkar was elected to the Dáil for Dublin West at first attempt in 2007. He has served as Minister for Transport, Tourism & Sport, Minister for Health, Minister for Social Protection and and served as Taoiseach from 2017–2020. Leo lives in Dublin with his partner Dr Matthew Barrett.

To be Irish means to be part of a global family, to believe in something bigger than ourselves, to belong. People talk about Irish identity changing in the last few decades, but the truth is that we have always been a diverse people, with multiple identities, connected by thousands of invisible threads into a vivid, multi-chromatic national tapestry. It's something that often confuses people from other countries. They think being Irish means drinking a certain brand of stout, practicing a particular religion, or having a certain skin colour, but we have never been defined simply by what we have in common. Our strength has always come from our diversity, our willingness to adapt and evolve, and our ability to pass on this spirit of hope to a new generation.

For over a thousand years we have travelled to far off shores, sometimes for work, sometimes for adventure, sometimes to find a new home. In the same way, our island has become a new home for visitors from around the globe. Our nation of migrants includes pre-Celtic tribes from Spain and Celts from Central Europe, Roman citizens from Britain (like our patron Saint Patrick), Vikings from Denmark and Norway (who founded Dublin and Cork and many other cities on our island), French-speaking Normans, and English and Scottish planters. Even an Indian doctor who married an Irish nurse while both were migrants in the UK. Each brought a new infusion of knowledge, culture and wealth to Ireland enriching us before becoming more Irish than the Irish themselves.

I was born in the Rotunda and grew up in West Dublin and it never occurred to me that I was anything else except Irish. This was my home and my heritage. As I grew older, however, I realised that some others viewed me as different, because of my surname, because of my skin colour, because of differences that I had never imagined would affect my Irishness. Being Irish came to mean more to me precisely because some people tried to deny it to me.

Every nationality likes to think it is unique, but there is something distinctive about being Irish. It can be seen in the behaviour of Irish people when we travel abroad. We look out for each other and act like ambassadors for our country, earning respect and admiration, instead of being the source of shame.

We seek out connections with home, whether the reassuring comfort of an Irish cup of tea, or a packet of proper crisps, or keeping in touch with what is going on at home. It means feeling strangely delighted when we see someone at an international sporting event wearing a GAA jersey.

The people who shout loudest about someone not being Irish enough, who cling to a rigid conception of identity, and attempt to deny it to others are cowards who are afraid of what being Irish really means. They are insecure about their own identity and try to over-compensate by lashing out at others. They are really at war with themselves.

There is no one version of Irishness. Our strength comes from each other, everyone bringing their own talents, ideas and dreams. We draw inspiration from the past, but we are not bound by it. We are all colours and backgrounds, every religion and none.

Some of us do not drink, we like different kinds of music, we follow foreign sports as well as our own, and we eat our dinner in the middle of the day as well as in the evening. We disagree about politics and have our occasional fights. But when it matters most, we are there for each other. It's there in the camaraderie and good behaviour when we travel abroad for major sporting occasions. It's seen at home when we look out for each other during a pandemic.

Being Irish means our nationality is never a burden. It's the opposite. It lifts us up, it provides a sense of belonging and, in the darkest of times, it gives us a feeling of hope. To me being Irish simply means that you are someone who calls Ireland 'home'.

Hilary Wakeman

Hilary Wakeman is a retired priest, still officiating in the Church of England, and the author of *Saving Christianity: New Thinking for Old Beliefs*. Her most recent book consists of the diary of her first year in Ireland, *A Different World: An English Vicar in West Cork*, which came out in September 2021. She lives in Norfolk in the UK.

Nowhere else is like Ireland ...

I needed permission to use a photo of two West Cork children for my recent book, but I couldn't contact the mother, couldn't even remember her name. My West Cork son-in-law knew who I meant. He didn't know her name either, but he would recognise her if he saw her. From here in England, I asked him to look out for her so he could show her the photo and ask her permission. A couple of days later I got a call from him. He had been driving through a busy street and he saw her on the footpath opposite. He stopped the car, leapt out, crossed the road to her, showed her the photo, had a bit of a chat, got her permission, thanked her effusively and got back in his car. All this time the traffic behind him waited patiently. He thought it had taken maybe four minutes.

You wouldn't do that in England. Or any of the other countries I've lived in. Nowhere else is like Ireland. And I miss it.

Over a quarter of a century ago I left the Church of England parish and moved to Ireland with my husband and one of our adult children to be the Rector of a Church of Ireland parish in the southwest. I wish I could say it was like coming home, but although my mother was Irish I only knew Ireland as a tourist: Dublin and the west coast. It would take a while to become 'home' because it was all so strange. It felt as if we had moved back in time fifty years or so.

One thing I remember are the cakes: I was amazed – and delighted – that almost every church or community gathering ended with homemade cakes. Almost every tea-time visit with parishioners involved at least a homemade cake. Sherry or whiskey was sometimes included.

I loved the way children of all ages chatted to their bus drivers or their teachers as if they were all human beings. In fact, there was never a shortage of conversation at any level. Buying something, even in Cork City, could mean getting into fascinating discussions with the shop staff.

Local shops were homely: my hairdressers was in two tiny cottage-style rooms at the top of the main street, and in winter the front room luxuriated in an open fire and all-round conversation. Everybody seemed to know everybody. And to an English ex-vicar, accustomed to often fairly anonymous twenty-minute crematorium funerals, the three-day funerals there, with the whole community taking part, were a beautiful way of helping people to start the long process of bereavement.

A lot has changed in that quarter of a century. For example, my hairdresser now has a beautiful silver-decor salon in the middle of Main Street. But there is still that beautiful way of doing funerals. And children still talk to adults like human beings. And there is always conversation. I love it. I miss it. My Irish passport is in my bag, ready to go any day now.

Shona Weymes

Shona Weymes lives in Dublin and was accredited as a Humanist Celebrant and a HSE registered Solemniser of Marriages in 2017. She has been a lifelong Humanist, since before she knew there was a name for her personal beliefs, and is a proud member of the Humanist Association of Ireland since 2014. She received an MA in Cognitive Science from UCD and also trained as an actor at the Liverpool Institute for Performing Arts.

Being Irish with humanist views in 2021 is a strange, conflicting, terrifying, hopeful, challenging and interesting time. During Covid we have witnessed the unsettling influence that misinformation spread by social media can have. We have seen divisions being nurtured by those with insular viewpoints. We have witnessed the devastating impact that social inequality has had on those most vulnerable financially, socially and, on a personal level, emotionally during lockdown. Over the last number of years we have faced a range of challenges produced by our economic system. We have seen multiple housing crises, we have seen skyrocketing numbers of homelessness. All exacerbated by a failure to protect our society from exploitation by vulture funds. These difficulties are being exploited by the lowest common denominator, to assign blame, sow discord and inflame tensions.

There have been opportunities for great hope and love too. The struggles which have faced the world, as well as our country and communities, during the past year have shown us what we can achieve collectively. We've re-learned to appreciate the people who keep our country going, the frontline and essential workers who risk their lives for us.

Growing up in Ireland I don't think it occurred to me that we could change things. In the 1980s and 90s, I remember feeling that everything was just the way it was and that was the end of it. It was the same bunch of cronies who did whatever it was they did, and the rest of us just had to get on with it.

> *Then, something happened. Suddenly there was hope. A realisation that change could happen, and it could be good. Things started shifting, people were talking about the kind of country they wanted to live in, and how to achieve it. It became real. Peace. No more traffic diversions or closed streets or shops because of bomb scares.*

As a nation we used our voices to loosen the grip of sectarianism, exclusion and division. We are still an evolving society and we continue to set out markers signifying the kind of country we wish to live in. We continually strive to create a country which represents our shared humanity through compassion, tolerance and respect.

It has been an interesting time to live through. There is a feeling that it's now acceptable and even a responsibility to stand up, speak up and show up to be counted when there's a change you want in how your country is run. Since I have been able to vote, we have collectively and constitutionally made marriage an equal right, repealed the Eighth Amendment, and repealed blasphemy offences. We have debated and protested, we have sought and achieved meaningful change.

We have been and continue to be challenged. This has highlighted areas in which we can still strive to create a more ethical and democratic society. A society for all people equally, reflected in not just our ideals, but also in how we care for the most vulnerable. As I write there are protests happening about religious orders being gifted control of our maternity services by the State, the same orders that have been responsible for atrocities in our past. We still have the education provided for our youth by the State being administered mainly under catholic dogma. People talk about 'Catholic Ireland' but we have roundly rejected that idea time and time again, and it's time that our so-called secular state provides secular services.

There are strides to make in how we treat those seeking refuge. Culturally we have become a more diverse society, and we are quick to pat ourselves on the back. We have a long way to go yet. There has been a rise in racism in Ireland, the flames of which have been fanned by those who wish to exploit it for their own gain – a tactic we've seen employed worldwide by the far right. Being Irish should help provide us with a better view. We should use our history to remember what it's like to seek a better a life, to be the oppressed.

There must also be a shared focus on dealing with the challenges of climate change. We must not shirk our responsibility to clean up the mess we've made of our planet. We are facing a tipping point, and it may be that it requires reimagining and even dismantling the current economic system in the interests of life itself.

As we move forward we face these challenges together and for the benefit of everyone.

I have great hope for the future with all we have learned about ourselves, what we have already achieved, and what we choose about how we wish to live.

I can't wait to see what we do next.

Keith Wood

Keith Wood is a former Irish international rugby captain and winner of the World Rugby Player of the Year Award in 2001. Keith's business interests are based in Killaloe and incorporate investments in Leadership, Communication, Media, Clean Tech and Sports Technology at a local and global level. Keith is a Patron of the Special Olympics.

Wearing the Green Jersey

For a time, I donned the green jersey, as did my father before me. I did so with pride as a representative of our country. I would like to believe that I did so with some success but not at a level to match my own or my country's ambition. If I have regrets, they are relative, as you do what you can with the skills, tools and knowledge you have at your disposal at a given time. I did have great joy, however, watching our team flower after I had left the field. This success was the Ireland we yearned and toiled for, and I could enjoy it vicariously, albeit recognising that I had a hand in it but also didn't. That fact never lessened the pride I felt.

That time coincided with the Celtic Tiger, which spawned a more arrogant commercial and political Ireland, a brash lack of sense of nation where donning the green jersey took on a different tone, a different meaning, a disparaging of our national colour. We were all tarred with that brush, and if some deserved it, our country did not. This was a strange time where we believed there was new wealth in our pockets. It wasn't real, however, and we lost our way. The wealth was a mirage, lost in a sea of debt. This was a lesson for the ages, and we hope we never have to learn it again.

So, as we embark on our second century as a republic, what would we wish for our identity to be, what could we hope to stand for? Do we have an aspiration to learn from past mistakes and carve out a new identity for Ireland and Irishness in a global society? Is there a place for national pride in a global world? I remember the satisfaction I had in wearing the green, the pressure and responsibility, the humility, but overwhelmingly the pride.

In the future, what will we, as a country, be able to look back at with pride? I love the original meaning of wearing the green, a celebration and support of those that represented our country. I would like it extended to incorporate something Ireland and her citizens have achieved, not just on the sporting fields but also encompassing our whole society: from business, technology, engineering, arts and literature to civic duty, social equality and sustainability.

In Healthy Ireland, we worked on having a definition of what it meant to be Irish. Our declaration 'that to be Irish was to be healthy in body and mind' is a step in the right direction. If we go beyond health and view the whole of Irish society, how might we define ourselves? What if we look at the whole board, the whole gamut of what we want Irishness to be? We are a small island with a small population. For such a small nation, we have a high level of influence on the global stage. From cigarette bans to plastic bags to social equality legislation, we may not be first through the gate, but we are incredibly comprehensive when we get going. We are innovative and entrepreneurial and not shy of a bit of hard work. Our small stature as a country is part of our charm and essential to our opportunity for change in the coming decades.

If we enact real change, can we do it in such a way that it can be described as being a definable Irish way? Working together as a statement of what it means to be Irish; healthy, under our own roofs, sustainable and green, a blend of the old ways and the new. We should be looking at an Irish solution for Ireland, not for alacrity or cute-hoorism but for sustainable excellence. We need to recognise where we have come from and have an understanding to look for mitigation to safeguard what is essentially Irish. Essentially Irish but better for this changing century. We can't fall into the trap of demonising our way of life, but we can change it, improve it, maybe even understand it better. We are and have been a rural society and we have to bring a higher sense of balance between our urban and rural selves with a respect for both, because we need both to be in harmony to succeed as a country.

> *We need to protect that way of life and make it fit for purpose in a more climate-sensitive fashion. Ireland is a perfect size to stress test new ways, new ideas, new innovations. Whatever works, I would hope we use our influence and communication skills that we are famous for and export those solutions all over the world. Now that is donning the green jersey.*

My father died when he was fifty and I was ten. I turn fifty as this book comes out. My only memory of his advice was a one-liner, 'never be afraid of being proud of what you are good at.' We could be great at being Irish, we could celebrate it, and we could be proud of it too.

Paddy Logue

Paddy Logue was the editor of the precursor to and inspiration for this volume, *Being Irish: Personal Reflections on Irish Identity Today*, published by Oak Tree Press in 2000. For many years he worked in the European Union PEACE programmes in peace and conflict impact assessment. He is now eighty years of age and in remission from throat cancer.

Afterword:
Looking Back, Looking Forward

Growing up my identity was summed up in two words: Irish Catholic. Two natures in one person. They were intrinsically linked, although one or other aspect might come to the fore depending on the circumstances. The Irish flickered when asked my address by RUC foot patrols and, hoping to get away with it, I named the district: Creggan. 'And where is that?' I named the city: Derry. 'Never heard of that place' was the usual reply. Then there was a long stand on the pavement, much scoffing from the RUC until I said 'Londonderry' or the RUC got bored.

When Pope John XXIII convened the Second Vatican Council, I felt proud to be a Catholic. And excited. There was the promise of change in Ireland where, although I didn't understand it fully at the time, Christ and Caesar were hand in glove.

I lived in the cities of Leeds, Liverpool and London in the early seventies. I became fond of the English with whom I worked and socialised. They were liberal on identity and rights issues and committed to social justice and equality. They were patriotic English, but in no way nationalistic. By the time I returned to Ireland a few years later, I had lost both the religious bit of my identity and the narrow nationalist bit, but had gained a global perspective on social justice, equality and, importantly, humanism.

The humanist identity train was not crowded in Ireland at that time. It is now. Census returns in both jurisdictions show a steady increase in the numbers indicating no religious affiliation or refusing to answer the question. Surveys reveal a rapid decline in the numbers who consider religion important in their lives. This is the most striking difference in the current volume of *Being Irish* compared to the 2000 edition. How do we meet the equality and justice needs of this new and growing demographic?

A radical approach is needed both to free up religion from publicly funded, state roles in health and education the better to do good for its adherents; and to change the ethos of the state the better for it to do good for all citizens equally. It requires a friendly separation of church and state which respects 'freedom of thought, conscience, religion, opinion and expression' as set out in Articles 18 and 19 of the Universal Declaration of Human Rights. Such a separation limits the involvement of the church in matters of the state, and equally limits the interference of the state in church matters. It is an idea whose time has come.

The ceasefires of 1994, the 1998 Agreement, and the European Union PEACE programmes created a safe context for reflecting on our recent history and our identities. I came face to face with the victims of the Northern Ireland conflict which included the bereaved, the injured, families, women, the LGBTQ+ community, former security force personnel, former political prisoners, and many others. The individual stories spun a web of hurt, loss, regret, despair, learning and, for some, redemption.

In one workshop a former loyalist prisoner was cajoled by a group of nationalists. 'Just admit that you are Irish, and we can all get together as Irish citizens and sort this country out.' He replied: 'I am British for the very same reason that you are Irish. You feel Irish. I feel British.' Identity is couched in terms of sentiment. Citizenship is a legal construct.

At another conference a woman from an African country, overlooked for some time by the chairman who was distracted by the clamour of men jockeying for attention, eventually managed to be heard. 'In my country, it wasn't the war that divided us, it was injustice.' She sat down. There was a brief pause, the clamour resumed, and her insight was lost in a chorus of competing war stories.

Important as these and other similar discussions were to the evolution of my Irish identity in the twenty-three years since the 1998 Agreement, they do not compare in significance to the headline events that have taken place throughout Ireland in the same period. The economic crash of 2008 and its austerity aftermath; the ongoing increase in immigration and asylum seekers; the unprecedented coming together in government of Fine Gael and Fianna Fáil; the ups and downs of the power-sharing Executive in Northern Ireland; the implications of the 2016 English Brexit referendum, including 'the border in the Irish Sea'; the resignations of three Unionist leaders in the space of a few weeks; and, of course, Covid-19.

But by far the most significant events, where justice and equality rhymed, were the two referendums on same-sex marriage in 2015 and on the repeal of the abortion ban in 2018. I consider the latter the most important vote taken in Ireland in my lifetime. It is having a seismic impact on Irish identity, on how we see ourselves, and on how we want to be portrayed to the outside world. It is a harbinger of both a new kind of Ireland and a new Irish identity. It is a call to action to forge in the smithy of democratic negotiation a new secular constitution. It is an invitation to relish the joy, pride and humanity of a common identity liberated from a nightmarish history of division, bigotry and superstition.

Bringing these twins to birth is the task facing patriotic and progressive people in Ireland in the coming years.